# MELTDOWN

What Plane Crashes, Oil Spills, and
Dumb Business Decisions Can Teach Us
About How to Succeed at Work and at Home

## CHRIS CLEARFIELD
## and ANDRÁS TILCSIK

PENGUIN BOOKS

PENGUIN BOOKS
An imprint of Penguin Random House LLC
penguinrandomhouse.com

First published in the United States of America by Penguin Press,
an imprint of Penguin Random House LLC, 2018
Published in Penguin Books 2019

ISBN 9780735222632 (hardcover)
ISBN 9780735222656 (paperback)
ISBN 9780735222649 (ebook)

Printed in the United States of America
3  5  7  9  10  8  6  4  2

DESIGNED BY NICOLE LAROCHE

PENGUIN BOOKS

MELTDOWN

Chris Clearfield is a former derivatives trader who worked in New York, Hong Kong, and Tokyo. He is a licensed commercial pilot and has written about complexity and failure for *The Guardian*, *Forbes*, and the *Harvard Kennedy School Review*. He lives in Seattle.

András Tilcsik holds the Canada Research Chair in Strategy, Organizations, and Society at the University of Toronto's Rotman School of Management. The United Nations named his course on organizational failure the best course on disaster risk management in a business school. He holds a PhD in organizational behavior from Harvard and lives in Toronto.

To whistleblowers, strangers, and leaders
who listen. We need more of you.

To Linnéa, Torvald, and Soren

—CHRIS CLEARFIELD

To my parents and Marvin

—ANDRÁS TILCSIK

# CONTENTS

**meltdown** / 'mɛlt·daʊn / *noun*

**1:** an accident in a nuclear reactor in which the fuel overheats and melts the reactor core; may be caused by earthquakes, tsunamis, reckless testing, mundane mistakes, or even just a stuck valve

**2:** collapse or breakdown of a system

Prologue

# A DAY LIKE ANY OTHER

"It was the quotation marks around
'empty' that got me."

## I.

It was a warm Monday in late June, just before rush hour. Ann and David Wherley boarded the first car of Metro Train 112, bound for Washington, DC, on their way home from an orientation for hospital volunteers. A young woman gave up her seat near the front of the car, and the Wherleys sat together, inseparable as they had been since high school. David, sixty-two, had retired recently, and the couple was looking forward to their fortieth wedding anniversary and a trip to Europe.

David had been a decorated fighter pilot and Air Force officer. In fact, during the 9/11 attacks, he was the general who scrambled fighter jets over Washington and ordered pilots to use their discretion to shoot down any passenger plane that threatened the city. But even as a commanding general, he refused to be chauffeured around. He loved taking the Metro.

At 4:58 p.m., a screech interrupted the rhythmic click-clack of the wheels as the driver slammed on the emergency brake. Then came a cacophony of broken glass, bending metal, and screams as Train 112 slammed into something: a train inexplicably stopped on the tracks. The impact drove a thirteen-foot-thick wall of debris—a mass of crushed seats, ceiling panels, and metal posts—into Train 112 and killed David, Ann, and seven others.

Such a collision should have been impossible. The entire Washington Metro system, made up of over one hundred miles of track, was wired to detect and control trains. When trains got too close to each other, they would automatically slow down. But that day, as Train 112 rounded a curve, another train sat stopped on the tracks ahead—present in the real world, but somehow invisible to the track sensors. Train 112 automatically accelerated; after all, the sensors showed that the track was clear. By the time the driver saw the stopped train and hit the emergency brake, the collision was inevitable.

As rescue workers pulled injured riders from the wreckage, Metro engineers got to work. They needed to make sure that other passengers weren't at risk. And to do that, they had to solve a mystery: *How does a train twice the length of a football field just disappear?*

# II.

Alarming failures like the crash of Train 112 happen all the time. Take a look at this list of headlines, all from a single week:

**CATASTROPHIC MINING DISASTER IN BRAZIL**

**ANOTHER DAY, ANOTHER HACK: CREDIT CARD STEALING MALWARE HITS HOTEL CHAIN**

**HYUNDAI CARS ARE RECALLED OVER
FAULTY BRAKE SWITCH**

**STORY OF FLINT WATER CRISIS, "FAILURE OF
GOVERNMENT," UNFOLDS IN WASHINGTON**

**"MASSIVE INTELLIGENCE FAILURE" LED
TO THE PARIS TERROR ATTACKS**

**VANCOUVER SETTLES LAWSUIT WITH
MAN WRONGFULLY IMPRISONED
FOR NEARLY THREE DECADES**

**EBOLA RESPONSE: SCIENTISTS BLAST
"DANGEROUSLY FRAGILE GLOBAL SYSTEM"**

**INQUEST INTO MURDER OF SEVEN-YEAR-OLD
HAS BECOME SAGA OF THE SYSTEM'S FAILURE
TO PROTECT HER**

**FIRES TO CLEAR LAND SPARK VAST WILDFIRES AND
CAUSE ECOLOGICAL DISASTER IN INDONESIA**

**FDA INVESTIGATES E. COLI OUTBREAK AT
CHIPOTLE RESTAURANTS IN WASHINGTON
AND OREGON**

It might sound like an exceptionally bad week, but there was nothing special about it. Hardly a week goes by without a handful of meltdowns. One week it's an industrial accident, another it's a bankruptcy, and another it's an awful medical error. Even small issues can wreak great havoc. In recent years, for example, several airlines have grounded their entire fleets of planes because of glitches in their technology systems, stranding passengers for days. These problems may make us angry, but they don't surprise us anymore. To be alive in the twenty-first century is to rely on countless complex systems that profoundly affect our lives—from the electrical grid and water treatment plants to transportation systems and communication networks to healthcare and the law. But sometimes our systems fail us.

These failures—and even large-scale meltdowns like BP's oil spill in the Gulf of Mexico, the Fukushima nuclear disaster, and the global financial crisis—seem to stem from very different problems. But their underlying causes turn out to be surprisingly similar. These events have a shared DNA, one that researchers are just beginning to understand. That shared DNA means that failures in one industry can provide lessons for people in other fields: dentists can learn from pilots, and marketing teams from SWAT teams. Understanding the deep causes of failure in high-stakes, exotic domains like deepwater drilling and high-altitude mountaineering can teach us lessons about failure in our more ordinary systems, too. It turns out that everyday meltdowns—failed projects, bad hiring decisions, and even disastrous dinner parties—have a lot in common with oil spills and mountaineering accidents. Fortunately, over the past few decades, researchers around the world have found solutions that can transform how we make decisions, build our teams, design our systems, and prevent the kinds of meltdowns that have become all too common.

This book has two parts. The first explores why our systems fail. It reveals that the same reasons lie behind what appear to be very different events: a social media disaster at Starbucks, the Three Mile Island nuclear accident, a meltdown on Wall Street, and a strange scandal in small-town post offices in the United Kingdom. Part One also explores the paradox of progress: as our systems have become more capable, they have also become more complex and less forgiving, creating an environment where small mistakes can turn into massive failures. Systems that were once innocuous can now accidentally kill people, bankrupt companies, and jail the innocent. And Part One shows that the changes that made our systems vulnerable to accidental failures also provide fertile ground for intentional wrongdoing, like hacking and fraud.

The second part—the bulk of the book—looks at solutions that we can all use. It shows how people can learn from small errors to find out where bigger threats are brewing, how a receptionist saved a life by speaking up to her boss, and how a training program that pilots initially dismissed as "charm school" became one of the reasons flying is safer than ever. It examines why diversity helps us avoid big mistakes and what Everest climbers and Boeing engineers can teach us about the power of simplicity. We'll learn how film crews and ER teams manage surprises—and how their approach could have saved the mismanaged Facebook IPO and Target's failed Canadian expansion. And we'll revisit the puzzle of the disappearing Metro train and see how close engineers were to averting that tragedy.

We came together to write this book from two different paths. Chris started his career as a derivatives trader. During the 2007–2008 financial crisis, he watched from his trading desk as Lehman Brothers collapsed and stock markets around the world unraveled. Around the same time, he began to train as a pilot and developed a very personal interest in avoiding catastrophic mistakes. András comes from the world of research and studies why organizations struggle with complexity. A few years ago, he created a course called Catastrophic Failure in Organizations, in which managers from all sorts of backgrounds study headline-grabbing failures and share their own experiences with everyday meltdowns.

Our source material for the book comes from accident reports, academic studies, and interviews with a broad swath of people, from CEOs to first-time homebuyers. The ideas that emerged explain all sorts of failures and provide practical insights that anyone can use. In the age of meltdowns, these insights will be essential to making good decisions at work and in our personal lives, running successful organizations, and tackling some of our greatest global challenges.

# III.

One of the first people we interviewed for this book was Ben Berman, a NASA researcher, airline captain, and former accident investigator who also has an economics degree from Harvard. In many ways, Berman explained, aviation is an ideal laboratory in which to understand how small changes can prevent big meltdowns.

Though the likelihood of a failure on an individual flight is vanishingly small, there are more than one hundred thousand commercial flights per day. And there are lots of noncatastrophic failures, occasions when error traps—things like checklists and warning systems—catch mistakes before they spiral out of control.

But still, accidents happen. When they do, there are rich sources of data about what went wrong. Cockpit voice recorders and black boxes provide records of the crew's actions and information about what was going on with the airplane itself, often all the way to the point of impact. These records are critical to investigators like Berman—people who dig through the human tragedy of crash sites to prevent future accidents.

On a beautiful May afternoon in 1996, Berman was in New York City with his family when his pager went off. Ben was on the National Transportation Safety Board's "Go Team," a group of investigators dispatched in case of a major accident. He soon learned the grim details: ValuJet Flight 592, carrying more than one hundred passengers, had disappeared from radar ten minutes after takeoff from Miami and crashed into the Florida Everglades swamp. A fire had broken out on board—that much was clear from the pilots' radio calls to air traffic control—but what had caused it was a mystery.

When Berman arrived at the accident site the next day, the smell of jet fuel still lingered in the air. Debris was scattered over the dense marshes, but there was no sign of the fuselage or anything else that looked like an airplane. The fragmented wreckage was buried under waist-high water and layers of saw grass and swamp muck. Sneakers and sandals floated on the surface.

While search crews combed the black swamp water, Berman assembled his team at the Miami Airport and began to interview people who had handled the flight on the ground. One by one, ramp agents came to the ValuJet station manager's office, where the investigators had set up for the day. Most interviews went something like this:

> BERMAN: What did you notice about the plane?
> RAMP AGENT: Nothing special, really . . .
> BERMAN: Anything unusual when you were servicing the plane? Or when you were helping with the pushback? Or any other time?
> RAMP AGENT: No, everything was normal.
> BERMAN: Did *anything* at all draw your attention?
> RAMP AGENT: No, really, there was nothing at all.

No one had seen anything.

Then, while sipping coffee between interviews, Berman noticed something interesting in a stack of papers on the station manager's desk. The bottom of a sheet stuck out from the pile, with a signature on it. It was Candalyn Kubeck's; she was the flight's captain. Berman pulled the stack from the tray and leafed through the sheets. They were nothing special, just the standard flight papers for ValuJet 592.

But one sheet caught his attention:

---

**SabreTech**™

### SHIPPING TICKET                    NO: 01041

SHIP TO: VALUJET AIRLINES, CONCOURSE C, GATE 28, HARTSFIELD AIRPORT, ATLANTA, GA, 30320

DATE: 5/10/96

VIA: VALUJET (COMAT)

| ITEM | QTY: | U/M | PART NUMBER | SERIAL NUMBER | COND. | DESCRIPTION |
|------|------|-----|-------------|---------------|-------|-------------|
| 1 | 5 | EACH | "5 BOXES" | | | OXY CANISTERS |
| | | | | | | "EMPTY" |

---

It was a shipping ticket from SabreTech, an airline maintenance contractor, listing ValuJet "COMAT"—company-owned materials— that were on the plane. Berman was intrigued. There had been a fire on the plane, and here was a document saying there had been oxy canisters on board. And there was something else: "It was the quotation marks around 'empty' that got me," Berman told us.

The investigators drove over to SabreTech's office at the airport and found the clerk who had signed the shipping ticket. They learned that the items described on the ticket as oxy canisters were actually chemical oxygen generators, the devices that produce oxygen for the masks that drop from overhead compartments if a plane loses cabin pressure.

"So, were these empty?" Berman asked.

"They were out of service—they were unserviceable, expired."

This was a big red flag. Chemical oxygen generators create tremendous heat when activated. And, under the wrong conditions, the otherwise lifesaving oxygen can stoke an inferno. If the boxes contained expired oxygen generators—ones that reached the end of their approved lives—rather than truly empty canisters, a powerful time bomb might have been loaded onto the plane. How could this happen? How did this deadly cargo find its way onto a passenger jet?

The investigation revealed a morass of mistakes, coincidences, and everyday confusions. ValuJet had bought three airplanes and hired SabreTech to refurbish them in a hangar at Miami Airport. Many of the oxygen generators on these planes had expired and needed to be replaced. ValuJet told SabreTech that if a generator had not been *expended* (that is, if it was still capable of generating oxygen), it was necessary to install a safety cap on it.

But there was confusion over the distinction between canisters that were *expired* and canisters that were not *expended*. Many canisters were expired but not expended. Others were expired and expended. Still others were expended but unexpired. And there were also replacement canisters, which were unexpended and unexpired. "If this seems confusing, do not waste your time trying to figure it out—the SabreTech mechanics did not, nor should they have been expected to," wrote the journalist and pilot William Langewiesche in the *Atlantic*:

> Yes, a mechanic might have found his way past the ValuJet work card and into the huge MD-80 maintenance manual, to chapter 35-22-01, within which line "h" would have instructed him to "store or dispose of oxygen generator." By diligently pursuing his options, the mechanic could have found his way to a different part of the manual and learned that "all serviceable and unserviceable (unexpended) oxygen generators (canisters) are to be stored in an area that ensures that each unit is

not exposed to high temperatures or possible damage." By pondering the implications of the parentheses he might have deduced that the "unexpended" canisters were also "unserviceable" canisters and that because he had no shipping cap, he should perhaps take such canisters to a safe area and "initiate" them, according to the procedures described in section 2.D.

And this just went on: more details, more distinctions, more terms, more warnings, more engineer-speak.

The safety caps weren't installed, and the generators ended up in cardboard boxes. After a few weeks, they were taken over to SabreTech's shipping and receiving department. They sat there until a shipping clerk was told to clean up the place. It made sense to him to ship the boxes to ValuJet's headquarters in Atlanta.

The canisters had green tags on them. Technically, a green tag meant "repairable," but it's unclear what the mechanics meant by it. The clerk thought the tag meant "unserviceable" or "out of service." He concluded that the canisters were empty. Another clerk filled out a shipping ticket and put quotation marks around "empty" and "5 boxes." It was just his habit to put words between quotation marks.

The boxes traveled through the system, step by step, from the mechanics to the clerks, from the ramp agents to the cargo hold. The flight crew didn't spot the problem, and Captain Kubeck signed the flight papers. "As a result, the passengers' last line of defense folded," wrote Langewiesche. "They were unlucky, and the system killed them."

THE INVESTIGATIONS into Washington Metro Train 112 and ValuJet 592 revealed that these accidents were rooted in the same cause: the increasing complexity of our systems. When Train 112 crashed, Jasmine Garsd, a producer at National Public Radio, happened to be riding a few cars back from the impact. "The train collision was like a very fast movie coming to a screeching halt," she recalled. "I think in moments like these you come to realize two things: how tiny and vulnerable we are in this world of massive machines we've built, and how ignorant we are of that vulnerability."

But there is hope. In the past few decades, our understanding of complexity, organizational behavior, and cognitive psychology has given us a window into how small mistakes blossom into massive failures. Not only do we understand how these sorts of accidents happen, but we also understand how small steps can prevent them. A handful of companies, researchers, and teams around the world are leading a revolution to find solutions that prevent meltdowns—and don't require advanced technologies or million-dollar budgets.

In the spring of 2016, we arranged for Ben Berman to speak to a room full of people interested in the risk management lessons of aviation. It was an incredibly diverse group: HR professionals and civil servants, entrepreneurs and doctors, nonprofit managers and lawyers, and even someone from the fashion industry. But Berman's lessons cut across disciplines. "System failures," he told the group, "are incredibly costly and easy to underestimate—and it's very likely that you'll face something like this in your career or your life." He paused and looked out at the audience. "The good news, I think, is that you can make a real difference."

Part One

# FAILURE ALL AROUND US

## Chapter One

# THE DANGER ZONE

"Oh this will be fun."

## I.

The Ventana Nuclear Power Plant lies in the foothills of the majestic San Gabriel Mountains, just forty miles east of Los Angeles. One day in the late 1970s, a tremor rattled through the plant. As alarms rang and warning lights flashed, panic broke out in the control room. On a panel crowded with gauges, an indicator showed that coolant water in the reactor core had reached a dangerously high level. The control room crew, employees of California Gas and Electric, opened relief valves to get rid of the excess water. But in reality, the water level wasn't high. In fact, it was so low that the reactor core was inches away from being exposed. A supervisor finally realized that the water level indicator was wrong—all because of a stuck needle. The crew scrambled to close the valves to prevent a meltdown of the reactor core. For several terrifying minutes, the plant was on the brink of nuclear disaster.

"I may be wrong, but I would say you're probably lucky to be alive," a nuclear expert told a couple of journalists who happened to be at the plant during the accident. "For that matter, I think we might say the same for the rest of Southern California."

Fortunately, this incident never actually occurred. It's from the plot of *The China Syndrome*, a 1979 thriller starring Jack Lemmon, Jane Fonda, and Michael Douglas. It was sheer fiction, at least according to nuclear industry executives, who lambasted the film even before it was released. They said the story had no scientific credibility; one executive called it a "character assassination of an entire industry."

Michael Douglas, who both coproduced and starred in the film, disagreed: "I have a premonition that a lot of what's in this picture will be reenacted in life in the next two or three years."

It didn't take that long. Twelve days after *The China Syndrome* opened in theaters, Tom Kauffman, a handsome twenty-six-year-old with long red hair, arrived for work at the Three Mile Island Nuclear Generating Station, a concrete fortress built on a sandbar in the middle of Pennsylvania's Susquehanna River. It was 6:30 on a Wednesday morning, and Kauffman could tell that something was wrong. The vapor plumes coming from the giant cooling towers were much smaller than normal. And as he was receiving his security pat down, he could hear an emergency alarm. "Oh, they're having some problem down there in Unit Two," the guard told him.

Inside, the control room was crowded with operators, and hundreds of lights were flashing on the mammoth console. Radiation alarms went off all over the facility. Shortly before 7:00 a.m., a supervisor declared a site emergency. This meant there was a possibility of an "uncontrolled release of radioactivity" in the plant. By 8:00 a.m., half of the nuclear fuel in one of the plant's two reactors had melted, and by 10:30 a.m., radioactive gas had leaked into the control room.

It was the worst nuclear accident in American history. Engineers struggled to stabilize the overheated reactor for days, and some officials feared the worst. Scientists debated whether the hydrogen bubble that had formed in the reactor could explode, and it was clear that radiation would kill anyone who got close enough to manually open a valve to remove the buildup of volatile gas.

After a tense meeting in the White House Situation Room, President Carter's science aide took aside Victor Gilinsky, the commissioner of the Nuclear Regulatory Commission, and quietly suggested that they send in terminal cancer patients to release the valve. Gilinsky looked him over and could tell he wasn't joking.

The communities around the plant turned into ghost towns as 140,000 people fled the area. Five days into the crisis, President Carter and the First Lady traveled to the site to quell the panic. Wearing bright yellow booties over their shoes to protect themselves from traces of radiation on the ground, they toured the plant and reassured the nation. The same day, engineers figured out that the hydrogen bubble posed no immediate threat. And once coolant was restored, the core temperature began to fall, though it took a whole month before the hottest parts of the core started to cool. Eventually, all public advisories were lifted. But many came to think of Three Mile Island as a place where our worst fears almost came to pass.

The Three Mile Island meltdown began as a simple plumbing problem. A work crew was performing routine maintenance on the nonnuclear part of the plant. For reasons that we still don't totally understand, the set of pumps that normally sent water to the steam generator shut down. One theory is that, during the maintenance, moisture accidentally got into the air system that controlled the plant's instruments and regulated the pumps. Without water flowing to the steam generator, it couldn't remove heat from the reactor core, so the temperature increased and pressure built up in the reactor. In response, a small pressure-relief valve automatically opened, as designed. But then came another glitch. When pressure returned to normal, the relief valve didn't close. It stuck open. The water that was supposed to cover and cool the core started to escape.

An indicator light in the control room led operators to believe that the valve was closed. But in reality, the light showed only that the valve had been *told* to close, not that it *had* closed. And there were no instruments directly showing the water level in the core, so operators relied on a different measurement: the water level in a part of the system called the pressurizer. But as water escaped through the stuck-open valve, water in the pressurizer appeared to be *rising* even as it was falling in the core. So the operators assumed that there was too much water, when in fact they had the opposite problem. When an emergency cooling system turned on automatically and forced water into the core, they all but shut it off. The core began to melt.

The operators knew something was wrong, but they didn't know what, and it took them hours to figure out that water was being lost. The avalanche of alarms was unnerving. With all the sirens, klaxon horns, and flashing lights, it was hard to tell trivial warnings from vital alarms. Communication became even more difficult when high radiation readings forced everyone in the control room to wear respirators.

And it was unclear just how hot the core had become. Some temperature readings were high. Others were low. For a while, the computer monitoring the reactor temperature tapped out nothing but lines like these:

```
??????????????????????????????????????????????????????????????????????????????
??????????????????????????????????????????????????????????????????????????????
??????????????????????????????????????????????????????????????????????????????
??????????????????????????????????????????????????????????????????????????????
??????????????????????????????????????????????????????????????????????????????
??????????????????????????????????????????????????????????????????????????????
```

The situation was nearly as bad at the Nuclear Regulatory Commission. "It was difficult to process the uncertain and often contradictory information," Gilinsky recalled. "I got lots of useless advice from all sides. No one seemed to have a reliable grip on what was going on, or what to do."

It was a puzzling, unprecedented crisis. And it changed everything we know about failure in modern systems.

# II.

Four months after the Three Mile Island accident, a mail truck climbed a winding mountain road up to a secluded cabin in Hillsdale, New York, in the foothills of the Berkshires. It was a hot August day, and it took the driver a few tries to find the place. When the truck stopped, a lean, curly-haired man in his mid-fifties emerged from the cabin and eagerly signed for a package—a large box filled with books and articles about industrial accidents.

The man was Charles Perrow, or Chick, as his friends called him. Perrow was an unlikely person to revolutionize the science of catastrophic failure. He wasn't an engineer but a sociology professor. He had done no previous research on accidents, nuclear power, or safety. He was an expert on organizations rather than catastrophes. His most recent article was titled "Insurgency of the Powerless: Farm Worker Movements, 1946–1972." When Three Mile Island happened, he was studying the organization of textile mills in nineteenth-century New England.

Sociologists rarely have a big impact on life-and-death matters like nuclear safety. A *New Yorker* cartoonist once lampooned the discipline with the image of a man reading the newspaper headline "Sociologists on Strike!!! Nation in Peril!!" But just five years after that box was delivered to Perrow's cabin, his book *Normal Accidents*—a study of catastrophes in high-risk industries—became a sort of academic cult classic. Experts in a range of fields—from nuclear engineers to software experts and medical researchers—read and debated the book. Perrow accepted a professorship at Yale, and by the time his second book on catastrophes was published, the *American Prospect* magazine declared that his work had "achieved iconic status." One endorsement for the book called him "the undisputed 'master of disaster.'"

Perrow first got interested in meltdowns when the presidential commission on the Three Mile Island accident asked him to study the event. The commission was initially planning to hear only from engineers and lawyers, but its sole sociologist member suggested they also consult Perrow. She had a hunch that there was something to be learned from a social scientist, someone who had thought about how organizations actually operate in the real world.

When Perrow received the transcripts of the commission's hearings, he read all the materials in an afternoon. That night he tossed and turned for hours, and when he finally got to sleep, he had his worst nightmares since his army days in World War II. "The testimony of the operators made a profound impression on me," he recalled years later. "Here was an enormously, catastrophically risky technology, and they had no idea what was going on for some hours. . . . I suddenly realized that I was in the thick of it, in the very middle of it, because this was an organizational problem more than anything else."

He had three weeks to write a ten-page report, but—with the help of graduate students who sent boxes of materials to his cabin—he wound up cranking out a forty-page paper by the deadline. He then put together what he would later describe as "a toxic and corrosive group of graduate research assistants who argued with me and each other." It was, Perrow recalled, "the gloomiest group on campus, known for our gallows humor. At our Monday meetings, one of us would say, 'It was a great weekend for the project,' and rattle off the latest disasters."

This group reflected Perrow's personality. One scholar described him as a curmudgeon but called his research a "beacon." Students said he was a demanding teacher, but they loved his classes because they learned so much. Among academics, he had a reputation for giving unusually intense but constructive criticism. "Chick's critical appraisals of my work have been the yardstick by which I've judged my success," wrote one author. "He has never failed to produce pages and pages of sometimes scathing remarks, usually well reasoned, and always ending with something like 'Love, Chick' or 'My Usual Sensitive Self.'"

## III.

The more Perrow learned about Three Mile Island, the more fascinated he became. It was a major accident, but its causes were trivial: not a massive earthquake or a big engineering mistake, but a combination of small failures—a plumbing problem, a stuck valve, and an ambiguous indicator light.

And it was an accident that happened incredibly quickly. Consider the initial plumbing glitch, the resulting failure of the pumps to send water to the steam generator, the increasing pressure in the reactor, the opening of the pressure relief valve and its failure to close, and then the misleading indication of the valve's position—all this happened in just *thirteen seconds*. In less than ten minutes, the damage to the core was already done.

To Perrow, it was clear that blaming the operators was a cheap shot. The official investigation portrayed the plant staff as the main culprits, but Perrow realized that their mistakes were mistakes only in hindsight—"retrospective errors," he called them.

Take, for example, the greatest blunder—the assumption that the problem was too much water rather than too little. When the operators made this assumption, the readings available to them didn't show that the coolant level was too low. To the best of their knowledge, there was no danger of uncovering the core, so they focused on another serious problem: the risk of overfilling the system. Though there were indications that might have helped reveal the true nature of the problem, the operators thought these were due to instrument malfunction. And that was a reasonable assumption; instruments *were* malfunctioning. Before investigators figured out the bizarre synergy of small failures that had occurred at the plant, the operators' decisions seemed sensible.

That was a scary conclusion. Here was one of the worst nuclear accidents in history, but it couldn't be blamed on obvious human errors or a big external shock. It somehow just emerged from small mishaps that came together in a weird way.

In Perrow's view, the accident was not a freak occurrence, but a fundamental feature of the nuclear power plant as a *system*. The failure was driven by the *connections* between different parts, rather than the parts themselves. The moisture that got into the air system wouldn't have been a problem on its own. But through its connection to pumps and the steam generator, a host of valves, and the reactor, it had a big impact.

For years, Perrow and his team of students trudged through the details of hundreds of accidents, from airplane crashes to chemical plant explosions. And the same pattern showed up over and over again. Different parts of a system unexpectedly interacted with one another, small failures combined in unanticipated ways, and people didn't understand what was happening.

Perrow's theory was that two factors make systems susceptible to these kinds of failures. If we understand those factors, we can figure out which systems are most vulnerable.

The first factor has to do with how the different parts of the system interact with one another. Some systems are linear: they are like an assembly line in a car factory where things proceed through an easily predictable sequence. Each car goes from the first station to the second to the third and so on, with different parts installed at each step. And if a station breaks down, it will be immediately obvious which one failed. It's also clear what the consequences will be: cars won't reach the next station and might pile up at the previous one. In systems like these, the different parts interact in mostly visible and predictable ways.

Other systems, like nuclear power plants, are more complex: their parts are more likely to interact in hidden and unexpected ways. Complex systems are more like an elaborate web than an assembly line. Many of their parts are intricately linked and can easily affect one another. Even seemingly unrelated parts might be connected indirectly, and some subsystems are linked to many parts of the system. So when something goes wrong, problems pop up everywhere, and it's hard to figure out what's going on.

To make matters worse, much of what goes on in complex systems is invisible to the naked eye. Imagine walking on a hiking trail that winds down the edge of a cliff. You are only steps away from a precipice, but your senses keep you safe. Your head and eyes are constantly focusing to make sure you're not making missteps or veering too close to the edge.

Now, imagine that you had to navigate the same path by looking through binoculars. You can no longer take in the whole scene. Instead, you have to move your attention around through a narrow and indirect focus. You look down to where your left foot might land.

Then you swing the binoculars to try to gauge how far you are from the edge. Then you prepare to move your right foot, and then you have to focus back on the path again. And now imagine that you're *running* down the path while relying only on these sporadic and indirect pictures. That's what we are doing when we're trying to manage a complex system.

Perrow was quick to note that the difference between complex and linear systems isn't sophistication. An automotive assembly plant, for example, is anything but unsophisticated, and yet its parts interact in mostly linear and transparent ways. Or take dams. They are marvels of engineering but weren't complex by Perrow's definition.

In a complex system, we can't go in to take a look at what's happening in the belly of the beast. We need to rely on indirect indicators to assess most situations. In a nuclear power plant, for example, we can't just send someone to see what's happening in the core. We need to piece together a full picture from small slivers—pressure indications, water flow measurements, and the like. We see some things but not everything. So our diagnoses can easily turn out to be wrong.

And when we have complex interactions, small changes can have huge effects. At Three Mile Island, a cupful of nonradioactive water caused the loss of a thousand liters of radioactive coolant. It's the butterfly effect from chaos theory—the idea that a butterfly flapping its wings in Brazil might create the conditions for a tornado in Texas. The pioneers of chaos theory understood that our models and measurements would never be good enough to predict the effects of the flapping wings. Perrow argued something similar: we simply can't understand enough about complex systems to predict all the possible consequences of even a small failure.

# IV.

The second element of Perrow's theory has to do with how much slack there is in a system. He borrowed a term from engineering: *tight coupling*. When a system is tightly coupled, there is little slack or buffer among its parts. The failure of one part can easily affect the others. Loose coupling means the opposite: there is a lot of slack among parts, so when one fails, the rest of the system can usually survive.

In tightly coupled systems, it's not enough to get things *mostly* right. The quantity of inputs must be precise, and they need to be combined in a particular order and time frame. Redoing a task if it's not done correctly the first time isn't usually an option. Substitutes or alternative methods rarely work—there is only one way to skin the cat. Everything happens quickly, and we can't just turn off the system while we deal with a problem.

Take nuclear power plants. Controlling a chain reaction requires a specific set of conditions, and even small deviations from the correct process (like a stuck-open valve) can cause big problems. And when problems arise, we can't just pause or unplug the system. The chain reaction proceeds at its own pace, and even if we stop it, there is still a great deal of leftover heat. Timing also matters. If the reactor is overheating, it doesn't help to add more coolant a few hours later—it needs to be done right away. And problems spread quickly as the core melts and radiation escapes.

An aircraft manufacturing plant is more loosely coupled. The tail and the fuselage, for example, are built separately, and if there are problems in one, they can be fixed before attaching the two parts. And it doesn't matter which part we build first. If we run into any problems, we can just put things on hold and store incomplete products, like partially finished tails, and then return to them later. And if we turn off all the machines, the system will stop.

No system fits perfectly into Perrow's categories, but some systems are more complex and tightly coupled than others. It's a matter of degrees, and we can map systems based on these dimensions. Perrow's initial sketch looked something like this:

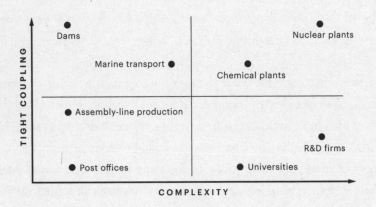

Toward the top of the chart, dams and nuclear plants are both tightly coupled, but dams are (at least traditionally) much less complex. They comprise fewer parts and provide fewer opportunities for unforeseen and invisible interactions.

Near the bottom of the chart, post offices and universities are loosely coupled—things need not be in a precise order, and there is a lot of time to fix problems. "In the post office, mail can pile up for a while in a buffer stack without undue alarm," Perrow wrote, because "people tolerate the Christmas rush just as students tolerate lines at fall registration."

But a post office is less complex than a university. It's a fairly straightforward system. A university, in contrast, is an intricate bureaucracy filled with a bewildering array of units, subunits, functions, rules, and people with different agendas—from researchers and teachers to students and administrators—often linked in messy, unpredictable ways. With decades of experience in this system, Perrow wrote vividly about how an ordinary academic incident—the decision not to grant tenure to an assistant professor who is popular with students and community members but has published too little—might create tricky and unexpected problems for a dean. But thanks to loose coupling, there is a lot of time and flexibility to deal with such issues, and the incident won't damage the rest of the system. A scandal in the sociology department doesn't usually affect the medical school.

The danger zone in Perrow's chart is the upper-right quadrant. It's the combination of complexity and tight coupling that causes meltdowns. Small errors are inevitable in complex systems, and once things begin to go south, such systems produce baffling symptoms. No matter how hard we try, we struggle to make a diagnosis and might even make things worse by solving the wrong problem. And if the system is also tightly coupled, we can't stop the falling dominoes. Failures spread quickly and uncontrollably.

Perrow called these meltdowns *normal accidents*. "A normal accident," he wrote, "is where everyone tries very hard to play safe, but unexpected interaction of two or more failures (because of interactive complexity) causes a cascade of failures (because of tight coupling)." Such accidents are normal not in the sense of being frequent but in the sense of being natural and inevitable. "It is normal for us to die, but we only do it once," he quipped.

Normal accidents, Perrow admits, are extremely rare. Most disasters are preventable, and their immediate causes aren't complexity and tight coupling but avoidable mistakes—management failures, ignored warning signs, miscommunication, poor training, and reckless risk-taking. But Perrow's framework also helps us understand these accidents: *complexity and tight coupling contribute to preventable meltdowns, too*. If a system is complex, our understanding of how it works and what's happening in it is less likely to be correct, and our mistakes are more likely to become combined with other errors in perplexing ways. And tight coupling makes the resulting failures harder to contain.

Imagine a maintenance worker who accidentally causes a small glitch—by closing the wrong valve, for example. Many systems absorb such trivial failures every day, but Three Mile Island shows just how much damage small failures can do under the right conditions. Complexity and coupling create a danger zone, where small mistakes turn into meltdowns.

And meltdowns don't just include large-scale engineering disasters. Complex and coupled systems—and system failures—are all around us, even in the most unlikely places.

# V.

In the winter of 2012, Starbucks launched a social media campaign to get coffee lovers in the holiday spirit. It asked its customers to post festive messages on Twitter using the hashtag #SpreadThe Cheer. The company also sponsored an ice rink at the Natural History Museum in London, which featured a giant screen to display all the tweets that included the hashtag.

It was a smart marketing idea. Customers would generate free content for Starbucks and flood the internet with warm and fuzzy messages about the upcoming holidays and their favorite Starbucks drinks. The messages wouldn't just appear online but also on a big screen visible to many ice skaters, coffee drinkers at the ice rink café, museumgoers, and passersby. And inappropriate messages would be weeded out by a moderation filter, so the holiday spirit—and its association with warm Starbucks drinks—would prevail.

It was a Saturday evening in mid-December, and everything at the ice rink was going well—for a while. Then, unbeknownst to Starbucks, the content filter broke, and messages like these began to appear on the giant screen:

> I like buying coffee that tastes nice from a shop that pays tax. So I avoid @starbucks #spreadthecheer

> Hey #Starbucks. PAY YOUR FUCKING TAX #spreadthecheer

> If firms like Starbucks paid proper taxes, Museums wouldn't have to prostitute themselves to advertisers #spreadthecheer

> #spreadthecheer Tax Dodging MoFo's

The messages were referring to a recent controversy that involved the use of legal tax-avoidance tactics by Starbucks.

Kate Talbot, a community organizer in her early twenties, took a photo of the screen with her phone and tweeted it with these words: "Oh dear, Starbucks have a screen showing their #spreadthecheer tweets at the National History Museum." Soon enough Talbot's own tweet showed up on the screen. So she sent another one: "Omg now they are showing my tweet! Someone PR should be on this . . . #spreadthecheer #Starbucks #payyourtaxes."

News of the ongoing fiasco spread quickly over Twitter and encouraged even more people to get involved. "Turns out a Starbucks in London is displaying on a screen any tweet with the #spreadthecheer hashtag," one man tweeted. "Oh this will be fun."

The avalanche of tweets was unstoppable.

Will Starbucks #SpreadTheCheer this Christmas by
stopping to exploit workers and starting to contribute some
tax? #taxavoidance #livingwage

Dear @StarbucksUK, was it clever to have a screen at a
museum showing all tweets to you? #spreadthecheer
#payyourtaxes

Smash Starbucks! Vive la revolution, you have nothing to
lose but your overpriced milky coffee drowned in syrup
#spreadthecheer

Maybe starbucks should hire a minimum-wage, no benefits
or paid lunch breaks "barista" to monitor and vet tweets
first for #spreadthecheer.

Talk about a PR fail. #spreadthecheer

Starbucks found itself in Chick Perrow's world.

Social media is a complex system. It's made up of countless people with many different views and motives. It's hard to know who they are and what they will make of a particular campaign. And it's hard to predict how they might react to a mistake like the glitch of Starbucks' moderation filter. Kate Talbot responded by taking a photo of the screen and sharing it. Others then reacted to the news that any tweet using the right hashtag would be displayed at a prominent location. And then traditional media outlets reacted to the blizzard of tweets. They published reports of how the PR stunt backfired, so the botched campaign became mainstream news and reached even more people. These were unintended interactions between the glitch in the content filter, Talbot's photo, other Twitter users' reactions, and the resulting media coverage.

When the content filter broke, it increased tight coupling because the screen now pulled in any tweet automatically. And the news that Starbucks had a PR disaster in the making spread rapidly on Twitter—a tightly coupled system by design. At first, just a few people shared the information, then some of their followers shared it, too, and then the followers of those followers, and so on. Even after the moderation filter was fixed, the slew of negative tweets continued. And there was nothing Starbucks could do to stop them.

A campaign for holiday cheer seems as far from a nuclear power plant as you can get, but Perrow's ideas still apply. In fact, we can see complexity and coupling in all sorts of places, even at home. Take Thanksgiving dinner, something we don't usually think of as a system. First, there's the travel: the days before and after the holiday are some of the busiest travel days in the year. In the United States, Thanksgiving is always the fourth Thursday in November; in Perrow's terms, that means there's little slack—there's only a one-day window for the holiday. The massive amount of travel also creates complex interactions: cars on the roads create gridlock, and the network structure of air travel means that bad weather at a major hub—like Chicago, New York, or Atlanta—can cause a ripple effect that strands travelers around the country.

Then there's the dinner itself. Many houses have only one oven, so the classic roasted or baked Thanksgiving dishes—the turkey, casseroles, and pies—are linked. If a casserole or the turkey takes longer than expected, that delays the rest of the meal. And the dishes depend on one another. Stuffing often cooks inside the turkey, and gravy comes from the roasted bird's juices. A simple meal like spaghetti with meat sauce doesn't have these kinds of interconnections.

It's also hard to tell what's going on inside the system—that is, whether the turkey is done cooking or still has hours left to go. To solve this problem, some companies add a safety mechanism—a small plastic button stuck in the turkey that pops out when the bird is done cooking. But these buttons, like many safety systems, are unreliable. More experienced cooks use a meat thermometer as an indicator of what's going on inside the turkey, but it's still hard to pinpoint the amount of time needed.

The meal is also tightly coupled: for the most part, you can't pause the cooking process and return to it later. Dishes keep cooking and the guests are on their way. Once a mistake has been made—once the turkey is overcooked or an ingredient missed—you can't go back.

Sure enough, as Perrow might predict, the whole meal can easily spiral out of control. A few years ago, the gourmet food magazine *Bon Appétit* asked its readers to share "their craziest Thanksgiving food disaster stories." The response was overwhelming. Hundreds of people wrote in with all kinds of culinary failures, from flaming turkeys and bland batches of gravy to stuffing that tasted like soggy bread crumbs.

False diagnoses are a common problem. People worry that their turkey will be undercooked when in fact it's already as dry as a bone. Or they worry about burning the turkey only to find out it's still raw on the inside, which means the stuffing inside the bird is also undercooked. Sometimes both problems happen at the same time: the breast meat is overdone, but the thighs are undercooked.

With the clock ticking, complexity often overwhelms cooks. They make a mistake without even realizing it's a mistake until much later—when their guests sit down and taste the food. "Hundreds of you sent in stories about accidentally using the wrong ingredient in your pies, gravies, casseroles and more," the magazine noted. "Our favorite iteration was a reader who accidentally used Vicks 44 [a potent cough syrup] instead of vanilla in her ice cream."

To avoid Thanksgiving disasters, some experts recommend simplifying the part of the system that's most clearly in the danger zone: the turkey. "If you break down the turkey into smaller pieces and cook them separately, you'll have a higher margin for success," says chef Jason Quinn. "It's easier to cook white meat perfectly than trying to cook white meat and dark meat perfectly at the same time." The stuffing, too, can be made separately.

As a result, the turkey becomes a less complex system. The various parts are less connected, and it's easier to see what's going on with each of them. Tight coupling is also reduced. You can roast some parts—the drumsticks and wings, for example—earlier. Then there is more space in the oven later on, and it's easier to monitor the breast meat to make sure that it's roasted to perfection. If unexpected issues arise, you can just focus on the problem at hand—without having to worry about a whole complex system of white meats, dark meats, stuffing, and all.

This approach—reducing complexity and adding slack—helps us escape from the danger zone. It can be an effective solution, one we'll explore later in this book. But in recent decades, the world has actually been moving in the opposite direction: many systems that were once far from the danger zone are now in the middle of it.

Chapter Two

# DEEP WATERS, NEW HORIZONS

"People have been jailed when it is obvious a
complex computer system is at fault."

## I.

When Erika Christakis hit send on an email to the students in her residential college, she didn't expect that it would spur a controversy across the Yale University campus, garner national attention, and drive aggrieved students to confront her and her husband, Professor Nicholas Christakis. She and Nicholas were co-masters at Yale's Silliman College, a residential community that housed more than four hundred students and included a library, a movie theater, a recording studio, and a dining hall.

In the days before Halloween in 2015, Yale's Intercultural Affairs Committee sent an email urging students to avoid racially and culturally insensitive Halloween costumes. The email came amid a broader conversation about race and privilege in the United States, spurred by the shooting of black men by police, the mass shooting of nine black worshipers in a South Carolina church by a white supremacist, and conversations and protests led by Black Lives Matter activists.

The Halloween controversy ensnared Erika and Nicholas when Erika, an expert in early childhood development, responded to the committee's email about appropriate costumes. Though Erika's email acknowledged the committee's concerns, it questioned whether a fiat from administrators restricting the behavior of students was the right solution. "Have we lost faith in young people's capacity—in your capacity—to exercise self-censure, through social norming, and also in your capacity to ignore or reject things that trouble you . . . What does this debate about Halloween costumes say about our view of young adults, of their strength and judgment?"

In response, a group of students posted an open letter and launched a petition calling for Nicholas and Erika to resign from their position as co-masters. A few days later, the controversy escalated. Nicholas was walking across the Silliman courtyard when a group of students confronted him about his support of Erika's email and demanded an apology.

Nicholas told them that his obligation was to listen to the students, not to apologize. He explained his position:

> I have said that I am sorry for causing you pain . . . that's different than the statement that I'm sorry for what I said. I stand behind free speech . . . Even when it's offensive, especially when it's offensive . . . I *agree* with the content of your speech. I am as against racism as you are. I am as against social inequality as you are. I have spent my life addressing these issues. . . . But that is different than the freedom of speech, the right to defend people to say whatever they want, including you.

But the crowd grew agitated. Someone yelled: "He doesn't deserve to be listened to!"

Another student began to talk, and when Nicholas interjected, she shouted him down: "Be quiet!"

She argued that the master's primary obligation was to create a safe space for students in the college, not to foster a climate of discussion. When Nicholas disagreed, she lost her temper. "Why the fuck did you accept the position? Who the fuck hired you?" she shouted. "You should not sleep at night! You are disgusting!"

WHAT'S SURPRISING is not the content of this debate but how quickly it moved into the national spotlight. A visiting activist shot a video of the confrontation and posted it online. What, in years past, would have stayed on campus exploded on social media.

And social media affected the real world. Ultimately, Erika and Nicholas resigned from their positions as co-masters. The viral video also came to haunt the student who had lost her temper. She was labeled the "Shrieking Girl," her identity was outed, and she was pilloried for her privilege; one website revealed that her family lived in a $700,000 house in a wealthy town in Connecticut. Amid all this, comment sections exploded with racist and threatening language. And the story quickly spread to the international media, from Hong Kong to Hungary. It wasn't the kind of publicity Yale needed.

When Chick Perrow published his treatise on system failures in 1984, the technology that drove this controversy didn't exist. Today, smartphone videos create complexity because they link things that weren't always connected—in this case, a university courtyard and the international spotlight. When combined with the amplifying power of social media, such videos become part of a tightly coupled system: shared at lightning speed, impossible to take down.

In 1984, the university was an obvious example of a loosely

coupled system. Today, that's not so clear. And it's not just universities. Since Perrow's initial analysis, many of the systems that he had classified as linear or loosely coupled have become complex and tightly coupled. All sorts of systems are moving into the danger zone.

Take dams, which Perrow saw as tightly coupled but low on complexity. If something went wrong, a dam might flood and devastate a downstream region. But dams, Perrow argued, are simple, linear systems with few unexpected interactions, which keeps them out of the danger zone. That's no longer the case.

If you visited a dam in the 1980s, you probably would have been shown around by a dam tender—someone who lived near the dam and was responsible for its safety. These days you might not run into anyone. Operators sit in faraway control rooms—which look a lot like the ones in a nuclear power plant—and make decisions without directly seeing the dam.

A federal dam inspector named Patrick Regan recently reassessed Perrow's analysis and found that, since the 1990s, new technologies and regulations have completely changed the way dams are operated. When a dam tender ran things, dams were simple. If water needed to be released so it didn't overflow the dam, a tender would walk up to the dam crest and push a switch to open the gates. Tenders could see with their own eyes if the right gate was indeed moving or not.

But today, a remote operator clicks a virtual button on a computer screen and then "gets a signal that the gate is moving from some form of position sensor," Regan wrote. "If the sensor is giving erroneous data, the operator has no real knowledge if the gate is moving or how far it is moving."

You can probably guess the consequences. At a California dam, for example, when a position switch fell off a gate, the remote operators got confused about the gate's position and didn't realize how much water they were releasing. People were stranded down-stream, and though tragedy was avoided, it was the beginning of a classic system accident. All it took was a small mechanical failure and a misleading indicator, and the system was soon slipping out of control.

Dams today, Regan argues, inhabit the same complex and tightly coupled danger zone that nuclear power plants do. Dam operators run an intricate system and rely on indirect indicators. The implications, Regan writes, are troubling: "As the systems that control our dams get more complex, the probability of a failure increases."

# II.

In his 1984 book, Perrow paid little attention to finance. The financial system didn't even make it into his matrix of complexity and coupling. But over the next three decades, finance became a perfect example of a complex and tightly coupled system. Take the crash of 1987, when the stock market fell by more than 20 percent in a single day. In the lead-up to the crash, many large investors began using portfolio insurance, a trading strategy that made the stock market more complex because it created unanticipated links between different investors. It also increased coupling because once prices started to drop, portfolio insurance programs automatically sold more stock, pushing prices even lower.

That same kind of price spiral affected the hedge fund Long-Term Capital Management (LTCM) a decade later. The massive fund had borrowed $100 billion from firms across Wall Street to invest in assets—like high-yield Russian bonds—that were cheap relative to LTCM's computer models. As a result, LTCM sat at the center of a complex financial web. In the fall of 1998, when Russia defaulted on its debt, that web began to unravel. Ultimately, the Federal Reserve had to organize a $3 billion bailout to contain the crisis.

Ten years after that, mortgage derivatives and credit default swaps created complexity and coupling that caused the collapse of Lehman Brothers and spurred the global financial crisis. And things could have been a lot worse. As Andrew Ross Sorkin detailed in his book *Too Big to Fail*, the whole system nearly unraveled because of the deep and opaque connections between banks.

In 2010, Perrow said in an interview that the financial system "exceeds the complexity of any nuclear plant I ever studied." Then, in the summer of 2012, complexity and tight coupling caused a meltdown at one of Wall Street's biggest trading firms.

AUGUST 1, 2012, should have been a slow summer day on Wall Street. There was no big news from the ongoing European debt crisis, and no important economic indicators were to be released. But when the New York Stock Exchange opened, the stock price of the Swiss pharmaceutical company Novartis went crazy. It exploded at the open and then moved sharply down. Within just ten minutes, almost a full day's worth of Novartis shares changed hands, and orders continued to flood into the market.

At a tiny office in a neoclassical skyscraper just off Wall Street, an automated trading system bought thousands of shares of Novartis before it hit a built-in risk limit and stopped trading. The system beeped loudly and grabbed John Mueller's attention. Mueller, an MIT-trained computer scientist, had designed most of his firm's trading platform, which made money by trading hundreds of stocks at very high speeds.

*What the hell is going on?* Mueller pulled up information about Novartis on his Bloomberg Terminal. Though the stock price had taken a hit, Novartis had made no announcements that might have explained why. And Mueller wasn't alone in his confusion: the strange behavior puzzled traders like him all over Wall Street.

The spreadsheet on Mueller's monitors showed two opposing views of the world. In red, it showed losses from his earlier purchases, as the price of Novartis continued to drop. Another column, in green, showed his model's prediction: the price was *too low*, and Mueller should buy as many shares as he could. As his eyes darted between the two columns, Mueller saw what other traders had also started to notice: the same kind of baffling moves were happening in all kinds of stocks, from General Motors to Pepsi. That meant that the problem probably had to do with something other than the individual companies themselves. Soon enough, trading floors across Wall Street buzzed with rumors; one theory was that something had gone wrong at a well-known trading firm called Knight Capital.

Tom Joyce, Knight's CEO, lay sprawled on his sofa watching *SportsCenter*. TJ, as everyone calls him, would normally have been at Knight's office in Jersey City. But that day, he was at his home in the posh commuter town of Darien, Connecticut, recovering from surgery with ice and a heavy wrap around his knee.

At around ten o'clock, he got a call from his head of trading. "Have you been watching CNBC? We've had a trading error—it's a big one." A computer glitch—the details were still sketchy—caused Knight to accumulate an unwanted $6.5 *billion* position during the first half hour of trading. TJ reeled from the implications: a position of this size was a regulatory nightmare and might threaten Knight's very existence.

For nearly thirty minutes, Knight's trading system had gone haywire and sent out hundreds of unintended orders per second in 140 stocks. Those very orders had caused the anomalies that John Mueller and traders across Wall Street saw on their screens. And because Knight's mistake roiled the markets in such a visible way, traders could reverse engineer its positions. Knight was a poker player whose opponents knew exactly what cards it held, and it was already all in. For thirty minutes, the company had lost more than $15 million *per minute*.

In the car on the way to the office, TJ made one of the most important calls of his career. He tried to convince Mary Schapiro, the chair of the Securities and Exchange Commission, that Knight's trades should be reversed because they were clearly erroneous. An IT worker at Knight hadn't correctly copied a new version of the firm's trading software to all of its servers. "It was as legitimate an error as you could hope for," TJ argued. Schapiro needed to discuss this with her staff. An hour later she called back: the trades would stand.

TJ winced as he pulled himself out of the car and grabbed his crutches. As the elevator ascended to his office, he wondered how such a trivial error could have crippled Knight. How could a single employee's carelessness cost the firm $500 million?

Though a small software glitch caused Knight's failure, its roots lay much deeper. The previous decade of technological innovation on Wall Street created the perfect conditions for the meltdown. Regulation and technology transformed stock trading from a fragmented, inefficient, relationship-based activity to a tightly connected endeavor dominated by computers and algorithms. Firms like Knight, which once used floor traders and phones to execute trades, had to adapt to a new world.

In 2006, the majority of stock trading became automated when the United States introduced something called Regulation National Market System, or Reg NMS. Though pundits casually refer to the "stock market" as if it were a unified whole, the U.S. market is actually composed of more than a dozen exchanges, each of which has slightly different rules but can execute trades in any U.S. stock.

Reg NMS brought two major changes. First, it took humans out of the loop by mandating that exchanges execute orders quickly and automatically. Before that, an investor's order might have sat for minutes, waiting for a human to match it with another investor and consummate the trade manually. Second, Reg NMS leveled the playing field by requiring that exchanges connect to and honor each other's markets. Imagine that an investor sends an order to the New York Stock Exchange (NYSE) to buy 100 shares of IBM. In the past, that order would have been stuck on the NYSE even if another exchange offered shares for a lower price. But Reg NMS required all exchanges to send their orders to other exchanges that displayed better prices. This created a truly national market.

Though few outside of Wall Street had heard of Knight Capital, it handled orders from small investors, sent through brokers like E-Trade, Fidelity, and TD Ameritrade, and large investors like pension funds. These orders came to Knight's servers, where a piece of computer code called a Smart Order Router determined how they should be handled: whether Knight should send them directly to an exchange, match them against orders in its own internal trading systems, or handle them in some other way.

Knight kept updating its technology to reflect changes in the markets. Because of Reg NMS, the number of stock exchanges ballooned. And existing exchanges, like Nasdaq and the NYSE, were always tweaking their rules to attract a broad spectrum of customers, from professional traders and massive pension funds to individuals investing a small nest egg.

The shift to an all-electronic marketplace was a revolution in finance. The use of computers drove down costs, increased the speed of trading, and gave traders a lot more control over their orders. But Reg NMS also created a more complex and tightly coupled market, which led to some surprising events. On May 6, 2010, for example, the markets experienced the so-called flash crash, in which a small disruption quickly spread to hundreds of stocks that plunged sharply, some to as low as a penny, only to recover moments later. It was one of the strangest days in Wall Street history, and that's saying something.

Then Knight caused the latest headline-grabbing meltdown.


IT'S HARD TO pinpoint the precise origin of Knight's failure, but October 2011 isn't a bad place to start. That month, the NYSE proposed a new way for small investors to trade: the Retail Liquidity Program (RLP). The program created a sort of shadow market for small-scale investors, allowing them to trade at prices that might be better than the rest of the market by a fraction of a penny. As they did many times a year, Knight's programmers modified their trading software to give their customers access to the new program.

Clients had to be able to specify that they wanted their orders to participate in the RLP. To facilitate this, Knight's programmers added a "flag" to their system. This flag, one of many that could indicate special handling for an order, told Knight's system to route the order to the RLP. A flag is like a "FRAGILE" sticker on a package: it doesn't affect the contents of the package, but it signals that it needs special handling. When firms like Fidelity sent RLP orders to Knight, they would include the flag, perhaps represented by the capital letter P (for the "P" in RLP), in a special part of the order:

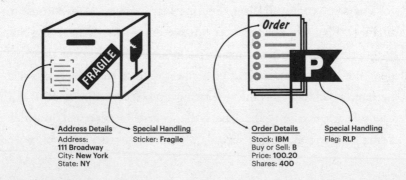

Address Details
Address:
111 Broadway
City: New York
State: NY

Special Handling
Sticker: Fragile

Order Details
Stock: IBM
Buy or Sell: B
Price: 100.20
Shares: 400

Special Handling
Flag: RLP

When Knight's Smart Order Router processed an incoming order with this flag, it would route it to the part of its system that knew what to do with RLP orders:

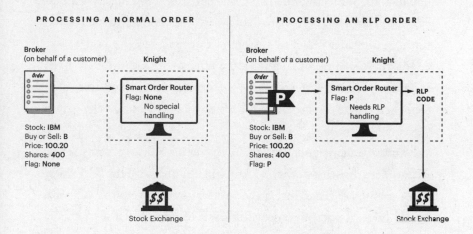

**PROCESSING A NORMAL ORDER**

Broker
(on behalf of a customer)　　　Knight

Order

Smart Order Router
Flag: **None**
　　No special
　　handling

Stock: **IBM**
Buy or Sell: **B**
Price: **100.20**
Shares: **400**
Flag: **None**

Stock Exchange

**PROCESSING AN RLP ORDER**

Broker
(on behalf of a customer)　　　Knight

Order
P

Smart Order Router
Flag: **P**
　　Needs RLP
　　handling

RLP
CODE

Stock: **IBM**
Buy or Sell: **B**
Price: **100.20**
Shares: **400**
Flag: **P**

Stock Exchange

For many years, Knight had used the same flag to specify a different order type: a so-called Power Peg order. When a trader sent a Power Peg order, Knight's system would divide it into smaller batches and send it out as a series of orders; the goal was to reduce price movements that might result from a large order. Power Peg was an old technology, and Knight stopped supporting it in 2003. But programmers didn't remove the code from the trading system; they just made it inaccessible. A few years later, another change meant that the Smart Order Router could no longer track the trades made by Power Peg orders. This shouldn't have mattered—after all, Power Peg had already been disabled—and no one noticed the error.

These seemingly innocuous steps—the launch of the RLP, the persistence of the Power Peg functionality, the inability to track Power Peg trades, and the reuse of the Power Peg flag—created the conditions for a financial meltdown. A few days before the RLP program started, an IT worker at Knight rolled out the new version of the trading software. To make sure there were no problems, he initially did this on only a few of Knight's servers. Everything was OK, so he rolled out the RLP code on all eight servers. Or at least he intended to. Somehow, he missed one of the servers. Seven computers were running the updated software, but the eighth server was running the older version—the one with the Power Peg code.

On the morning of August 1, hundreds of RLP orders arrived at Knight's trading systems. On seven servers, these orders were handled correctly and sent to the NYSE as RLP orders. On the eighth server, all hell broke loose.

When the market opened at 9:30, the server started processing the RLP orders that customers had sent. But it didn't have the RLP code, so for each RLP order, instead of sending one order to the NYSE at a fixed price, it sent out order after order, hundreds per second, and used the defunct Power Peg code to determine the price. It flooded the NYSE with orders in more than a hundred companies, including Ford, General Motors, Pepsi, and, as John Mueller saw, Novartis.

Though the filled orders didn't show up in Knight's regular systems, they were captured by a monitoring program that tracked stray trading. But that program didn't show much detail about where the positions were coming from, so managers didn't understand the gravity of the mistake. And, like the computer at Three Mile Island that printed out only question marks, Knight's monitoring program quickly fell behind.

By the time Knight fixed the problem, it was already on the brink of bankruptcy.

KNIGHT'S MELTDOWN couldn't have happened thirty years ago. Before computers dominated trading, the majority of transactions happened face-to-face on the floors of stock exchanges. This made trading easier to understand and reduced the chance of complex, unexpected interactions. When something strange did happen, like a client calling in an unusually large order, traders could double-check things before executing the trade, which made the market loosely coupled. And if there was a misunderstanding, traders could have a discussion and simply cancel the incorrect trades. But the rise of computer-based trading made modern finance complex, opaque, and unforgiving.

When TJ arrived at the office, he and his executive team worked to secure emergency funding from their trading partners as the price of Knight's own stock plunged. The day after the meltdown, TJ, hurt knee and all, appeared on Bloomberg Television to reassure investors. "Technology breaks. It ain't good. We don't look forward to it. But technology breaks."

TJ scrambled to save the company. Over the weekend, he secured a big cash injection. A few months later, Knight announced that it was merging with Getco, a former rival. Shortly after the merger, TJ left the combined company.

"I don't think anyone is impervious to having problems," TJ told us. "Everybody's smarter, runs faster, and jumps higher in hindsight. Leading up to the error, we took tons of reasonable measures." But those measures weren't enough. Firms like Knight had moved much farther into the danger zone than anyone realized.

## III.

April 20, 2010, started as a good day for Caleb Holloway, a lanky twenty-eight-year-old floorhand on one of the world's most sophisticated oil rigs. Holloway and his colleagues were about to finish drilling a challenging exploration well in the BP-controlled Macondo Prospect, and everyone was looking forward to being done. That morning, the rig boss, Jimmy Harrell, called Holloway into his office. There, in a small ceremony in front of the rig's leaders, he presented the young floorhand with a silver watch, a reward for spotting a worn bolt during a recent inspection.

Less than twelve hours later, Holloway narrowly escaped death. Mud and oil, propelled by the immense pressure from the well, shot into the air high above the rig, the Deepwater Horizon. A few minutes later, the engines ignited a cloud of gas. Crew members launched half-empty lifeboats or jumped into the dark waters of the Gulf of Mexico sixty feet below. Others never made it off the rig; eleven people died. Before it sank, the Deepwater Horizon burned for two days, shooting flames so high that observers saw them from thirty miles away.

Over the next three months, oil gushed, unchecked, through the mile-deep wellhead. Finally, eighty-seven days after the explosion, BP sealed the well. But by then, nearly five million barrels of oil had spilled into the Gulf and formed a massive, moving slick.

DEEPWATER HORIZON wasn't just a clever name. The year before it exploded, the rig drilled the then-deepest oil well ever, under a mile of seawater and five miles of earth. Companies like BP, which leased the rig, needed to drill deep to exploit new sources of oil. But drilling so deep pushed the envelope on complexity and tight coupling. BP ventured farther and farther into the danger zone. And at a cost of a million dollars a day, Deepwater Horizon didn't come cheap, so BP engineers pushed the rig to finish up its work at Macondo and move on to its next project.

The blowout wasn't caused by a worn bolt or anything a deckhand would have caught during a safety inspection. It all came down to BP's failure to manage the complexity of its well.

Just as radioactivity makes it hard to observe the core of a nuclear reactor directly, the high-pressure, underwater environment obscured what was going on inside the well. Drillers couldn't just "send a guy down" to see what was happening miles below the earth. Instead, they had to rely on computer simulations and indirect measurements like well pressure and pump flow.

So when BP made a series of risky decisions—like ignoring worrisome pressure readings and skipping cement integrity tests—complexity hid the resulting problems. Horizon's crew was operating on the razor's edge of catastrophe, but they didn't know it.

As the crew battled the blowout, complexity struck again. The rig's elaborate emergency systems were just too overwhelming. There were as many as thirty buttons to control a single safety system, and a detailed emergency handbook described so many contingencies that it was hard to know which protocol to follow. When the accident began, the crew was frozen. The Horizon's safety systems paralyzed them.

And the rig, having drilled into the Gulf's unstable geological formations, was tightly coupled. When disaster struck, the system couldn't just be turned off, fixed, and restarted. The oil and gas had nowhere to go but up.

Deepwater Horizon was a marvel of engineering that pushed the frontiers of drilling. But even far into the danger zone, it still relied on an approach to safety that was better suited to a simpler, more forgiving environment.

Transocean, the company that owned the rig, did care deeply about certain aspects of safety. "Safety meeting after safety meeting after safety meeting," Holloway recalled. "We had weekly safety meetings, we had daily safety meetings."

The crew even helped make a rap video about hand safety on the deck. It went like this:

> *An incident-free workplace*
> *All the time, everywhere*

*It all starts with planning*
*And keeping your hands clear*
*A motorman working on motors*
*Keep 'em clear!*
*A roustabout landing them lifts*
*Keep 'em clear!*
*A roughneck trippin' on pipe*
*Keep 'em clear!*

BP, too, was vigilant about slips, falls, and other injuries. As one former engineer explained, "Senior BP management focused so heavily on the easy part of safety—holding the hand rails, spending hours discussing the merits of reverse parking, and the dangers of not having a lid on a coffee cup—but were less enthusiastic about the hard stuff, investing in and maintaining their complex facilities."

*They spent more time worrying about coffee spills than oil spills.*

This approach sounds absurd, but it made sense to these companies. Burnt hands, slips and falls, and car accidents mean lost work time and cost a firm a lot of money. Injuries like these are also easy to track, so one can handily compile statistics about incident rates and safety improvements and measure how they affect the bottom line. Fewer incidents produce visible results—lower costs and higher profits—quarter after quarter. Those results create an illusion of safety. Incredibly, that illusion persisted even after the Deepwater Horizon accident. "Notwithstanding the tragic loss of life in the Gulf of Mexico, we achieved an exemplary statistical safety record as measured by our total recordable incident rate and total potential severity rate," Transocean wrote in a securities filing. "As measured by these standards, we recorded the best year in safety performance in our company's history, which is a reflection on our commitment to achieving an incident-free environment, all the time, everywhere."

*The best year in safety performance? An exemplary safety record?* They were involved in the worst accident in the industry's history, but by their standards, it was the safest year ever.

Maybe they didn't have the right standards. Maybe, in fact, their whole approach needed to change.

AS OUR SYSTEMS CHANGE, so must our ways of managing them. Knight, BP, and Transocean used an outdated approach. Knight, for one, didn't view itself as a technology company, even though technology formed the core of its business. This approach might have worked when floor traders dominated finance. But that's not the era in which Knight traded.

Similarly, BP's and Transocean's approach to safety might have worked in a simpler system, like a routine onshore drilling operation. There, an emphasis on worker incident rates and maintenance details like worn bolts might have done the trick. But Deepwater Horizon was a complex offshore rig. It operated squarely in the danger zone.

When Perrow published *Normal Accidents* in 1984, the danger zone he described was sparse: it included systems like nuclear facilities, chemical plants, and space missions. Since then, all kinds of systems—from universities and Wall Street firms to dams and oil rigs—have become more complex and tightly coupled.

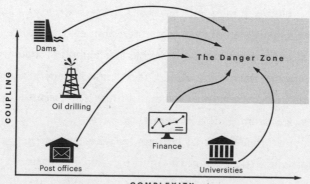

No system seems immune to this shift, not even those that used to be the epitomes of simplicity and loose coupling. Consider the humble post office. In 1984, Perrow placed it in the safest corner of his matrix, far from the danger zone. It was one of the most unlikely systems to go crazy. But even that's changed.

# IV.

In the early 2000s, the Post Office in the United Kingdom rolled out a fancy new IT system called Horizon. It cost a billion pounds and was proudly called "one of the biggest IT projects ever implemented in Europe." But a few years later, the system would be the subject of widespread discussions in the British Parliament, and newspapers would appear with headlines like these:

**DECENT LIVES DESTROYED BY THE POST OFFICE**

**POST OFFICE UNDER FIRE OVER IT SYSTEM**

**SUBPOSTMASTERS FIGHT TO CLEAR NAMES IN THEFT AND FALSE ACCOUNTING CASE**

In the United Kingdom, the Post Office is a semiprivate company that lets people not only mail letters but also access their bank accounts and pensions, top off prepaid cell phones, and pay bills. Outside of big towns, the Post Office contracts with franchisees called sub-postmasters, mostly small business owners who provide these services from their own shops.

The Post Office designed Horizon to manage hundreds of products and reduce the amount of time that sub-postmasters spent on bookkeeping. And by many measures the system was successful. But soon after its implementation, some sub-postmasters complained that Horizon had accounting problems, reported shortfalls in cash and stamps by mistake, and caused ATMs to behave strangely. The breadth of Horizon's capabilities may have been a part of the reason: according to the *Financial Times*, an independent forensic review found "exceptionally complex systems that had trouble linking with other systems; a lack of proper training; and a business model that gave sub-postmasters all the responsibility for dealing with any problems." It turns out that Horizon was both complex and tightly coupled.

Tom Brown had seen a lot as a sub-postmaster; he'd been in the job for three decades and had been held up at gunpoint five times. Yet he struggled with Horizon. When he contacted the Post Office, he was told, "No problem. It will be sorted out."

But at the next audit, he was accused of stealing £85,000. The police arrested him and searched his home and car. Though the case was dropped five years later, Brown's reputation was dragged through the mud. He lost his business, his home, and more than £250,000.

Despite the anomalies that some sub-postmasters reported, the Post Office has remained "fully confident that the Horizon computer system in its branches, and all the accounting processes around it, are absolutely accurate and reliable at all times." Indeed, in a response to a fact-checking request, the Post Office expressed concern about being included in a book about system failures, noting that Horizon is used "across 11,600 branches by postmasters, agents, and their many thousands of staff to process six million transactions successfully every day, including on behalf of the UK's high street banks."

Convinced of the system's accuracy, the Post Office accused some sub-postmasters of theft, fraud, and false accounting and demanded that they pay back alleged shortages. In some cases, it even brought criminal charges. Here's the story of Jo Hamilton, who used to run a Post Office from a village shop and faced a £2,000 discrepancy:

> I had to remortgage the house and repay the money. Originally, I was charged with stealing. They said if I repaid and pleaded guilty to 14 counts of false accounting, they would drop the theft, so the decision was made that I was less likely to go to prison for false accounting than I was for theft, so that's what I did. If I didn't plead guilty, they would have charged me for theft. I couldn't prove I didn't take anything, they couldn't prove I did, and at the time they told me I was the only person that had ever had problems with Horizon.

After some Members of Parliament raised concerns with the Post Office, it appointed an outside forensic accounting firm, Second Sight, to conduct an investigation. Second Sight found that the problems might have been due to unexpected interactions in the system: "an unusual combination of circumstances such as power and communication failures, or errors at the counter."

It also found that shortfalls might be explained by sophisticated attacks on ATMs perpetrated by cybercriminals who installed malware to circumvent built-in software controls. In fact, many of the unexplained cash machine shortages reported by sub-postmasters occurred on externally located ATMs run by the Bank of Ireland, which suggested a possible vulnerability common to those machines. But the complexity of the Horizon system obscured these potential issues for years. During that time, a number of sub-postmasters ended up bankrupt or jailed.

Despite Horizon's bewildering complexity and the growing number of complaints, Post Office managers maintained their faith in the system, disputing the conclusions of the Second Sight report. "After two years of investigation, it remains the case that there is absolutely no evidence of any systemic issues with the computer system," they insisted. But the issue remains unsettled: the Post Office is defending a class-action lawsuit brought by more than five hundred sub-postmasters, and the Criminal Cases Review Commission is investigating several convictions in which Horizon may have played a role.

As one MP concluded, the idea that "sub-postmasters and sub-postmistresses, who have worked tirelessly in their local communities, for decades in some cases, have suddenly all worked out that they can defraud the system is complete and utter nonsense." Or as a former sub-postmaster commented, "Some people have been jailed when it is obvious a complex computer system is at fault."

Chapter Three

# HACKING, FRAUD, AND ALL THE NEWS THAT'S UNFIT TO PRINT

"They didn't have to lie. All they had to do was
to obfuscate it with sheer complexity."

## I.

In 2010, a charming New Zealander named Barnaby Jack took the stage at Black Hat, a hacker conference held annually in Las Vegas. To his right stood two automated teller machines, cash machines identical to those found in bars and corner stores the world over. Jack, a security researcher, had spent years exploring the small computers inside ATMs. Until recently, manufacturers had tended to equate ATM security with physical protections, taking steps like storing cash inside a safe and bolting down machines. But with a few clicks of his computer mouse, Jack was about to demonstrate how fragile the ATMs' security was. He was about to show a room full of hackers how to get rich quick.

The crowd listened intently as Jack sketched out the technical details in a PowerPoint presentation. Then the fun began. To attack the first ATM, Jack wrote a program to hack into it remotely.

Though the machine still functioned like a normal ATM and would let customers withdraw cash, it also saved a record of their card numbers and let Jack download them.

He also created a backdoor, a hidden way to access the system. When he walked over to the machine, inserted a fake ATM card, and pushed a button, the machine began dispensing bills indiscriminately—without linking the withdrawal to any bank account.

He then turned to a second ATM and plugged a USB memory stick into the computer at the heart of the machine. The computer loaded his program, displayed the word "JACKPOT!!" in flashing letters on the screen, and blared catchy slot machine music as it dumped bills onto the floor. The crowd erupted in cheers.

But Jack, hailed as a genius by his peers, didn't break into ATMs to steal money. He was a "white hat" hacker—he broke into systems to help make them more secure. Before going public, he would turn his results over to manufacturers so they could fix the problems he found.

But not all hackers are so friendly. A few weeks before Christmas in 2013, hackers stole forty million credit card numbers from shoppers at Target, one of the world's largest retailers. They used credentials stolen from a heating contractor to enter Target's computer network and break in to cash registers in nearly eighteen hundred stores. They installed software on the registers to monitor every transaction and steal customers' credit card information.

We don't usually think of cash registers as computers. But, like ATMs, that's essentially what they are. Target's registers were connected parts of a large, complex system, so once hackers found a vulnerability, they were able to exploit it in every store. When Target announced that it had been hacked, its sales fell sharply and, within months, its CEO resigned.

It was an embarrassing fiasco, but hacked cash registers don't put lives at risk. A hacked car, on the other hand, is a different story.

# II.

*Whatever happens, don't panic.*

Andy Greenberg was driving down the highway at 70 miles per hour when the accelerator in his 2014 Jeep Cherokee stopped working. He stomped on the gas, but nothing happened. As the Jeep slowed to a crawl in the right lane and tractor trailers whizzed past him, he shouted into his cell phone, "I need the accelerator to work. Seriously, it's fucking dangerous. I need to move!" But the Jeep's stereo had been turned up to full blast, and the hackers on the other end of the phone couldn't hear him over the blaring hip-hop.

*Don't panic.*

The good news was that Greenberg was in the Jeep to write a magazine story, and the hackers weren't trying to hurt him. Greenberg writes about technology and security for *Wired*. The two hackers, Charlie Miller and Chris Valasek, sat miles away in Miller's living room. They laughed as Greenberg struggled with the ailing Jeep. After years of research, the pair had figured out how to use the Jeep's cellular internet connection to attack computers inside the car. Those computers controlled everything from the windshield wipers to the speedometer and brakes. Greenberg was now their test subject. They were attacking his transmission.

Two years earlier, the pair had invited Greenberg to sit behind the wheel of a different car they'd hacked. Back then, their attacks required a data cable connecting their laptop to the car's internal network. Sitting in the back seat, they shifted the car into automatic parking mode, made its steering wheel jerk uncontrollably, and disabled the brakes. When the two released details of these attacks at the 2013 Black Hat conference, auto manufacturers downplayed the threat. After all, the hackers needed a physical connection to the car.

But Miller and Valasek eventually figured out how to attack cars remotely. The two-ton Jeep sported a state-of-the-art entertainment system that controlled everything from the radio to the car's navigation and air-conditioning. It also connected to the internet and ran applications that searched for cheap gas and displayed reviews of nearby restaurants.

That connection allowed Miller and Valasek to hack the Jeep from Miller's sofa. First, they figured out how to access the entertainment system through the cellular network. They then used it as a foothold to access the car's other thirty-odd computers. At high speeds, they could disable the transmission. At low speeds, they could cut off the brakes and take control of the steering.

Greenberg pulled off at the next exit ramp and restarted the Jeep. He had expected the harmless demonstrations the pair had shown him years earlier. But this time was different. The hackers weren't in the back seat. And they didn't know there was no place for him to pull off the highway when they killed the transmission.

Despite the scare, it was a great story for Greenberg. Three days after *Wired* published his account, Chrysler acknowledged the security flaw, issued a recall of 1.4 million vehicles, and sent owners a USB drive they could plug into their dashboard to update the software and close the backdoor. But there are always more vulnerabilities: just a few months later, Miller and Valasek figured out how to take control of steering, cause unintended acceleration, and slam on the brakes—all at high speeds.

"The real threat," Greenberg explained, "comes from malicious actors that connect things together. They use a chain of bugs to jump from one system to the next until they achieve full code execution." In other words, they exploit complexity: they use the connections in the system to move from the software that controls the radio and GPS to the computers that run the car itself. "As cars add more features," Greenberg told us, "there are more opportunities for abuse." And there will be more features: in driverless cars, computers will control everything, and some models might not even have a steering wheel or brake pedal.

It's not just cars, ATMs, and cash registers that are vulnerable. After his presentation in Las Vegas, Barnaby Jack turned his attention to medical devices. Using an antenna and a laptop, he built a device that could hack into insulin pumps from hundreds of feet away. He could take control of the pump and inject the entire reserve of insulin, with potentially lethal results. His hack even disabled the vibration that normally warned of impending injection.

Jack also hacked implantable defibrillators. He figured out how to control these pacemaker-like devices remotely and deliver an 830-volt shock to a patient's heart. The attack showed up in the television series *Homeland*, when terrorists hacked the fictional vice president's pacemaker to assassinate him. Critics called the plot far-fetched. But Jack thought the show actually made the attack seem *too difficult*. Others took the threat seriously, too. Years before *Homeland* aired, Vice President Dick Cheney had his cardiologist disable the wireless functionality in Cheney's implanted device to avoid just such an attack.

This transformation of cars and pacemakers from offline devices into complex, connected machines is nothing short of revolutionary. And it's just the tip of the iceberg. From jet engines to home thermostats, billions of new devices are now part of a network often called the Internet of Things, a huge, complex system vulnerable to both accidents and attacks.

Several manufacturers, for example, already make "smart" washers and dryers that connect wirelessly to the internet. These appliances do clever things, like automatically reordering detergent and monitoring the cost of electricity to run only when rates are low. So far, so good. But think about the risks. If our smart dryer has a security flaw, hackers might be able to access it remotely, reprogram the software to overheat the motor, and cause a fire. If even just a thousand homes in a medium-size city had a vulnerable dryer, a hacker could wreak havoc.

The Internet of Things offers us a sort of Faustian bargain. On the one hand, it can allow us to do more—travel in driverless cars, increase engine reliability on airplanes, and save energy in our homes. On the other hand, it creates a path for hackers to do harm in the real world.

Attacks on cars, ATMs, and cash registers aren't accidents. But they, too, originate from the danger zone. Complex computer programs are more likely to have security flaws. Modern networks are rife with interconnections and unexpected interactions that attackers can exploit. And tight coupling means that once a hacker has a foothold, things progress swiftly and can't easily be undone.

In fact, in all sorts of areas, complexity creates opportunities for wrongdoing, and tight coupling amplifies the consequences. It's not just hackers who exploit the danger zone to do wrong; it's also executives at some of the world's biggest companies.

# III.

What would you need to start a small business—say, a produce stand that sells potatoes?

Let's start with the basics. You need the stand itself and somewhere to put it. You need potatoes to sell, of course, so you need a supplier, someone you buy your potatoes from. And you'll need some cash to give customers change. Tuber Temptations, a purveyor of fine potatoes, is born.

Success! Your potatoes are delicious, and people can't get enough of them. Food critics rave: "Tuber Temptations Thrives!" Business booms. You open more stands and hire employees to staff them. You start selling different varieties of potatoes and branch out into the sweet potato market. You even take out a loan that allows you to set up more stands and expand faster. Life is good.

But things have also gotten more complex. When you started, you could see your whole business—your one cash register and all the potatoes that you owned—in a single glance. Now you're struggling to keep everything straight. You have to pay closer attention to the cash in the registers because other people are selling your potatoes, and you need to make sure they're being honest. You also have to monitor your inventory. You don't want to run out of popular potatoes, but you also don't want to have so many potatoes that they start to go bad. And you have to make loan payments to the bank every month, no matter how many potatoes you sell.

All businesses, from your potato stand to big banks, have to keep track of these kinds of details. But as a business becomes more complex, so do the ways it counts its income, expenses, assets, and debts. When you're counting bills in the cash drawer or potatoes on the stand, it's clear how many there are. But when a big business is counting income from a set of future transactions or trying to figure out the value of a complex financial product, there is much more room for ambiguity.

Most of the companies we hear about in the news, those that trade on a stock market, have to disclose everything that's material to their business. Teams of external accountants check those reports to make sure they meet accounting standards. But even with audits and public disclosures, a big company's business is much harder to understand than your potato stand's. In Perrow's framework, a large company is more like a nuclear reactor than an assembly line. What goes on in the inside isn't directly observable.

---

TAKE A LOOK at these awards, all won by one company.

Year 1: Most innovative company in America (*Fortune* magazine)
Year 2: Most innovative company in America (*Fortune* magazine)
Year 3: Most innovative company in America (*Fortune* magazine)
Year 4: Most innovative company in America (*Fortune* magazine)
Year 5: Most innovative company in America (*Fortune* magazine)
Year 6: Most innovative company in America (*Fortune* magazine)
Year 7: eBusiness of the Year Award (The MIT Sloan School
   of Management)

Which company do you think it was? Amazon? Google? Apple? Maybe General Electric?

What if you knew that the company's chief financial officer was also singled out as an innovator?

Year 5: CFO Excellence Award for Capital Structure
   Management
Year 6: CFO of the Year Award

Maybe something in finance then, like Goldman Sachs or Citibank? What if we added that, just a few years later, the CFO pled guilty to federal crimes?

His name was Andy Fastow. The company was Enron.

Perhaps no group exploited complexity to its advantage more than Fastow and his colleagues at the helm of the energy giant Enron. They used so much accounting sleight of hand that, when they finally revealed what was going on, the entire company collapsed in a matter of weeks. Investors lost billions, and many employee retirement accounts were wiped out. It also became clear that Fastow had used complex financial structures to hide Enron's debt, inflate its profits, and surreptitiously pay himself tens of millions of dollars. Fastow, Enron CEOs Ken Lay and Jeff Skilling, and a slew of other executives were convicted of federal crimes.

"One way to hide a log is to put it in the woods," said Michigan congressman John Dingell. "What we're looking at here is an example of superbly complex financial reports. They didn't have to lie. All they had to do was to obfuscate it with sheer complexity."

The executives at the center of the Enron saga used complexity in two ways. First, they used it to make money. Complicated rules governed Enron's markets, and the company's traders knew how to capitalize on those rules. For example, California had replaced its regulated electricity sector with a market governed by staggeringly complex rules. Enron's traders took advantage of these rules by devising trading strategies, with names like "Fat Boy" and "Death Star," to game the market.

One strategy exploited price caps in California. To try to keep electricity affordable, California's grid regulator could cap the price. Because Enron traders could look at power prices across the whole region, they might buy power for $250 in California and send it out of state, where they could sell it for $1,200 per unit. They also gamed forecasts for electricity demand and used fictional movements of electricity to get paid without actually moving any power. They merely made a series of commitments on paper that canceled each other out and, in doing so, made money without generating any electricity. Worse still, traders called power plants that Enron operated and asked them to shut down so the price of electricity would spike. "We want you guys to get a little creative and come up with a reason to go down," one trader phoned a plant operator.

"Like a forced outage type of thing?" the operator asked.

"Right."

These strategies caused rolling blackouts and power emergencies in California, and cost the state $40 billion in added energy costs.

Enron executives also used complexity in a second key way: to hide what was happening in the business. Though they had made a ton of money in California, the company as a whole hemorrhaged cash. It struggled with a series of costly and ambitious projects, many in developing markets. A failed power project in Dabhol, India, for example, cost a billion dollars.

In most companies, such projects would have raised red flags. But Enron saw the undertaking, which was the world's largest foreign investment in India, as groundbreaking. Enron executive Rebecca Mark put it this way: "We are in the business of doing deals. This deal mentality is central to what we do. It's never a question of finding deals but of finding the kind of deals we like to do. We like to be pioneers."

For executives like Mark, it didn't matter whether their deals made money. They were paid bonuses based on estimates of how well a project *would do* rather than on the actual cash that came in. Enron used a special type of accounting called mark-to-market to keep track of its finances. Mark-to-market accounting let Enron executives replace the messy reality on the ground (like a billion dollars in expenses with no cash coming in) with rosy projections from optimistic financial models. At the very moment they signed a twenty-year contract to sell power in India, they counted all the money that they projected would come in.

To see how they used mark-to-market accounting, let's step back into the world of our potato stand for a moment.

Our potato stand accounts for how much money it makes based on how much cash it has. When a customer buys a potato for a dollar, we add that money into our bank account and subtract one potato from our inventory. Pretty straightforward.

Now let's imagine that the price of potatoes, across the whole world, is going up. Potatoes that used to cost a dollar apiece now cost two dollars. For our business, using traditional accounting methods, this increase in price will only be realized when we sell a potato—instead of paying us a buck, each customer will now pay us two dollars per potato.

But if we used mark-to-market accounting, as soon as the price of potatoes increased, our accounts would reflect the result of that increase: if we had owned one hundred potatoes when the price increased by a dollar, mark-to-market accounting would make it look like we made $100, *without actually having any new cash come in*. We're keeping our books based on what our inventory of potatoes is worth, not based on how much cash we're actually collecting.

Mark-to-market accounting makes sense for businesses like banks because they own stocks, bonds, and derivatives, which are easy to value and can be easily traded. In theory, mark-to-market accounting adds transparency. If something that the bank owns, like a stock, falls in value, the bank's books reflect that immediately. That said, we probably shouldn't use mark-to-market accounting for our potato stand. And it might also seem strange for Enron, which started as a natural gas pipeline company.

But Jeff Skilling, who joined Enron from the consulting powerhouse McKinsey, worked hard to transform Enron with his big idea: the company would no longer focus on running pipelines. Instead, it would run a kind of virtual marketplace for natural gas itself. Enron would be a middleman that bought and sold contracts—promises for the later delivery of natural gas. This new Enron, Skilling argued, was a trading company that should be allowed to use mark-to-market accounting for its energy trading business. In 1992, regulators agreed, and Enron didn't look back. That year, it became the largest buyer and seller of natural gas in North America. And over the next few years, it started using mark-to-market accounting in almost all of its businesses.

It did make sense for Enron to use mark-to-market for commodities, like natural gas, in which there was actually a market. But even when there wasn't a market, Enron built models to estimate the "fair value" of its assets. When the company undertook a big project, it built a model that showed how much money it *would* earn from it. The model accounted for the cost of the project, but it also included the money Enron would make from it over the next several years or even decades. After applying a few simple formulas and moving the transaction to a special Enron-owned company, mark-to-market accounting let Enron executives treat the whole project as a profitable venture. Enron booked that "profit" immediately, without having received any payments. This buoyed the stock price and enriched executives like Rebecca Mark and Jeff Skilling. Mark-to-market let Enron's leaders convince themselves (and their shareholders) that they were doing better than they were.

But mark-to-market accounting didn't just increase complexity; it also turned Enron into a tightly coupled system. Under mark-to-market accounting, the company could take years of potential profits from a deal and record them immediately. That resulted in a bump in earnings for the quarter in which the deal was signed. But, because that revenue had already been recognized, it did not contribute to future earnings. Every quarter was a blank slate, and since investors expected growth, bigger and bigger deals had to be done. Even a short interruption in deals would shake investor confidence. There was no slowing down.

And Enron still needed real money—for salaries, to buy companies, and to build its ambitious projects. So it borrowed. But that could be risky. If investors knew how much debt it was accumulating, Enron might seem like it was on shaky financial ground. So it used convoluted transactions to hide the debt. At one point, for example, it borrowed nearly $500 million from Citibank. It then created a series of transactions—all between companies Enron itself owned—and exploited the accounting rules to make it look like the loan was actually profit. It was like getting a cash advance on a credit card, depositing the money in a checking account, hiding the fact that you even have that credit card, and pretending that the money was your salary. For a while, it looks like you're making a lot of money. But it's just an illusion. You still have to repay the loan. A month later, Enron reversed all the transactions and returned the money to Citibank along with a handsome fee. Over and over, Enron ran this shell game with its investors.

By the year 2000, Fastow and his predecessors had created over thirteen hundred specialized companies to use in these complicated deals. "Accounting rules and regulations and securities laws and regulation are vague," Fastow later explained. "They're complex. . . . What I did at Enron and what we tended to do as a company [was] to view that complexity, that vagueness . . . not as a problem, but as an opportunity." *Complexity was an opportunity.*

But in March 2001, the house of cards began to fall. Short seller Jim Chanos took a look at Enron's financial statements and made a bet against the company. He tipped off *Fortune* reporter Bethany McLean, who dug deeper and published a story under the headline "Is Enron Overpriced?" The subtitle read: "It's in a bunch of complex businesses. Its financial statements are nearly impenetrable."

The article tried to describe how Enron made money. "But describing what Enron does isn't easy," McLean wrote, "because what it does is mind-numbingly complex." One droll banker put it differently: "Running a pipeline business can't take much time—Enron seems to spend all its available man hours on various, convoluted financing schemes."

By that October, Enron had to revise its financial statements. It acknowledged $1 billion in losses it had ignored and erased nearly $600 million in bogus profits. In meetings with investment bankers, Enron executives revealed that the company's true debt was not $13 billion (as it had disclosed publicly) but more like $38 billion. The missing debt had been cleverly hidden in Enron's 1,300 special-purpose companies. Less than a month later, Enron filed for bankruptcy.

Enron's fall from grace produced a web of collateral damage. Arthur Andersen, the accounting firm that signed off on Enron's books, was indicted on federal charges and shut down. And it soon became clear that some of the world's biggest investment banks had helped Enron exploit complexity and deceive shareholders. Citibank and JP Morgan Chase each paid over $2 billion to regulators and shareholders for their part in the deceptions—this on top of the money they lost in the Enron bankruptcy itself.

And for Enron employees, the consequences were brutal. Twenty thousand people lost their jobs, and many also lost their retirement savings. There was no buffer in the system to protect them from the fallout.

IN 1927, Owen Young, the chairman of General Electric, gave an address at Harvard Business School—the very institution from which Enron CEO Jeff Skilling would graduate decades later. The law, Young said, "functions in the clear light of wrong doing—things so wrong that the community must protect itself against them." Opposite wrongdoing, he continued, lies rightdoing, "things which are so generally appealing to the conscience of all that no mistake could be made no matter how complicated the business."

For businesses, the difficulty lies in the shadowy in-between. "When business was simple and local, it was fairly easy for local public opinion to penetrate the shadowed area," Young said. "When business became complicated and widespread, it was in this area that all restraints were removed. It was in this shadowed space that troublesome practices were born."

At Enron, clever executives exploited the shadowy place between wrongdoing and rightdoing. As Fastow put it, "You have a complex set of rules, and the objective is to use the rules to your advantage." The same deals that got him his CFO of the Year award, he joked, also got him his prison ID card.

Of course, Enron wasn't the only company that used complexity to hide wrongdoing. Far from it. Similar accounting scandals rocked Japanese conglomerates Toshiba and Olympus, Dutch grocery chain Ahold, Australian insurance firm HIH, and Indian IT giant Satyam. More recently, Volkswagen exploited complexity to game emissions tests and hide the dangerous level of pollution from its "clean diesel" cars. But using complexity to cheat, as we will see, isn't limited to the corporate world.

# IV.

What do you notice about these articles from the *New York Times*? (The bold font is our emphasis.)

# RETRACING A TRAIL:
# THE INVESTIGATION

## U.S. Sniper Case Seen as a Barrier to a Confession

OCT. 30, 2002

State and federal investigators said today that John Muhammad had been talking to them for more than an hour on the day of his arrest in the sniper shootings, **explaining the roots of his anger,** when the United States attorney for Maryland told them to deliver him to Baltimore to face federal weapons charges and forcing them to end their interrogation.

**The investigators said an F.B.I. agent and a Maryland detective had begun to develop a rapport with Mr. Muhammad.** The other suspect, Lee Malvo, 17, being questioned by a Montgomery County detective, was not answering any questions, the investigators said.

"It did not look like the juvenile was going to talk," a local law enforcement official said. "But it looked like **Muhammad was ready to share everything, and these guys were going to get a confession.**"

...

# A NATION AT WAR: MILITARY FAMILIES

### Relatives of Missing Soldiers
### Dread Hearing Worse News

MARCH 27, 2003

**Gregory Lynch Sr. choked up as he stood on his porch here overlooking the tobacco fields and cattle pastures, and declared that he remained optimistic**—even though a military official had just come by to warn him to brace himself, that even worse news could be coming any day now.

It is hard to imagine, he says, any worse news than what he learned on Sunday night: his 19-year-old daughter, Pfc. Jessica Lynch, had been in the Army convoy that was ambushed in southern Iraq.

...

**Mr. Lynch seemed distracted as he stood on the porch of his hilltop home here looking into the tobacco fields and pastures.** He talked about the satellite television service that brought CNN and other cable news networks into his home, his family's long history of military service and the poor condition of the local economy.

...

# A NATION AT WAR: VETERANS

## In Military Wards, Questions
## and Fears From the Wounded

APRIL 19, 2003

Lance Cpl. James Klingel of the Marines finds himself lost in
thought these days when he is not struggling with the physical
pain, his mind wandering from images of his girlfriend back
in Ohio to the sight of an exploding fireball to the sounds of
twisting metal.

...

In the worst moments, though, Corporal Klingel, a scout,
**said he questioned the legitimacy of his emotional pain** as
he considered the marine in the next bed, Staff Sgt. Eric Alva,
a distance runner whose right leg was blown off by a land
mine, or Seaman Brian Alaniz, **a Navy medic down the hall
who lost his right leg** when a mine exploded under him as he
rushed to aid Sergeant Alva.

"It's kind of hard to feel sorry for yourself when so many
people were hurt worse or died," said Corporal Klingel, 21,
**who added that it was about time for another appointment
with a chaplain.**

...

These stories embody the style of the modern newspaper. They don't just report facts. They put us in the center of emotional stories. You are in the room with the frustrated investigators who resent the petty jurisdictional squabbles that got in the way of a confession; on the porch with a grieving father coping with the unknown fate of his daughter and reflecting on his life; and in the hospital room with a wounded marine, traumatized by his time in Iraq and struggling to come to grips with his emotional pain.

All these articles were written at a tense time in the United States, soon after the burst of the dot-com bubble and the terrorist attacks of 9/11. In October 2002, a sniper began killing people at random around Washington, DC, and in March 2003, the United States invaded Iraq. At the same time, newspapers struggled to adapt to the forces transforming their industry. The rise of the internet and the proliferation of free content undermined long-standing business models. Even though the *Times* had just won seven Pulitzer Prizes, the paper couldn't field enough reporters to cover the news.

But there's something else at work in these stories. They were all written by Jayson Blair, an ambitious young reporter. And they were all fabricated.

Blair, who started as an intern at the paper, impressed some of his bosses with the speed at which he churned out pieces and was soon promoted, eventually to a full-time reporter. But his performance was inconsistent. Editors criticized him for sloppy reporting. His correction rate was "extraordinarily high by the standards of the paper," according to one editor. And even as he put in long hours, he struggled with a drinking and drug problem. By April 2002, things had gotten so bad that Jonathan Landman, the metropolitan editor, wrote to two of his colleagues: "We have to stop Jayson from writing for the Times. Right now."

When Blair returned from a leave of absence, he seemed rehabilitated. Editors initially kept him on a tight leash and had him focus on shorter assignments. But Blair chafed under the restrictions and lobbied for a job in a different part of the paper. He moved from the metro to the sports desk, and then, amid the Washington sniper case, to the national desk. In Washington, his deception took off.

Blair's front-page exclusive on the interrupted sniper confession prompted controversy. Law enforcement officials publicly denied his conclusions, and veteran reporters raised concerns. It soon became clear that, contrary to what Blair wrote, investigators weren't on the verge of obtaining a confession—they were negotiating with the suspect about mundane matters like lunch and a shower.

Other articles fabricated trivial details. Blair never visited Gregory Lynch's house, which didn't overlook tobacco fields or cattle from a hilltop vantage point. It was in a valley with no tobacco in sight. And Blair's interview with the injured marine happened over the phone after the marine was home, not in the hospital, as Blair wrote in the article. Moreover, the marine and the navy medic named in the article were never in the hospital at the same time, and Blair simply made up the quotes.

But the *Times* didn't suspect the deception until a reporter at the *San Antonio Express-News* complained that Blair had plagiarized one of her articles. After that accusation, editors began to dig deeper.

At first, they assumed it was a simple case of plagiarism. Blair claimed he had mixed up his notes. But editors soon learned a stunning truth: not only had Blair plagiarized the story, but it also seemed he'd lied about having even taken the trip to Texas. "People would kill to get these assignments, to get a chance to go and talk to and write about people around the country," said the *Times*'s media editor. "And here was this guy that might not even have bothered to get on a plane?"

When a group of seasoned *Times* reporters investigated, they discovered that what started as sloppy reporting had transitioned into full-blown fraud. Blair emailed his editor with updates on in-person interviews he was conducting on the road—updates that, in reality, he sent from New York City. He expensed meals with sources who didn't exist and turned in receipts from Brooklyn restaurants when he was supposedly in Washington, DC. And he never submitted expenses for travel or hotels, even after filing months of articles from the road.

We might look at Blair and conclude that he's a bad apple. That's certainly part of the story. But William Woo, a journalism professor at Stanford and a retired editor, saw echoes of Chick Perrow's ideas in the fraud. "News organizations," he wrote, "are characterized by interactive complexity." Blair's deception was a failure of the system, Woo argued: he got away with it for so long because of the complexity of modern journalism.

Editors celebrate vivid writing, like Blair's account of the emotional scene on Gregory Lynch's West Virginia porch. But like the core of a nuclear power plant, the truth behind such writing is difficult to observe. And research shows that unobservability is a key ingredient to news fabrications. Compared to genuine articles, falsified stories are more likely to be filed from distant locations and to focus on topics that lend themselves to the use of secret sources, such as war and terrorism; they are rarely about big public events like baseball games. Indeed, Blair's stories were often filed remotely and covered sensitive topics using unnamed sources and private interviews. And the sheer volume of information flowing through the newsroom meant that, in essence, editors depended on Blair to fact-check himself.

Blair also exploited organizational complexity to hide his fraud. The *Times* had a notoriously fragmented newsroom. Editors from different desks feuded; some didn't even speak to each other. Blair found these cracks and slipped through them. When he moved to the national desk to cover the DC sniper, his new bosses didn't know that there had been concerns about his performance.

Blair gamed the complexity of the organization in other ways, too. Take his expense reports. It wasn't the job of the administrative assistants who processed his expenses to know where he was supposed to be writing from. And it wasn't the job of his editors, who actually sent him on assignment, to review his receipts. So the contradictions in Blair's expense reports went unnoticed.

The scandal undermined readers' trust in the paper and roiled an already dysfunctional newsroom. Complexity had struck again.

SO FAR IN this book, we've examined the shared DNA of nuclear accidents, Twitter disasters, oil spills, Wall Street failures, and even wrongdoing. Complexity and coupling make these failures more likely and more consequential, and our brains and organizations aren't built to deal with these kinds of systems. And though many of the systems we've looked at give us tremendous benefits, they also push us deep into the danger zone.

We can't turn back the clock and return to a simpler world. But there are things we can all do—some small, some big—to make meltdowns less likely. We can learn how to build better systems, improve our decisions, and make our teams more effective in the face of complexity.

How? That's the question we take up in the second part of the book.

Part Two

# CONQUERING COMPLEXITY

## Chapter Four

# OUT OF THE DANGER ZONE

*"La La Land!"*

## I.

Glitz. Glamour. Complexity. Confusion.

It's the conclusion of the 89th Academy Awards, and actors Warren Beatty and Faye Dunaway are about to hand out the final Oscar of the evening. Beatty opens the red envelope, takes out a card, and looks at it. He blinks rapidly. Eyebrows raised, he searches inside the envelope again, but it's empty. He looks again at the card in his hand.

"And the Academy Award . . ." He stares at the camera for a good three seconds. Again, he reaches inside the envelope. ". . . for Best Picture . . ." He looks at Dunaway, who laughs, chiding him, "You're impossible!"

She thinks it's a bit, that he's milking the moment. He's not. He glances down at the card again, blinks, and shows it to her, as if to say, *Take a look at this.* Dunaway sees the card, and exclaims, *"La La Land!"* The audience erupts in cheers. The *La La Land* ensemble streams on stage, and producer Jordan Horowitz starts his speech, "Thank you, thank you all. Thank you to the Academy. Thank you to . . ."

At that moment, only two people in the world know that a mistake

has been made: Brian Cullinan and Martha Ruiz. They're both partners at the accounting firm PricewaterhouseCoopers (PwC). In the
week leading up to the Oscars, they tabulated the votes and stuffed
the winning cards into envelopes for each category. At the start of
the show, Cullinan and Ruiz positioned themselves backstage—one
standing stage right, the other stage left. They had identical leather
briefcases with the letters PwC and a flashy Oscar logo on them.
Each briefcase had twenty-four envelopes in it, one for every award
category.

A few weeks before the show, Cullinan and Ruiz described the
setup in a blog post:

### If something were to happen to the ballots, what is the backup system?

You can't be too careful! We have two sets of results envelopes, each packed in its own briefcase—one for each of us.
The morning of the awards we arrive separately at the show.
LA traffic can be unpredictable! At the event, we are both
backstage to hand the envelopes to the presenters.

We also memorize Every. Single. Winner. In. Every. Single. Category. The winners' names are not typed into a computer or written down, to avoid potential lost slips of paper or
breaches of security.

During the show, the accountants hand the envelopes to the presenters. As Cullinan put it, "We have to make sure that when we reach
into our briefcase that we hand the right one. . . . It's not rocket science, but with all the things going on, you do have to pay attention."

Minutes before the flubbed Best Picture announcement, Ruiz
gave the Best Actress envelope to Leonardo DiCaprio, who announced Emma Stone's win for her role in *La La Land*.

Then Cullinan's attention slipped. He tweeted a picture of Emma

Stone backstage and, around the same time, handed Beatty the next envelope in his briefcase. But it wasn't the envelope for Best Picture. It was his *copy* of the Best Actress award, the twin of the envelope that Ruiz had given DiCaprio. The card inside looked something like this:

---

The
OSCARS.

**EMMA STONE**
**"LA LA LAND"**

_Actress in a Leading Role_

---

It wasn't until Beatty was on stage, once he opened the envelope, that he realized that something was wrong, and he wasn't sure what to do. He showed the card to Dunaway, as if to enlist her help, but all she saw was *La La Land*, and that's what she blurted out.

As the *La La Land* producers made their speeches, a stage manager in a headset moved amid the throng. Then the accountants arrived onstage. A bunch of red envelopes were passed back and forth. Two and a half minutes into the speeches, *La La Land* producer Jordan Horowitz retook the microphone. "Guys, I'm sorry, no, there's a mistake. *Moonlight*, you guys won Best Picture . . . this is not a joke." He held the correct card up to the camera:

---

The
OSCARS.

**"MOONLIGHT"**
**ADELE ROMANSKI, DEDE GARDNER**
**AND JEREMY KLEINER, PRODUCERS**

_Best Picture_

---

"*Moonlight*. Best Picture."

At the glitzy after-party, a reporter found Cheryl Boone Isaacs, the Academy president, sitting on a white sofa, staring at her phone. He asked her what had gone through her mind during the debacle. "Horror," she responded.

> I just thought, What? What? I looked out and I saw a member of Pricewaterhouse coming on the stage, and I was, like, Oh, no, what—what's happening? What what WHAT? What could possibly . . . ? And then I just thought, Oh, my God, how does this happen? How. Does. This. Happen.

Though this was an embarrassing moment for the Academy and PwC, no one died because of the mishap. In the scheme of things, it was a pretty minor system failure. But it still teaches us something important.

As Cullinan said before the fiasco, handing out cards to celebrities wasn't rocket science. But it *was* challenging. The winners were secret until the moment they were announced, which added to the drama—and the complexity. And the high-profile audience and live television broadcast made the whole event tightly coupled.

The system had three big weaknesses. First, the category names on the envelopes were hard to read. They were printed in subtle gold lettering on a red background, so it was difficult to notice that Cullinan had handed Beatty the Best Actress envelope instead of the Best Picture one. And, on the cards, the category was at the very bottom, in tiny font. The name of the award winner (Emma Stone) and the title of the movie (*La La Land*) were both printed in large font. When Beatty showed Dunaway the card, she took a brief glance and saw *La La Land* prominently displayed.

Second, the accountants had a surprisingly hard job. It was chaotic backstage and, as Cullinan presciently put it, "you do have to pay attention." Some of the presenters got their envelopes from Ruiz, others from Cullinan. And there were lots of distractions— Cullinan's temptation to tweet celebrity pictures among them.

But the most interesting weakness had to do with PwC's two-briefcase system. You can see the logic: having two copies of every envelope protected PwC from some of the failures that they foresaw, like one of the accountants losing a briefcase or the other getting stuck in traffic. But the redundancy, intended as a safety feature, *added complexity*. All those extra envelopes created the potential for unexpected interactions in the system. There were more things to keep track of, more moving parts, more distractions—more ways for failure to creep in.

Charles Perrow once wrote that "safety systems are the biggest single source of catastrophic failure in complex, tightly coupled systems." He was referring to nuclear power plants, chemical refineries, and airplanes. But he could have been analyzing the Oscars. Without the extra envelopes, the Oscars fiasco would have never happened.


DESPITE PERROW'S WARNING, safety features have an obvious allure. They prevent some foreseeable errors, so it's tempting to use as many of them as possible. But safety features *themselves* become part of the system—and that adds complexity. As complexity grows, we're more likely to encounter failure from unexpected sources.*

Redundancies aren't the only kind of safety feature that backfires. One study of bedside alarms in five intensive-care units found that,

---

* This is true on a larger scale, too. Passenger jets, for example, are required to carry supplemental oxygen as a safety feature for passengers, but that requirement contributed to the complexity that was at the center of the ValuJet Flight 592 crash we explored in the prologue.

in just one month, there were 2.5 million alerts, nearly four hundred thousand of which made some sort of sound. That's about one alert *every second* and some sort of beeping every eight minutes. Nearly 90 percent of the alarms were false positives. It's like the old fable: cry wolf every eight minutes, and soon people will tune you out. Worse, when something serious *does* happen, constant alerts make it hard to sort out the important from the trivial.

It's counterintuitive: safety features reduce safety. Few people are as attuned to this irony as Dr. Bob Wachter, a physician and writer at the University of California, San Francisco (UCSF). In his book *The Digital Doctor*, Wachter recounts the case of Pablo Garcia, a teenage patient who nearly died when a nurse accidentally gave him an enormous dose of an antibiotic.

In 2012, UCSF adopted a new computerized system. It was integrated with a futuristic room-sized pharmacy robot that sported mechanical arms and packaged medication from presorted drawers. Doctors and nurses hoped that the technology would eliminate clerical errors and improve patient safety. "Computerized ordering would make a doctor's handwriting as irrelevant as scratches on a record album," Wachter wrote. "A pharmacy robot could ensure that the right medication was pulled off the shelf, and that the dose was measured with a jeweler's precision. And a bar-coding system would render the final leg in this relay race flawless, since it would signal the nurse if she had grabbed the wrong medication or was in the wrong patient's room."

These are great safety features, and they eliminated many common errors. But they also added a lot of complexity. In Garcia's case, the trouble began when the interface of the ordering system—which was designed to eliminate clerical mistakes—confused a young pediatrician. She thought she'd ordered just one 160 mg pill. But she had actually entered the order as 160 mg/kg, so the system multiplied her dosage by Garcia's weight of 38.6 kilograms. *She ordered 38½ pills.*

A warning system kicked in, and an overdose alert appeared on the computer. But the doctor clicked out of it because unnecessary warnings popped up on the screen all the time. The pharmacist who checked the order (electronically, of course) also missed the mistake. The million-dollar pharmacy robot happily packaged the pills. And, though the nurse who came to Pablo Garcia's room had some doubts about the huge dose, another safety device, the bar-coding system, told her she was in the right room with the right patient. This put her worries to rest, and she had the boy take the pills—all 38½ of them.

Bells and whistles and redundancies eliminate some errors, but they also fuel complexity and can cause spectacular meltdowns. Yet when we react to big failures—even ones in which complexity played a role—we are tempted to add *even more* safety features. During a discussion about the overdose, one of Wachter's colleagues mused, "I think we need to build in just one more alert here." Wachter practically shouted in response: "The problem is that we have too many alerts. Adding another only makes it worse!"

He's right. The apparently obvious solution—piling on more and more safety features—doesn't work. So where does that leave us? How do we make systems better?

Diagnosis is a good first step. Perrow's complexity/coupling matrix helps us figure out if we are vulnerable to baffling accidents or unexpected acts of wrongdoing. "The matrix tells you where in your project or business you should expect a nasty surprise," said Gary Miller, a nuclear engineer turned management consultant who has become something of an evangelist for Perrow's framework at his firm.

Miller gave the example of a retailer that's planning to open a bunch of new stores. "Do you have a very tight launch schedule and no margin for error? That's tight coupling. Do you also have a complicated inventory system so it's very difficult to monitor things directly? That's complexity. If you have both, you know that a crazy failure will happen at some point, so you know you need to change things before you launch."

A crucial point, Miller argued, is that Perrow's matrix is helpful even though it doesn't tell us what exactly that "crazy failure" will look like. Simply knowing that a part of our system—or organization or project—is vulnerable helps us figure out if we need to reduce complexity and tight coupling and where we should concentrate our efforts. It's a bit like wearing a seatbelt. The reason we buckle up isn't that we have predicted the exact details of an impending accident and the injuries we'll suffer. We wear seatbelts because we know that something unforeseeable might happen. We give ourselves a cushion of time when cooking an elaborate holiday dinner not because we know *what* will go wrong but because we know that *something* will. "You don't need to predict it to prevent it," Miller told us. "But you do need to treat complexity and coupling as key variables whenever you plan something or build something."

Perrow's matrix tells us if we're headed for dangerous territory—and then it's up to us to change course. In the rest of this chapter, we'll explore how to do just that. We'll look at cases when people managed to make a system—an airplane, a climbing expedition, even a bakery—less complex or less tightly coupled.

## II.

"The Airbus A330 is unbelievably beautiful to look at, from nose to tail," writes KLM pilot Thijs Jongsma in a blog entry that amounts to a love letter to the airplane. "She stands extremely tall. When she's on the ground, she leans slightly forward, as if she's ready to break into a sprint at any moment. When she's cruising, the nose lifts a bit, all of which gives it just a little bit more elegance. . . . She's the most beautiful aircraft I've ever flown."

The cockpit, too, is a masterpiece. It has a sleek, streamlined design with just a few screens, an ergonomic layout, and a clever system of color coding for the various displays and panel lights. "Did I already mention that Porsche designed many of the instruments in the cockpit?" writes Jongsma. "It's no wonder that the shape, color, and lighting are so beautiful."

Then there is the ease of control. Instead of a yoke—a conventional control wheel in front of each pilot—the A330 features small sidestick controllers, which look like joysticks on a video game console.

The sidesticks are linked to the plane's computers, so once pilots give a command—a fifteen-degree right turn, for instance—they can just let go of the stick, and the plane will execute the task perfectly. And the sidesticks take up very little space and don't obstruct the instrument panel. "As there is no longer a steering wheel, there is space for a table which can be folded tidily under the instrument panel," writes Jongsma below a photo of his lunch neatly arranged on a tray table. "There is no other KLM aircraft that allows pilots to work and eat at a table!"

Now take a look at the cockpit of a Boeing 737:

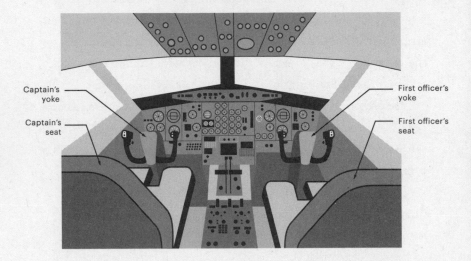

This cockpit has no sleek sidesticks, let alone tray tables. In front of each pilot, there is a large W-shaped control yoke mounted on a three-foot-tall control column. Pilots roll the plane by turning the yoke left or right. To lower the nose, they push the entire control column forward; to raise the nose, they pull the column back toward themselves. If necessary, they pull it all the way back—that's why their seats are split in the front. In comparison to the clever sidesticks in the Airbus, these controls seem oversized and awkward.

"When we fly the Boeing 737, we get these huge control wheels in front of us—and they're moving when either pilot moves them," says Ben Berman, the airline captain and accident investigator you met in the prologue. "The control wheels of the two pilots are physically connected, so if I turn mine left, the first officer's wheel also turns left. If I pull back hard, then the first officer's column will also move back and probably bump their knees or poke them in the belly."

As for a neatly arranged meal tray, forget about it. "The control wheel is so big that it's in your way when you're eating lunch," said Berman. "It makes you spill stuff on your shirt and tie all the time!"

In many ways, the Airbus A330 seems to have better design than the Boeing 737. It is ergonomic elegance versus bulky awkwardness—lunch served on a nifty tray table versus lunch spilled on your shirt. But if we look closer, it turns out there is something brilliant about the 737's old-school yoke and unwieldy control column.

In 2009, Air France Flight 447, an Airbus A330 carrying 228 people, crashed into the Atlantic Ocean, leaving no survivors. Five years later, AirAsia 8501—an Airbus A320 featuring a similar flight-control system as the A330—plunged into the Java Sea, killing all 155 passengers and seven crew members.

Those clever little sidesticks played a role in both accidents. Ultimately, both planes crashed because they went into an aerodynamic stall—a situation when the nose of the plane is pitched up at so steep an angle that there is not enough air flowing over the wings and, as a result, not enough "lift" to hold up the plane. There is a simple remedy for a stall: push the plane's nose down! But in both cases, a junior pilot, gripped by confusion and panic, *pulled back* on the sidesticks, raising the nose even higher. And in both cases, the other pilot failed to spot this fatal error.

"The two sidesticks don't move together, and the other pilot's sidestick is in a dark corner on the other side, so you really don't see what your colleague is doing," says Captain Berman. "Even if you somehow managed to look over, you'd have to look right when your colleague is moving the stick—otherwise you won't see it."

This just wouldn't happen in a cockpit with those old-fashioned yokes that move together. If your copilot pulls back on that big control column, you can't miss it. It is literally in your face and likely hitting you in the stomach. And that reduces complexity because it makes what's happening clearly visible.

But you needn't go further than your car to appreciate the power of transparency. *Star Trek* actor Anton Yelchin died when he got out of his Jeep Grand Cherokee and the 4,500-pound car rolled down his driveway and pinned his body against a brick pillar. The cause of the accident was traced to the Jeep's gearshift design. With normal gearshifts, you can *feel* and *see* the shifter's position when you change gears. But in the Jeep, the driver simply pushed forward or backward on the sleek Monostable shifter to change gears, and then the shifter returned to the center. The lack of feedback confused hundreds of drivers, making them believe that they had put the car in park when it was actually in neutral or reverse.

There is value in elegant designs. They're beautiful to look at and fun to play with. But there is also tremendous value in being able to see the state of a system by simply looking at it. Transparent design makes it hard for us to do the wrong thing—and it makes it easier to realize if we *have* made a mistake. Transparency reduces complexity and gives us a way out of the danger zone.

The same goes for all sorts of systems, not just physical ones. Remember mark-to-market accounting, which obscured what Enron was up to? It turned the company into a black box. And trusting a black box—no matter how sleek and shiny—can cause disaster.

BRINGING DAYLIGHT into a system isn't always possible—and it isn't the only way to reduce complexity. Consider a climbing expedition to Mount Everest. There are many hidden risks, from crevasses and falling rocks to avalanches and sudden weather changes. Altitude sickness causes blurred vision, and overexposure to UV rays leads to snow blindness. And when a blizzard hits, nothing is visible at all. The mountain is an opaque system, and there isn't much we can do about that.

But there are other ways to reduce complexity. In the past, logistical problems plagued several Everest expeditions. There were delayed flights, customs issues at the border, problems with supply deliveries, money disputes with local porters, and various respiratory and digestive ailments that climbers had developed during the trek to base camp. Many of these problems had surfaced weeks before the real climb even began, and they seemed to be small problems at the time.

But these little things caused delays, put stress on team leaders, took time away from planning, and prevented climbers from acclimating themselves to high altitudes. And then, during the final push to the summit, these failures interacted with other problems. Distracted team leaders and exhausted climbers missed obvious warning signs and made mistakes they wouldn't normally make. And if the weather turns bad on Everest, a worn-out team that's running behind schedule stands little chance.

Once we realize that the real killer isn't the mountain but the interaction of many small failures, we can see a solution: rooting out as many logistical problems as possible. And that's what the best mountaineering companies do. They treat the boring logistical issues as critical safety concerns. They pay a lot of attention to some of the most mundane aspects of an expedition, from hiring logistical staff who take the burden off team leaders to setting up well-equipped base camp facilities. Even cooking is a big deal. As one company's brochure put it, "Our attention to food and its preparation on Everest and mountains around the world has led to very few gastrointestinal issues for our team members."

Mountaineers understand that risk often comes from the complex interaction of small failures. Logistical improvements can't make Everest completely safe, but they make expeditions less complex and prevent a bunch of small failures that might otherwise blossom into a disaster.

It turns out that the solutions that work on Everest can also help us manage everyday situations where the stakes are lower, like hosting a Thanksgiving dinner. The problem there, too, is that a combination of small problems can cause big failures. Juggling the cooking alongside other tasks, from cleaning the bathroom to setting the table, adds stress and causes distractions. Harried hosts make silly mistakes, like the *Bon Appétit* reader from Chapter One who made her ice cream with cough syrup instead of vanilla.

Instead of just focusing on the cooking itself—the culinary equivalent of the summit push—we can look at the whole event as a system. Just like expedition companies, we can work to take care of small details before they become distractions. Before the big day, we can rake the yard and clean the bathroom. We can also make sure that we have all the ingredients we need: not just the obvious ones, but also things like salt, olive oil, and tin foil. By treating these mundane issues as key to a successful meal, we can prevent a Thanksgiving disaster.

In other systems, people have found a way to reduce complexity by removing unnecessary bells and whistles. Think back to the Boeing cockpit and take a look at the list below. It's a list of failures that can affect a large, multiengine jet. Which of these would you expect to trigger a high-level alert in the cockpit?

- Engine fire
- The approach to landing has begun but the landing gear is not down
- Impending aerodynamic stall
- Engine stops running

They all sound pretty bad, don't they?

But only one of these situations triggers the full arsenal of alarms in a modern Boeing cockpit. When an aerodynamic stall is imminent, red warning lights come on and a red text message appears on a cockpit screen. The control columns shake violently and loudly. Pilots see and hear and feel the warnings.

Other than a stall, nothing—not even an engine fire—activates all these alerts. An engine fire is a serious event, of course, but it might not affect the flight path immediately. Because of that, it triggers red warning lights, red text messages, and a distinctive bell sound, but doesn't shake the control columns.

There's an even lower level of alerts, called an "advisory," which produces an amber text message on the screen but nothing else, not even warning lights. Low fluid in one of the hydraulic systems falls into this category. Pilots need to know about it because they have to monitor the fluid quantity, but the situation is not urgent. If the fluid runs out completely, they will get a higher-level caution alert that illuminates more amber lights and makes more noise.

The principle is simple: don't overwhelm people by making a warning system—or, indeed, any system—more complex than it needs to be. Cut what you don't need and prioritize what you keep.* This is called a hierarchy of alerts. In the past, as planes were becoming more and more complex, warning lights began to appear all over the cockpit, and alarms were going off all the time. Thanks to the hierarchical approach, most flights these days don't have any alerts, and pilots are unlikely to be overwhelmed by trivial warnings.

No wonder that other industries are starting to take notice. "We formed a committee to review all of our alerts, pruning them one by one," writes Bob Wachter about his hospital's efforts to create a hierarchy of alerts. "This is painstaking work, the digital equivalent of weeding the lawn."

---

* Boeing engineers work very hard to trigger the right reactions, which sometimes requires an even more nuanced approach. For example, an engine that quits during the early portion of the takeoff roll requires quick reactions by the pilots to stop the airplane on the runway, so the warnings include red warning lights, a red text message, and a synthetic voice shouting "ENGINE FAIL." A few seconds later, as the plane accelerates, there isn't enough runway to stop, so the airplane automatically inhibits all these warnings except the text message. This is done to avoid triggering the pilots into trying to stop the plane when that cannot be done. And if an engine fails while the plane is in stable cruising flight, it only sets off amber lights, a beep sound, and an amber text message.

Sometimes, of course, it's impossible to reduce complexity—we can't always make things more transparent, get rid of small failures, and trim excessive safety features. But even in those cases, we can try to make things more loosely coupled.

Gary Miller, the management consultant you met earlier in this chapter, once worked on a project to revitalize a small chain of bakery cafés. The owners had been planning to open several new locations while also rolling out new menu offerings and a fresh look in their existing bakeries.

"It was a bakery—it's as different from Three Mile Island as it gets." Miller chuckled. "But in some ways, if you think about it, it wasn't that different."

He thought the renewal plan was too complex and tightly coupled. The new menu was long and complicated, and it meant that the company had to rely on an intricate network of suppliers. "They had these byzantine contracts with a bunch of new suppliers," Miller said. "Everything—breads, soups, sauces, fruit, drinks—was coming from different places, and it was hard to figure out how to navigate it all. Even the new store design was very complex." What's more, the timetable for the renewal plan was aggressive. The owners wanted to implement the whole transformation in all existing locations at the same time, while also opening several new bakeries. There was little margin for error.

Miller tried to convince the owners to remove some of the complexity—shorten the menu, streamline the supply chain, and simplify the new store design. But the owners wouldn't budge. They had already signed most of the necessary contracts, and they loved the new menu and design. Miller then tried something different. "I convinced them to slow down, relax the timetable, and not do all the stores all at once. It took a while, but they finally said OK."

Sure enough, given all the complexity, the launch didn't go perfectly. But because the plan now had some slack in it, the company was able to deal with the problems. "There were some rocky weeks," Miller reflected, "but it wasn't a disaster."

WHAT WE'VE SEEN in this chapter is that there are ways to simplify our systems, make them more transparent, and add slack to them. But this approach has limits. Flying will always have elements of complexity and coupling in it, as will medicine, deepwater drilling, and finance. You can probably think of plenty of reasons why the same is true in your own field and your own life.

Complexity and coupling, of course, have upsides. The bakery Gary Miller worked with benefited from a more complex and complete menu that gave customers more choices. When companies optimize their supply chains so that they don't have a lot of goods just sitting around, that saves money—but it also increases coupling. And many of the most useful technologies that shape how we live and work today are both complex and tightly coupled. There's no easy way out of the danger zone.

The good news is that we can be smarter about how we work, think, and live in this new world. Though we can't fundamentally change most systems, we can change *how we navigate within them*. In the coming chapters, we'll explore how we can make better decisions in the face of complexity; how we can learn from warning signs to find out where trouble is brewing in our systems; and how we can change the way we work with others to prevent meltdowns in the danger zone.

Chapter Five

# COMPLEX SYSTEMS, SIMPLE TOOLS

"It's a special exercise to question your own intuitions."

## I.

A tiny village called Aneyoshi lies in a cedar-lined valley on Japan's northeast coast. On a forested hillside next to the village's only road stands a stone tablet, carved with a warning:

> *Dwellings built on high ground will ensure the*
> *peace and happiness of our descendants.*
>
> *Remember the calamity of the great tsunami.*
>
> *Do not build homes below this point.*

Villagers erected the rock slab in the 1930s after they had moved the village uphill in the wake of a devastating tsunami. Tsunami stones like this one dot the Japanese coastline. Some were erected after a tsunami in 1896; others are even older. But after World War

II, people largely ignored these old warnings. Japan's population boomed, coastal towns grew, and many communities moved from higher ground to the seaside.

On March 11, 2011, when a massive earthquake struck off the coast, water from the resulting tsunami surged up the Aneyoshi valley, but stopped just a few hundred feet below the stone. Downhill, the waves destroyed everything.

Two hundred miles south of Aneyoshi lies the Fukushima Daiichi Nuclear Power Plant. When the earthquake struck, the plant's reactors shut down. Emergency generators turned on and began to cool the still-hot nuclear fuel. Everything seemed to be working as planned.

But less than an hour after the quake, the tsunami hit. The waves went over the plant's seawall and flooded the generators. The cooling system failed, and the reactors began to overheat and, soon after, melt down. A few generators sat higher up on a hillside, but the switching stations that were supposed to send power from them also got flooded. The brute force of nature clashed with a complex modern system. The result: meltdowns in three reactors, several chemical explosions, and the release of radioactive material into the air.

It was the world's worst nuclear accident in twenty-five years. But it was preventable. The Onagawa Nuclear Power Plant, for example, was much closer to the epicenter of the earthquake, but it survived mostly unscathed—even as the tsunami destroyed the surrounding towns. The Onagawa plant shut down safely. In fact, during the tsunami, hundreds of people from nearby communities found refuge *at the plant.* "At that time," one of them recalled, "there was no better place than the nuclear plant." *There was no better place than the nuclear plant.*

What made Onagawa so different? Three Stanford researchers—Phillip Lipscy, Kenji Kushida, and Trevor Incerti—explored this very question. They found several factors at work, but one of the most critical was the height of Onagawa's seawall. As they put it, "The Onagawa power plant's 14 meter sea wall was adequate for a 13 meter tsunami, the same height as the tsunami that overwhelmed the 10 meter sea wall at Fukushima Daiichi." A higher wall, they wrote, "would have prevented or substantially mitigated the disaster at Fukushima Daiichi." A few meters would have made a huge difference.

Looking beyond Onagawa and Fukushima, Lipscy and his colleagues came to a chilling conclusion: Fukushima isn't unique. There are at least *a dozen* other nuclear power plants where the top of the seawall is lower than the highest recorded wave run-ups in the region. And these plants are all over the world: Japan, Pakistan, Taiwan, the United Kingdom, and the United States.

Imagine it's your job to decide how tall a nuclear power plant's seawall should be. How would you make that call? It's a difficult decision because it's the extremes that matter, not the averages. Obviously, you might say, you'd want the wall to be taller than the highest wave run-ups previously observed in the area. Fair enough, but then what? How much taller should it be?

It's a tough question. Adding height costs a lot of money, especially if you want the wall to be strong, not just tall. A 12-meter wall, which is shorter than the one in Onagawa, is already the size of a four-story building! And as the wall grows, more and more problems come up. Construction becomes more complex, people begin to complain about the views, maintenance costs skyrocket, and the wall soon becomes a big item on your list of things to worry about. Clearly, the wall can't be infinitely tall. So how do you decide?

You might say you'll make some calculations based on historical data on wave run-ups and maybe the output from tsunami models. But historical data don't always capture the worst case, and models have a lot of uncertainty. Because you can't build an infinitely tall wall, you try to come up with a number that you are *very sure* will work. You can't be 100 percent certain about it, but you can come up with an idea of the likely range of possible wave sizes. You can think about a reasonable range between the best case and the worst case. You might be, for example, 99 percent sure that the tallest wave to ever hit your wall will be between 7 and 10 meters. And then you make a decision about the wall's height based on that forecast.

Most of us don't make decisions about seawalls for nuclear plants, but this scenario should still feel familiar. We make forecasts like these all the time. It's the same kind of prediction that we make when we estimate the length of a project, or the time it will take to get to the airport on a day with bad traffic. We can't be 100 percent sure about these forecasts. To have perfect certainty, we'd have to say that the project will take between zero days and an infinite number of days to complete. That's not useful at all, so implicitly or explicitly, we use what's called a confidence interval—a range between a plausible best-case scenario and a plausible worst-case scenario. We might be 90 percent sure, for example, that our project will take two to four months to complete.

The trouble is that we're very bad at these forecasts. We draw the ranges too narrowly. As psychologists Don Moore and Uriel Haran put it, "Research on these types of forecasts finds that 90% confidence intervals, which, by definition, should hit the mark 9 out of 10 times, tend to include the correct answer less than 50% of the time." *When we are 90 percent sure about a forecast, we are right less than half of the time.* We feel very confident even though it's a toss-up. Likewise, when we are 99 percent confident, we end up being wrong much more often than 1 percent of the time. If you are 99 percent sure that the highest waves will be between 7 and 10 meters, you may be in for a nasty surprise.

Usually, when we're estimating something—like the length of a project—we focus on the two endpoints: we think about a likely best-case outcome (the project is done in two months) and a plausible worst-case scenario (it might take four months). Moore, Haran, and their colleague Carey Morewedge came up with a better method, which pushes us to consider a broader range of outcomes. It's called SPIES—an abbreviation of its full name: Subjective Probability Interval Estimates. Though it sounds a bit wonky, it's really quite simple. Instead of just thinking about the two endpoints, you estimate the probability of several possible outcomes—several intervals within the entire range of possible values. You first set up the intervals to cover *all* possible outcomes. Then, one by one, you think about how likely *each* interval is and write down your estimate. Like this:

| INTERVAL (Length of Project) | ESTIMATED LIKELIHOOD |
| --- | --- |
| Less than 1 month | 0% |
| 1–2 months | 5% |
| 2–3 months | 35% |
| 3–4 months | 35% |
| 4–5 months | 15% |
| 5–6 months | 5% |
| 6–7 months | 3% |
| 7–8 months | 2% |
| More than 8 months | 0% |

From these likelihood estimates, you can then estimate a confidence interval. If you want 90 percent confidence, for example, you'd ignore the intervals that give you a total of 5 percent probability on the lower end (the *less than 1 month* and the *1–2 months* intervals) and you'd also ignore the intervals that give you a 5 percent total probability on the higher end (the *6–7 months*, the *7–8 months*, and the *more than 8 months* intervals). Whatever is left is your 90 percent confidence interval: *2–6 months*. But you don't even need to make this last set of calculations. Moore and Haran created a nifty online tool where you can easily enter your intervals and estimates.* The tool does the rest of the work and computes range forecasts at any level of confidence you want. It's quick and easy.

Is SPIES perfect? No, but it does make a big difference. Here's Moore and Haran:

> Our studies consistently show that forecasts made using SPIES hit the correct answer more frequently than other forecasting methods. For example, in one study, participants used both [traditional] confidence intervals and SPIES to estimate temperatures. While their 90% confidence intervals included the correct answer about 30% of the time, the hit-rate of intervals produced by the SPIES method was just shy of 74%. Another study included a quiz of the dates in which various historical events occurred. Participants who used [traditional] 90% confidence intervals answered 54% of the questions correctly. The confidence intervals SPIES produced, however, resulted in accurate estimates 77% of the time.

By forcing us to consider the full range of possibilities, rather than just two endpoints, SPIES reduces our overconfidence and makes us less likely to overlook ostensibly improbable scenarios.

Unfortunately, the engineers at Tokyo Electric Power Company (TEPCO) who designed the Fukushima plant didn't consider the full range of possibilities. "TEPCO did not think a huge tsunami which exceeds anticipation could actually occur," a senior company official conceded after the accident. Despite the warnings of age-old tsunami stones and modern computer models, the company "did not have sufficient humility to consider the full impact of natural disasters."

---

* The SPIES tool is available at http://www.meltdownbook.net/spies

# II.

TEPCO's managers were overconfident. They also faced a tough challenge. Though they used sophisticated models to predict how big a tsunami would be, they didn't get a lot of feedback on how good their models actually were: most of the time, there were no tsunamis. Overall, of course, this was a good thing, but it made TEPCO's task harder.

TEPCO's engineers worked in what psychologists call a wicked environment. In such environments, it's hard to check how good our predictions and decisions are. It's like trying to learn how to cook without being able to taste the food. Without feedback, experience doesn't make us into better decision makers. We don't develop the skill to tell whether adding a tablespoon of salt will yield a bland soup or a salty mess.

Other types of problems—those in so-called kind environments—provide frequent feedback on how decisions turn out. In these environments, people *do* develop the ability to recognize patterns to make effective snap judgments. Chess masters, for example, quickly generate promising moves, while inexperienced players often miss the best opportunities, even after long deliberations. And meteorologists use their experience with the weather in a specific area to improve their forecasts. These experts get feedback all the time. Chess masters win or lose games, and weather forecasters regularly check the accuracy of their forecasts. They get to taste the metaphorical soup that they're making. Experts in kind environments can become the sort of intuition-wielding superheroes Malcolm Gladwell profiles in his book *Blink*, such as the fire captain who relies on his sixth sense to pull his men from a burning building before the floor collapses.

But people who work in wicked environments never get a chance to develop this kind of expertise. Research shows that their judgments don't get much better over time. In one experiment, for example, immigration officers accepted ID photos that didn't match the person they were looking at *one in seven times*. These experienced officers were just as bad as students who participated in the same experiment. Cops, too, aren't better at detecting lies than untrained students. And people in wicked environments often make decisions based on irrelevant factors. One study showed that during a busy day of hearing parole cases, judges—who rarely get independent feedback on their decisions—are much more likely to grant parole right after meal breaks. The difference was huge: the percentage of favorable rulings was around 65 percent right after a meal—but gradually dropped to nearly zero before the next break! Think about that for a moment: hunger isn't something that should affect an expert's judgment, is it?

To make things worse, experts who work on wicked tasks face little tolerance for errors. They are expected to be reliable, so it's hard for them to admit, discuss, and learn from mistakes. We don't mind a forecaster getting tomorrow's temperature wrong, but we don't want to think about cops arresting the wrong people and parole judges making arbitrary decisions.

It's not that firefighters and meteorologists are smarter than cops or judges. It's all about *what they have to do*. Meteorologists, for example, are good at short-term predictions of rainfall—something they get a lot of practice with—but they're not very good at predicting rare events like tornadoes. And even their rain forecasts are better in the winter (when the clouds that cause rain are stable) than in the summer (when heat causes big thunderheads to spring up).

Making decisions in complex systems is more like forecasting tornadoes and less like predicting rain. Complex systems are wicked environments: the effects of our decisions are hard to understand and learn from, and our intuition often fails us. The good news is that there are tools we can use when we need to stop following our instincts.

Consider how doctors diagnose a broken ankle when a patient limps into the emergency room. For a long time, physicians were misled by symptoms that didn't actually matter, like swelling. They ordered many more X-rays than they needed to, using them as a sort of diagnostic safety net. But those X-rays cost money—a lot of money when added up across everyone with an injured ankle—and exposed patients to unnecessary radiation. Doctors also *missed* severe fractures, skipping X-rays even when they were needed. They relied on their gut instincts, but they never got enough feedback to improve those instincts.

In the early 1990s, a team of Canadian physicians set out to change things. They ran a study to identify the factors that really mattered. The data showed that, by using only four criteria, doctors could cut the number of X-rays by a third but still catch every severe fracture. Take a look at what became known as the Ottawa Ankle Rules:

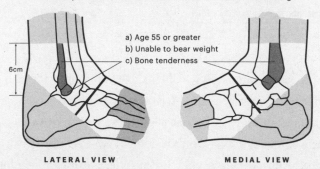

AN ANKLE X-RAY IS ONLY NECESSARY IF:

There is pain near the ankle bone AND one or more of the following

6cm

a) Age 55 or greater
b) Unable to bear weight
c) Bone tenderness

LATERAL VIEW          MEDIAL VIEW

Pain. Age. Weight bearing. Bone tenderness. Simple and predetermined, these criteria did much better than doctors' intuition.

Four simple questions turned every doctor into an expert diag-nostician.

Like the pre–Ottawa Ankle Rules doctors, we often use our gut instinct to make decisions with ad hoc, rather than predetermined, criteria. For example, think about how we usually pick who should run an important, high-risk project. We might consider a pool of potential project managers, intuitively compare them, and then make a choice. But that would be letting our gut feelings lead us astray in a wicked environment.

Instead, we should develop criteria based on *the project*. We first figure out the essential skills that the project manager will need to be successful. We then compare potential candidates along those criteria by simply scoring them with a 1, 0, or –1. If we're working with a group to make the decision, we independently score each per-son and then average the results. This gives us a numerical represen-tation of the overall strength of each person. Something like this:

| SKILL | AVERAGE RATING | | |
|---|---|---|---|
| | GARY | ALICE | SU-MI |
| Engineering understanding | 1 | 1 | .25 |
| Ability to connect with customer | -.25 | .5 | .75 |
| Ability to get internal buy-in | .5 | .75 | 1 |
| Total Score | 1.25 | 2.25 | 2 |

The process is simple, but it helps us avoid being blinded by a gregarious and personable employee who may lack the technical or organizational skills needed to succeed in the role (like Su-mi) or an engineering superstar who won't be able to connect with customers (like Gary). And, of course, your list of criteria can be much longer, and you might weight some items more heavily than others.

Lisa, a young mom in Seattle, and her husband used this method to find their first home. Before they started using predetermined criteria, they had looked at more than fifty houses but with no success. "Something about a house would really appeal to one of us but the other person wouldn't like it, and neither of us could explain their preference very well," Lisa told us. "And we were often fixated on little things—like ugly paint in a bedroom or some detail about the landscaping." Other times they became so smitten with a house that they forgot about their long-term goals. They imagined the fabulous dinner parties they could host and ignored the features of the house that made it unsuitable for a growing family. "What made it worse is that it's really tiring to go from house to house with a two-year-old," Lisa added. "You just want to be done. It's very easy to get tunnel vision."

After four futile months, the couple adopted a new approach. As the first step, they listed all the criteria that might matter to them, a dozen items ranging from the flow of the house to the quality of the neighborhood. Next, they prioritized the criteria using an online tool called a pairwise wiki survey. This tool randomly selected two criteria from their list, and each of them had to click on the item that they thought was more important:

---

## WHAT IS MORE IMPORTANT TO YOU?

Good flow                                    Quaint neighborhood

I can't decide

---

After making dozens of these choices, the tool calculated a score for each item, ranging from 0 (never preferred) to 100 (always preferred). "Good flow," for example, had a score of 79, which meant that it had a 79 percent chance of being chosen when paired with a randomly selected item from the list of criteria. The couple used these scores to weight the criteria.*

Then, when they saw a house, they independently gave a score of –1, 0, or +1 to each item. If they disagreed about a score, they took the average. The weighted sum gave them an overall score for each house. Here's an excerpt from their spreadsheet showing their actual ratings for a few houses:

| CRITERIA[†] | WEIGHT | HOUSE D | HOUSE J | HOUSE T |
|---|---|---|---|---|
| Functional features (3 bedrooms, guest space) | 89 | 1 | 1 | 1 |
| Good flow | 79 | 0.5 | 1 | 0.5 |
| Spaciousness | 73 | 0 | 1 | 1 |
| Potential for adding an Accessory Dwelling Unit | 67 | 1 | 1 | 1 |
| Connectedness with outdoors/natural environment | 62 | 1 | 1 | 0.5 |
| Feel of the home | 62 | 1 | -1 | 0.5 |
| Unlikely to need major maintenance | 61 | 1 | -0.5 | 1 |
| Value relative to price | 53 | 0 | 0 | 0.5 |
| Community feel of neighborhood | 65 | 0 | -1 | 0.5 |
| Quaint neighborhood | 57 | -1 | -1 | 0 |
| Neighbors | 54 | -1 | 0 | 0 |
| Total weighted score for house (maximum: 722) | | 269.5 | 155.5 | 450.5 |
| Total score for house as percentage (of 722) | | 37.3% | 21.5% | 62% |

Take a look at House D, for example. Lisa and her husband loved this house and gave it a bunch of +1 ratings. But, to their surprise, the total score ended up being quite low when they finished their calculations. "We liked many things about the house itself and almost fell in love with it," Lisa said. "But the scoring system made

---

* You can create your own pairwise wiki survey at www.allourideas.org.
† To simplify the process, the couple dropped a number of additional criteria that received very low ratings.

sure we also took into account the neighborhood, which wasn't a great one." Ultimately, the couple bought House T. Though it got fewer +1 scores than either D or J, it was solid on all dimensions and scored very well on some of the most heavily weighted items.

"This method helped us look past superficial details and our vague feelings," Lisa said. "It's just too complex to keep a dozen different criteria in mind at the same time, but with this tool, we could bring everything together into one whole picture. It also made our disagreements less emotionally charged—we were discussing concrete items rather than arguing over personal impressions."

Adding structure in this way doesn't make sense for every choice we make. But when facing an important decision in a wicked environment, it's a simple solution that makes a big difference.

## III.

In March 2013, when U.S. retail giant Target opened its first few stores in Canada, hundreds of curious shoppers and eager bargain hunters formed lines in the freezing predawn. Some people even camped out in tents. At 8:00 a.m., the doors opened. "I was going to be here at the grand opening of the Target, and I am! I'm so excited, so excited!" one woman said as she entered. Employees, wearing the company's traditional uniform of red shirts and khaki pants, clapped, cheered, and high-fived customers. "C'mon, guys, welcome to Target! C'mon, everybody, grab a cart!"

Target was well known in Canada long before it opened a single store, and Canadians would often cross the U.S. border to shop at its stores. To build up hype for its Canadian launch, Target aired a Canada-themed commercial during the Oscars. The company opened 124 stores in the country in less than nine months and entered every single Canadian province, even tiny Prince Edward Island.

Less than two years after its launch, Target closed all of its Canadian stores and pulled out of Canada. More than seventeen thousand people lost their jobs. By that time, Target Canada had racked up billions in losses. "Simply put, we were losing money every day," Target's CEO admitted. The Canadian press called the expansion a "spectacular failure," "an unmitigated disaster," and "the biggest failure of an American retailer in this country." It was a dramatic meltdown, so much so that a Canadian playwright has written a drama about it.

Target's expansion plan was bold. Rather than following a step-by-step approach, the company had acquired leases to more than one hundred retail spaces in a $1.8 billion real estate deal. There was pressure to launch as quickly as possible to avoid paying rent on empty stores. And landlords hated having large empty spaces in their malls, which ramped up the pressure even more. Target had committed itself to an ambitious timetable.

In other words, the Canadian expansion was a tightly coupled system from the start. "When you want to open that many stores in such a short period of time in a new country, the margin for error is very slim," said Joe Castaldo, a business journalist in Toronto who covered Target Canada's collapse. "So once one thing goes wrong, you don't have a lot of time to fix it because you have to open a new wave of stores in a couple of weeks."

The expansion was also complex. Moving to Canada required setting up a massive supply-chain management system to direct the flow of products from vendors to Target's warehouses, and from the warehouses to the stockrooms of stores and then to the store shelves. The system had to keep track of every single product and produce reliable data to help Target forecast demand, replenish stocks, and manage its distribution centers. In the United States, Target had a tried-and-true system for this. But Canada was different. The existing system would have required a lot of customization to work with French-language characters, the metric system, and the Canadian dollar. It just wasn't set up to work in another country.

In the interest of time, Target bought a ready-made supply-chain management system to use in Canada. It chose a German-made software that many retail experts considered the best in its class. It was a fancy, cutting-edge system, but it was hard to get used to. And few people at Target really understood it. Castaldo called it an "unforgiving beast."

To get the system up and running, employees had to enter data for seventy-five thousand different products. They often had dozens of fields to fill in for a single product, from product codes and measurements to the number of units that would fit into a shipping case. And this had to be done quickly, so there were plenty of opportunities for errors.

Sure enough, the employees made mistakes. These errors were mundane—typos, missed fields, product dimensions in inches rather than centimeters—but there were many of them. And the inventory management system wouldn't work properly unless it had accurate information for every product and the precise dimensions of every shelf in every store.

The myriad of little mistakes threw a big wrench in Target's supply chain. Products didn't flow to stores correctly, so when customers showed up, they found half-empty shelves. At the same time, because the expansion team overestimated demand, the warehouses were *overflowing* with goods. Target rented extra storage space, but that made it even harder to keep track of where everything was.

"Why did Target's distribution centers become so clogged so fast? Well, it turns out it doesn't take much for that to happen," Castaldo told us. "Everything needs to be moving in and out quickly to free up space for the next batch of goods, so one problem easily leads to another."

At one point, employees in the merchandising division spent two grueling weeks manually checking every line of product information in the system. But there were still too many errors. Stores were poorly stocked, shelves were empty, and customers got angry. And what managers in the Canadian head office saw on their computer screens didn't correspond to the reality on the ground—a sure sign of a complex system. "We almost didn't see what the customer was seeing," a former employee said. "We'd look on paper and think we're OK. Then we'd go to the store, and it's like, 'Oh my god.'"

The expansion turned into a huge mess. By early 2015, Target Canada was dead.

But in many ways, Target lost this battle much earlier—in 2011, when it signed the contract for store leases and committed itself to an aggressive timetable. Right around that time, Target's annual report described the anticipated risks of the Canadian move. It focused on a few generic factors, such as promotional programs, store remodeling efforts, and employee recruitment. There was no mention of the actual risks that would later thwart the expansion: the overly aggressive launch schedule, the complexity of the inventory system, the embarrassing data entry problems, and Canada's small quirks—like the metric system and the French characters—that turned into a huge pain. None of these things came up.

Of course, it's easy to be smart in hindsight. The rearview mirror, as Warren Buffett once supposedly said, is always clearer than the windshield. And hindsight always comes too late—or so it seems. But what if there was a way to harness the power of hindsight *before* a meltdown happened? What if we could benefit from hindsight in advance?

A COUPLE OF years ago, we surveyed sixty students a few weeks before their graduation from a top business school. It was a quick online survey with just one question. We gave the students a few minutes to write down what they saw as the greatest risks to the success of their school in the next few years. And we wanted to see if the wording of our question mattered, so we ran two slightly different versions of the survey. Half of the students saw our original question (Version #1), and the other half saw a tweaked version (Version #2).

Here's a random sample of the responses. Can you see any patterns?

| RESPONSES TO QUESTION VERSION #1 | RESPONSES TO QUESTION VERSION #2 |
| --- | --- |
| "Not enough practical training to students. We learn fewer hands-on skills than students elsewhere." | "Focusing too much on academics and too little on practical skills and career services." |
| "The program has a lot of competitors, and it cannot place students in good jobs every year." | "Academic scandals, such as students cheating in exams, damage the school's reputation." |
| "Our program does not combine classroom-based education with practical work experience." | "Artificial intelligence replacing many of the good entry-level jobs that our graduates used to go into." |
| "Few companies recruit from here compared to other schools. Not enough support for career preparation." | "Natural disaster damages the buildings. New laws make it too hard for foreign students to get visas." |
| "Competition from other schools and broader threats to the economy as a whole." | "More applied training at other schools. Online programs make in-person classes obsolete. The university's own economics department creates an applied program and absorbs our best students." |

As you can see, the responses to Version #1 are perfectly reasonable, though somewhat narrow. They're about external competition and the content of the program. They're classic student complaints: other schools do more, and the program isn't practical enough. These are sensible points, but check out the responses to Version #2. Here, too, the students talk about external competition and program content. But there is much more: *Cheating scandal! Natural disaster!*

*Artificial intelligence! Online education!* And the list goes on and on, from unexpected legal changes to competition from the university's own economics department. It's a more diverse set of risks. There are more out-of-left-field ideas.

So what's the difference between the two questions that led to these responses? The first one was a straightforward question you might ask when you try to get people to brainstorm about potential risks:

> Take a few minutes and think about the factors, trends, or events that pose the greatest threat to the viability and success of the school in the next two years—and write down everything that comes to mind.

The second version followed a different approach. It didn't focus on the risks that *might* come up. Instead, it asked people to imagine that it's two years later and a *bad outcome has already occurred*:

> Imagine that it's two years from today, and the school is really struggling. As a recent graduate, you constantly hear bad news about how things are going; in fact, the university might even eliminate the business program. Now, take a few minutes and imagine the factors, trends, or events that led to this outcome— and write down everything that comes to mind.

This question was based on a clever method called the *premortem*. Here's Gary Klein, the researcher who invented it:

> If a project goes poorly, there will be a lessons-learned session that looks at what went wrong and why the project failed—like a medical postmortem. Why don't we do that up front? Before a project starts, we should say, "We're looking in a crystal ball,

and this project has failed; it's a fiasco. Now, everybody, take two minutes and write down all the reasons why you think the project failed."

Then everyone announces what they came up with—and they suggest solutions to the risks on the group's collective list.

The premortem method is based on something psychologists call *prospective hindsight*—hindsight that comes from imagining that an event has already occurred. A landmark 1989 study showed that prospective hindsight boosts our ability to identify reasons why an outcome might occur. When research subjects used prospective hindsight, they came up with many more reasons—and those reasons tended to be more concrete and precise—than when they didn't imagine the outcome. It's a trick that makes hindsight work for us, not against us.

How? Here's an example from the study:

Consider predicting the winner of the first basketball game of a championship series. Before the game predicting the winner is based on general factors: match-ups between key players, team strengths and weaknesses, etc. . . . After the game it's a different story. The defeat of one team is explained both by these general factors and by specific events like Player A's early foul trouble, Player B's "off night," too much inactivity since the team won its previous series, etc.

*After the game, it's a different story.* If an outcome is certain, we come up with more concrete explanations for it—and that's the tendency the premortem exploits. It reframes how we think about causes, even if we just imagine the outcome. And the premortem also affects our motivation. "The logic is that instead of showing people that you are smart because you can come up with a good plan, you show you're smart by thinking of insightful reasons why this project might go south," says Gary Klein. "The whole dynamic changes from trying to avoid anything that might disrupt harmony to trying to surface potential problems."

Instead of asking, for example, how we can make Target's expansion work, we imagine that Target Canada has failed miserably. We then work hard to explain why it has failed—and we do all of this even before we decide about the expansion.

But you don't have to be considering a billion-dollar expansion to use the premortem. Jill Bloom, a smart and hardworking manager at a big technology company in Seattle, ran a premortem for a decision in her own life. After working in the same position for a couple of years, she was recruited into a new role. At first, she was excited: her new manager, Robert, seemed energetic and engaging, and she'd have the chance to work on big-picture questions. But it soon became clear that Robert was volatile rather than energetic. The role wasn't exactly what she expected, either: she did have the chance to work on strategic issues, but it was nearly impossible for her to get resources to put her ideas into practice. Worse, the team was constantly in crisis, and the irregular hours stressed her out.

Before she decided to join Robert's team, Bloom had put together a spreadsheet with the risks and benefits of the move. "But I missed some big risks, and I didn't go through the ones that I identified very deeply," she told us. "I didn't dive into them to assess whether they were real risks or not."

After a casual conversation about how unhappy she was with the change, another manager, Mary, asked if Bloom might be interested in joining her team. It was only a few months after her start with Robert's group, and Bloom worried that another move would set her back on the promotion ladder. To further complicate things, when he heard that she was considering a move, Robert offered her a different role in his team.

To decide between the roles—the new position that Robert offered and the one on Mary's team—Bloom sat down with her husband to run a premortem for each of her options. "We imagined that things *had* gone wrong a year from now and tried to figure out what led to it," Bloom told us. The premortems gave her a short list of concrete factors to consider when comparing the jobs, like the manager's style, team culture, and her ability to drive projects forward.

Armed with the list, she gathered as much information as she could. "You don't have time in a thirty-minute informational interview to trawl through twenty questions. The premortems helped me focus on my top few risks and ask specific questions about them." She then used the factors from the premortem as her criteria to compare the jobs. "Scoring each job based on these risks helped me figure out what really mattered to me. Moving to a new team might be a setback for my promotion timeline because I'll have to prove myself again. But when I compared that to my day-to-day interest in the work, I realized that Mary's team was actually much lower risk."

As decision time approached, both teams put a lot of pressure on her. "It felt overwhelming," Bloom told us. "I needed something to help me take a step back and dissect the decision." Using the premortem and predetermined criteria helped her do just that. Ultimately, she decided to join Mary's team, and the new role turned out to be a much better fit.

Daniel Kahneman, one of the founders of behavioral economics and the author of *Thinking, Fast and Slow*, recommends that we use tools to handle big, messy decisions in wicked environments. SPIES, predetermined criteria, and the premortem won't eliminate errors. But they do provide an interruption to business as usual and prompt us to approach our choices systematically.

As Kahneman put it, "Most decision makers will trust their own intuitions because they think they see the situation clearly. It's a special exercise to question your own intuitions." But, in wicked environments, questioning intuition is just what we need. Take Target. Based on their intuition from years of opening stores in the United States, Target executives expected that they would be successful in Canada. But they had never gotten feedback on an international expansion. So when they signed the billion-dollar Canadian lease, they were flying blind.

Instead of trusting their intuition, Target's leaders should have used the techniques we have seen in this chapter. SPIES could have helped them avoid overly optimistic sales forecasts. Like the first-time home buyers, they would have benefited from predetermined criteria to help them evaluate their big decision. And, like Jill Bloom and her husband, they could have run a premortem to identify concrete obstacles to their success. These tools help us navigate all kinds of wicked environments. We struggle in complex systems, but adding a little bit of structure to our decisions gives us a fighting chance.

Chapter Six

# READING THE WRITING
# ON THE WALL

"Yes, it keeps me up at night. Yes, it makes me emotional.
These are my kids. These are everybody's kids."

## I.

In the summer of 2014, LeeAnne Walters noticed raised red bumps on her kids' skin every time they'd soaked in the bathtub or played in the backyard pool. A few weeks later, the kids' hair started falling out in big clumps, and one of her three-year-old twins stopped growing. In November, the tap water in LeeAnne's home turned an ugly brown color. She bought cases of bottled water for cooking, drinking, and teeth brushing. Soon the family began to limit their showers, and LeeAnne started bathing her two youngest kids in bottled water that she heated on the stove. *What in the world was wrong with her water?*

For months, her complaints to officials in her hometown of Flint, Michigan, fell on deaf ears. At one public meeting, where she brought bottles of brown water from her tap, city officials called her a liar for claiming that the water had come from her house. But after

LeeAnne made a video of her son's rash and showed it to his doctor, the pediatrician wrote a note urging the city to test her water. When Mike Glasgow, the city's utilities administrator, came to LeeAnne's house to take a look, he noticed an orange tint to the water. Worried about corrosion, he sampled the water for lead.

About a week later, Glasgow called LeeAnne with the results. His message was simple: *Don't let anyone drink the water.* The lead level was dangerously high.

There is no safe amount of lead in water, but the Environmental Protection Agency views anything above 15 parts per billion (ppb) as requiring corrective action. In LeeAnne's house—even though all the plumbing was new and a water filter had been installed—the lead level was 104 ppb. Glasgow confessed that he'd never seen a number that high. The next week he ran new tests: by then, the lead level had jumped to 397. Later, when an independent lab tested the water without the filter, the measurements averaged 2,500 ppb. One test measured 13,500 ppb.

A few months before LeeAnne's kids broke out in rashes, the once-prosperous city of Flint had started drawing its water from the Flint River instead of buying it from nearby Detroit, as it had done for over forty years. It did this for one reason: to save money.

At a ceremony in the spring of 2014, Flint's mayor pushed a small black button that closed the valve to Detroit's water supply and started Flint's water treatment experiment. City and state officials toasted with clear glasses of Flint water. "Water is an absolute vital service that most everyone takes for granted," the mayor said. "It's a historic moment for the city of Flint to return to its roots and use our own river as our drinking water supply."

During the ceremony, city officials said that there shouldn't be any difference in water quality. But when people started complaining, they changed their tune and argued that the taste *might* be different because the water was harder. And when complaints poured in—the water tasted and smelled foul—officials tried a series of small fixes, like using fire hydrants to flush some of Flint's aging pipes.

Routine tests soon revealed that there wasn't enough disinfectant in the water. This allowed bacteria like *E. coli* to grow and meant that residents had to boil their water. In response, workers added much more chlorine—*too much*, in fact. The level of dangerous disinfectant by-products then rose, forcing the city to notify its customers and prompting the state to buy bottled water for its employees in Flint. As the city struggled to manage the *E. coli* issue, health officials noticed an outbreak of Legionnaires' disease, a bacterial lung infection. Their investigation suggested that the source of the outbreak was the city's water.

General Motors, which had a massive factory only five minutes from LeeAnne's house, also noticed problems. At around the same time that LeeAnne's kids started getting rashes, water was rusting the engine blocks the plant manufactured. At first, GM's solutions weren't too different from those that LeeAnne tried. The company installed water filters and then brought in huge trucks filled with water—the industrial equivalent of buying bottled water from the grocery store. When that didn't work, GM switched the plant's water supply to a nearby town.

Unlike GM, LeeAnne Walters couldn't switch her water supply. And as for her kids, the damage had been done. When she took her twins to the doctor after getting the lead results from Mike Glasgow, she found that one of them had already suffered lead poisoning. Even slightly elevated lead levels in toddlers can lower IQ, reduce lifetime earnings, and cause persistent behavioral problems.

After lead was discovered in LeeAnne's house, state officials tried to sweep the problem under the rug. They told LeeAnne that the lead in her water was coming from her house's plumbing. But LeeAnne's pipes had been entirely replaced a few years earlier with new plastic pipes that met modern safety standards.

All across the city, the same corrosion that rusted GM's engines was corroding Flint's old pipes and poisoning residents' water. Eventually, as LeeAnne continued her complaints, Flint officials replaced the aged pipe that connected her house to the water main. Her lead levels immediately fell.

Despite all the data—the water's taste and smell, the bacterial outbreaks, the boil-water advisories, the astronomical lead levels at LeeAnne's house, and the corrosion at the GM plant—state officials steadfastly insisted that Flint's water was safe to drink and denied that there was an issue.

Beyond just ignoring warning signs, officials *designed* their sampling procedures to reduce the amount of lead they would detect. Take a look at the following letter that Flint's water utility sent to some of its customers:

---

## DRINKING WATER LEAD & COPPER
## SAMPLING INSTRUCTIONS

Dear Resident:

Thank you for helping to monitor for lead and copper in your drinking water. It is important that you follow these instructions so that we may collect an accurate measurement of the lead and copper in your drinking water. This sample is supposed to represent the water you would typically drink and the faucet from where you would drink the water. Call your water supply if you have any questions.

1. Select a faucet in the KITCHEN or BATHROOM that is commonly used for drinking. DO NOT sample from a laundry sink or a hose spigot as these samples cannot be used by your utility.

2. Flush the COLD water for at least 5 minutes. Let the water sit for at least 6 hours **before** you plan to collect the sample. If you have a single handle faucet, turn it to the COLD side. DO NOT use this faucet again until it is sampled.

3. Wait at least 6 hours before collecting your sample but we do not recommend sampling if the faucet has sat idle for more than 12 hours.

4. Fill the sample bottle to the neck with the "first draw" of COLD water from the faucet that you flushed at least 6 hours previous.

---

The letter came with a small bottle for taking the sample, which the utility would later pick up and analyze.

This setup is common in the United States, where environmental regulations require utilities to gather samples from homes with the highest risk of lead contamination—those serviced by old pipes that contain lead. But the letter sent to Flint residents was different. It contained a deception hiding in plain sight. Take a look at Step 2 again!

By opening their faucets for five minutes the night before sampling, residents flushed the water from their pipes and temporarily cleaned out much of the lead from their home's plumbing system. One expert compared this practice to thoroughly vacuuming a room the night before sampling it for dust.

And the sample bottles had such a narrow mouth that residents couldn't turn on their taps all the way when taking samples. This further biased the results because the weaker flow of water dislodged less lead from the pipes. On top of all this, instead of focusing on high-risk homes, the water utility mostly sampled houses that didn't have any lead pipes or lead service lines.

When all that wasn't enough, Michigan officials decided that the lead measurements in LeeAnne's house were invalid. Because her house had a water filter, the test didn't technically adhere to federal standards—which had been designed to prevent utilities from using filtered water to *decrease* lead measurements. By excluding the results from LeeAnne's house, state officials were able to keep the overall lead level for the city just under the threshold that would trigger federal attention. And Flint didn't have to notify residents that there was a problem.

In the meantime, the water had poisoned not just LeeAnne's children but also kids all over the city. Here's LeeAnne:

> It was not just about my family. It's never been, and it never will be. What about all the other families, all the other kids in Flint? How do you sit by, and let people be hurt, and know about it and do nothing . . . ? When I have four-year-olds asking me if they're going to die, because they're poisoned . . . I have twins. One's 56 pounds. One's 35. He hasn't grown in a year. He's still having issues with the anemia. . . . Yes, it keeps me up at night. Yes, it makes me emotional. These are my kids. These are everybody's kids.

WHEN FLINT started sourcing its own water from the Flint River, state officials decided to forgo treating it with chemicals to control corrosion—despite the fact that it was a standard practice in water systems. That decision saved the city about *sixty dollars per day.* That's not a typo. It's not sixty dollars per resident—it's sixty dollars *per day,* or about $20,000 a year for a system that cost $5 million to run each year. That's less than half of the yearly cost of a lab technician. In contrast, researchers estimate that the cost of poisoning a *single child* with lead, when considering only the direct economic consequences on wages, is $50,000. In Flint, nine thousand kids drank the contaminated water. Michigan's budget allocated hundreds of millions of dollars to the city's ongoing water issues. More money will be needed if the city needs to replace its entire water infrastructure.

Complexity and coupling made Flint's crisis much worse. As the city transitioned from a well-tested system to a brand-new source of water, state officials encountered a series of difficult-to-foresee interactions—between bacteria, the chemicals used to treat those bacteria, corrosive chemicals, and aging lead pipes. And the nature of water systems meant that officials had to rely on imperfect and indirect indicators. Flint officials didn't have a good map of the city's pipes, for example, so most houses from which they took water samples didn't even have lead pipes. Plus, lead is invisible, and getting results from measurements can take weeks. There's also tight coupling: once lead is in the water, it can't be removed, and the damage to children who ingest it is irreversible.

All too often, when we deal with a complex system, we assume that things are working just fine and discard evidence that conflicts with that assumption. A state official who oversaw Flint's move to its own water supply remarked at the changeover ceremony that "When the treated river water starts being pumped into the system, we move from plan to reality. The water quality speaks for itself." He was right—the water quality did speak for itself. But without a systematic way to track problems, Michigan officials ignored warning signs. In fact, they didn't just miss the forest for the trees; they flat-out denied that they were standing in the woods.

Charles Perrow argues that this sort of denial is far too common. "We construct an expected world because we can't handle the complexity of the present one, and then process the information that fits the expected world, and find reasons to exclude the information that might contradict it. Unexpected or unlikely interactions are ignored when we make our construction."

That's exactly what happened in Flint.

# II.

Not far from the center of Washington, DC, a nondescript building houses the Operations Control Center for the Washington Metro System. Operators sit at desks arranged around an enormous screen with a real-time map and dozens of camera feeds showing train tracks and tunnel entrances.

The engineers who designed the Metro system in the 1970s incorporated a feature to automatically track trains. To do this, they divided the entire track system into a bunch of blocks. Some blocks were only 40 feet; others were as long as 1,500 feet. Each block had equipment to detect trains.

It was a clever system. A transmitter at one end of a block generated an electrical signal. A receiver at the other end of the block listened for that signal. When the block was empty, the rails themselves transmitted the signal from transmitter to receiver. But when a train entered the block, the circuit changed. The train's wheels connected the rails together, creating a path for the signal that skipped the receiver by sending it straight to the ground. So when the receiver lost the signal, the system knew that a train was there and marked the track as occupied. And it used this information to automatically manage the speed of trains and prevent collisions.

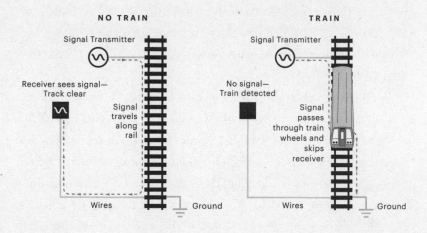

**NO TRAIN**

Signal Transmitter

Receiver sees signal—
Track clear

Signal
travels
along
rail

Wires          Ground

**TRAIN**

Signal Transmitter

No signal—
Train detected

Signal
passes
through train
wheels and
skips
receiver

Wires          Ground

But the system aged. Metro started to replace old components, but even so, the underlying technology was out of date. The system couldn't track the location of a specific train; it could only tell whether a section of track was occupied.

These complications came to a head in 2005. During a busy rush hour, three trains came within a few feet of colliding deep under the Potomac River. In a busy section of track, something caused the automatic system to fail, and only luck and quick action by train drivers saved the day.

By coincidence, an engineer overheard a discussion of the near collision. He took a look at the data for the track block in question and realized that the sensors had failed to detect the trains when they were in the middle of the block. He immediately sent workers down to the tracks. Over the next several days, as engineers troubleshot the problem, workers stood there to make sure that the track was clear before the control room allowed another train to enter.

The engineers had to figure out why the 900-foot-long block lost track of trains. They learned that the train detection signals were somehow making it from the transmitter to the receiver *even when a train occupied the block*. They suspected that there was a short circuit somewhere, but the problem went away before they could find it.

Even though the problem seemed to be fixed, the engineers replaced all the components of the circuit. But they still needed to make sure that the issue wouldn't occur elsewhere in the system. So they came up with a testing procedure: going forward, when maintenance crews worked on the track detection circuits, they would lay a large metal bar between the rails to simulate a train's wheels and make sure the block saw itself as occupied. Because the problem was intermittent, the crews needed to test the track in three places: near the transmitter, in the middle of the track, and by the receiver.

The engineers also developed a computer program to look for disappearing trains, and they ran it once a week. When they were satisfied that everything was working as it should, they gave the tool to their colleagues in the maintenance group and recommended that they use it once a month during rush hour.

The Metro engineers had found a needle in the haystack and, unlike the Flint officials, they acted on the warning signs they saw. They fixed the problem. And then they came up with testing procedures and a way to monitor the system so they would know if the needle popped up again. *They'd figured it out.*

But then the organization forgot about the problem. No one used the testing procedures or ran the program to look for disappearing trains.

Flash-forward to June 2009. As part of an upgrade program, workers replaced some of the components in track segment B2-304. The work didn't go well. After replacing components and tweaking the transmitter and receiver multiple times, the block's detection circuit still didn't work consistently. The workers stayed to see if the track detected the first train that passed after they finished their work. While they continued troubleshooting, they saw one more train pass by. They told the operations center that there were still issues, and then they left.

The operations center opened a work order for the section of the problematic track, but the work order just sat in the system. For the next five days, nearly every train that rode over that section of track disappeared from the track sensors, but no one noticed. When the trains got past the misbehaving segment of track, the system detected them, and everything looked normal again.

The fact that Metro missed the problems with segment B2-304 and failed to use the testing procedures or the program that its engineers developed wasn't simple carelessness. In a simple system, it's easy to keep track of important things, but in a complex and tightly coupled system, that's not the case. In the danger zone, it might not even be clear which things matter, and we don't have the luxury of missing important details.

On June 22, 2009, at the start of the evening rush hour, Train 214 arrived at the faulty section of track and disappeared like every train that had come before it. As had happened for the previous five days, when the track circuit lost detection, the train automatically started to slow down. But unlike all the trains that had come before it, 214 was unlucky. Before entering the block, the driver had been driving the train at a slower-than-normal speed because he liked to control precisely where it stopped at station platforms. When Train 214 started to slow down, it lacked the momentum to clear the troubled block of track. It came to rest entirely within the faulty track segment and completely disappeared from the system.

Train 214 was followed by Train 112, which carried David Wherley—the retired Air Force officer we met at the start of the

## THE DISAPPEARING TRAIN

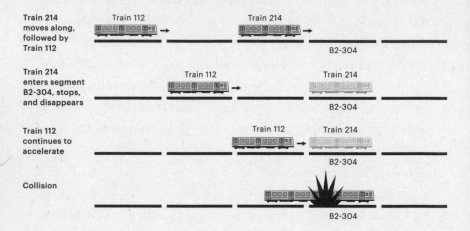

book—his wife, Ann, and many others. The automatic train control system saw the track ahead of Train 112 as clear and sent it a command to accelerate. At 4:58, as Train 112 rounded a corner, the driver saw the stalled train ahead and hit the emergency brake. But it was too late. A thirteen-foot-thick wave of debris—seats, poles, and ceiling panels—spilled into the train and shrank the first car from 75 feet to 12 feet.

Train 112 hit a phantom, a ghost that wasn't supposed to be there. Nine people died because the Metro system was so complex that it couldn't even keep track of the problems its engineers already knew how to fix.

## III.

There is an industry that has figured out how to avoid disaster by learning from warning signs: commercial aviation. At the beginning of the jet age, in the late 1950s, commercial airplanes crashed at a rate of about forty fatal accidents per one million departures. Within a decade, this had improved to fewer than two crashes in every million departures. In recent years, that number has improved even more—to about two crashes for every *ten million* departures. Per mile, driving is a hundred times riskier.

Much of this progress comes from paying attention to small errors, anomalies, and close calls—the very things officials ignored in Flint and the Washington Metro system. Airlines figured out how to learn not only from accidents that had happened but also from accidents that *could* have happened but *did not*.

There's a joke among pilots that a bird perched on the nose of an airliner looking back into the cockpit would see only the tops of the pilots' heads. That's because pilots juggle the need to look outside the airplane with the need to take care of a bunch of things inside the cockpit. During the busy portions of a flight, they often have their heads down, looking at maps, programming the navigation computers, and monitoring the flight instruments.

On a clear day in the cockpit of an airplane, pilots can see for hundreds of miles. But when it's cloudy, they can't see anything. They fly using the instruments in the cockpit, and they navigate by following a set of invisible highways made up of radio waves broadcast from radio beacons on the ground. Airplanes carry radio receivers that pilots can tune to these beacons. Like highways for cars (think I-5 on the West Coast of the United States or the M-20 running out of London), these highways have their own names. To fly from Seattle to San Francisco, for example, pilots might be on a flight plan that takes them along J589 to J143. Once these highways bring them to the general vicinity of their destination, they fly what's called an instrument approach that guides them to the airport. Each instrument approach is defined by a detailed set of instructions read from an instrument approach plate—a printed chart that shows altitudes, turn-by-turn instructions, and information about what radio beacons pilots should use. These plates specify how a plane should fly to a point where it's ready for landing, aligned with a runway and only a few hundred feet above the ground.

Through all this, air traffic controllers play an important role. They sequence planes for landing and ensure that planes don't collide with each other. They tell pilots how they should approach an airport and on which runway they will land.

Instrument flying happens in Perrow's danger zone. Low clouds, fog, and darkness obscure what's going on outside the airplane. Pilots rely on indirect sources of information: the flight instruments, radio navigation beacons, instrument approach plates, and discussions with controllers. And the system is tightly coupled. Once a plane takes off, pilots can't simply pull over to the side of the road as we can with a car; they have to keep flying until they land. And mistakes, if not caught in time, are hard to recover from.

On the morning of December 1, 1974, Trans World Airlines Flight 514 took off from Columbus, Ohio, and headed toward Washington National Airport with ninety-two people on board. It was a nasty day: cloudy and snowy, with high winds near Washington, DC. In the cockpit sat Richard Brock, a longtime captain, first officer Lenard Kresheck, and flight engineer Thomas Safranek.

The flight would take an hour to complete. But a few minutes after takeoff, an air traffic controller told the crew that the wind was too strong to land at National Airport. Captain Brock decided to divert to Dulles, a bigger airport about thirty miles west of National. The flight proceeded as normal, and about fifteen minutes later, when the plane was still about fifty miles northwest of Dulles, another air traffic controller cleared the crew to fly an instrument approach to Runway 12.

The crew "briefed the approach": they read aloud from the approach plate to Runway 12 and set up the aircraft to follow its detailed instructions. The approach plate had a bird's-eye view with altitudes, the location of the airport, and where the crew should start to descend. It also showed the position of Mount Weather— 1,764 feet high and 25 miles from the airport—and how high the plane should be flying to avoid it.

The approach plate also had a profile view that looked something like this:

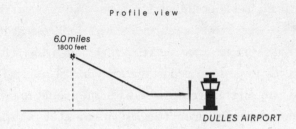

APPROACH PLATE

Profile view

6.0 miles
1800 feet

DULLES AIRPORT

The only point the profile view showed was at 1,800 feet, 6.0 miles from the airport. This indicated that, once the plane was six miles from Dulles, the crew should start descending from 1,800 feet until they could see the airport and land. But the profile view left out a big part of the picture: it didn't tell the crew anything about their altitude farther away from the airport.

When air traffic control cleared TWA 514 for the approach, the plane was northwest of a point on the map called Round Hill. As it descended through the turbulent clouds, the crew discussed the next steps.

CAPTAIN: 1,800 [feet] is the bottom.

FIRST OFFICER: Start down.

ENGINEER: We're out here quite a ways. I better turn the heat down.

FIRST OFFICER: I hate the altitude bumping around . . .
    gives you a headache after a while. . . . You can feel
    that wind down here now.
CAPTAIN: You know, according to this dumb sheet [the
    bird's-eye view of approach plate], it says that 3,400
    [feet] to Round Hill is our minimum altitude.

The flight engineer asked the captain where he saw that, and the captain replied, "Well, here. Round Hill."

The captain had noticed that, for planes coming from the west, the bird's-eye view showed a course line with 3,400 feet as the minimum altitude. But the crew wasn't on that course line. They were flying directly toward the airport, but they hadn't received any instructions from air traffic control on when they could descend. The profile view, which showed only the last six miles before the airport, didn't resolve the ambiguity.

Everyone spoke at the same time: "Well, but . . . when he clears you, that means you can go to your . . . initial approach. . . . Yeah, your initial approach altitude."

The captain was right: 1,800 feet was dangerously low because of Mount Weather, which was shrouded in clouds. But the discussion assuaged his concern, and he dropped the matter. The plane continued to descend.

"Dark in here," the flight engineer said. "And bumpy, too," the first officer responded. The ninety-two people on Flight 514 had one minute left to live.

CAPTAIN BROCK and his colleagues weren't the only people confused that day. Only half an hour earlier, another flight, also coming from the northwest, received the same instrument approach clearance. As with Flight 514, this other flight's clearance lacked any sort of altitude restriction—the requirement to fly at, for example, 3,400 feet until passing Mount Weather. This suggested that the pilot could descend down to 1,800 feet. But the captain of that flight happened to ask air traffic control a simple follow-up question: What was the lowest altitude at which to fly at that point? The controller clarified, and the plane landed just fine.

But the crew of Flight 514 misunderstood the approach. Their mental model didn't match reality. In the years since the accident, researchers have learned a lot about how the brain deals with ambiguous situations. When there isn't enough information to resolve a question, we feel discordance, and the brain works quickly to fill in the gaps so that it can replace dissonance with harmony. In other words, *it makes stuff up.*

It wasn't clear what the crew should do. They weren't flying along a normal course. The "dumb sheet" told them not to descend. But air traffic control had cleared them for the approach. To deal with this ambiguity, they invented a rule: "When he clears you, that means you can go to your initial approach altitude."

They couldn't see the mountain they were approaching, but they did glimpse patches of ground through the clouds. Their ground proximity radar sounded a warning horn. But it was too late; seconds later, they flew the plane into the granite slopes of Mount Weather. From the side, their final flight path looked like this:

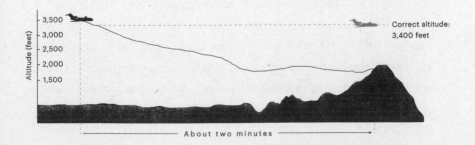

After the crash of Flight 514, the Federal Aviation Administration (FAA) revised the instrument approach plate. Take a look at the changes:

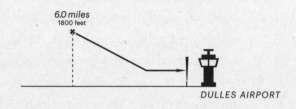

ORIGINAL PROFILE VIEW

6.0 miles
1800 feet

DULLES AIRPORT

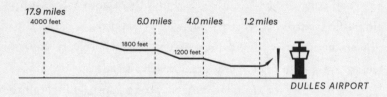

REVISED PROFILE VIEW

17.9 miles
4000 feet

6.0 miles      4.0 miles      1.2 miles

1800 feet

1200 feet

DULLES AIRPORT

Instead of indicating that the crew should descend to 1,800 feet six miles from the airport and leaving the instructions up to that point open to interpretation, the new profile view specified that planes should remain at 4,000 feet until they were 17.9 miles away. This depiction is unambiguous.

The crew's mistakes weren't due to negligence or incompetence. Rather, the pilots were confused about a subtle point regarding the services that air traffic control provided. When the controller cleared Flight 514 for the approach, the pilots expected that the controllers would provide an altitude restriction if one was needed. Air traffic control didn't think that one was needed.

The U.S. National Transportation Safety Board (NTSB) listened to hours of testimony about the role of the crew and air traffic controllers in the accident and concluded that "pilots have become so accustomed to receiving assistance from the controllers that, unless advised by the controller, they do not know what type of services they are or are not receiving."

Of course, it was easy to be smart in hindsight. But some people, it turns out, had figured out the problem well before the accident. They knew that the confusion about approach clearances was a disaster waiting to happen—and they even knew about the danger that lay in wait for pilots in the mountains near Dulles.

In 1974, United Airlines started an internal safety awareness program to get pilots to report incidents and suggestions related to safety. A crew could report the issues anonymously, and the airline promised that it would never use the information against the pilots—and that it would fight like hell to avoid turning their identities over to the FAA. Two months before the crash of Flight 514, United received a scary report from a crew that had just landed at Dulles.

Air traffic control had cleared the United flight, inbound from the northwest, on the same approach to Runway 12 that would later doom Flight 514. Like Brock, the United captain misinterpreted the approach plate and descended to 1,800 feet. The United crew *made the exact same mistake* that the TWA pilots did. But they got lucky. They missed Mount Weather and landed normally.

Still, the United crew thought that something might have been amiss. When they arrived at their gate, they reviewed the approach and realized that they had descended too early. It seemed like this was exactly the type of information that United was looking to gather, so they submitted a report.

The airline investigated the issue and sent a notice to its pilots:

---

The extensive use of radar vectoring, in terminal areas, had led to some misunderstanding on the part of flightcrews. Recent events prompt these reminders:

1. The words "cleared for approach" generally put the flightcrew on their own.

2. Don't start down to final approach fix altitude without reviewing other altitude minimums.

3. Inbound minimum altitudes to outer fixes are on the [approach] plates.

4. Flightcrews should thoroughly familiarize themselves with the altitude information shown on approach and/or area charts for the terminals into which they are operating. This includes minimum segment altitude (MSA) information.

---

Flight crews: you're on your own. Don't descend without understanding everything about the altitudes on the approach plate. These four bullet points, sent out *weeks* before the TWA crash, contained the antidote to Captain Brock's confusion. But United's safety awareness program was an internal initiative, so the notice didn't go out to the FAA, pilots at TWA, or any other airline. If it had, it might have saved ninety-two lives.

# IV.

To prevent failure in a complex system, we have to find a bunch of needles in a big haystack. United was on to something with its safety awareness program. It generated a map showing where some of those needles hid. But the program didn't go far enough—the map didn't get to all the right people.

Witnesses who testified during the Flight 514 investigation recommended that the FAA create an industry-wide system to collect anonymous safety reports and give immunity to anyone who used it. Six months later, the Aviation Safety Reporting System (ASRS) was born.

The ASRS, run by an independent unit at NASA, collects thousands of reports a month from pilots, military operators, air traffic controllers, mechanics, and anyone else involved in the aviation industry. Beyond getting immunity for a mistake, it's a point of pride for pilots to submit ASRS reports. They know the reports make air travel safer.

The reports are stored in a searchable database that anyone can access, and NASA highlights safety trends in its monthly newsletter, *Callback*. A recent issue, for example, described a report from a crew that received a last-minute runway change, which necessitated an overly aggressive descent to a lower altitude. The crew couldn't make the altitude in time, so they submitted a report. In response, the FAA changed the approach procedure.

Another issue of *Callback* described the dangers of complacency: from a pilot of a small plane who overlooked a checklist's instructions to switch fuel tanks (and had to land on a highway when he ran one of the fuel tanks dry) to a mechanic who destroyed an engine by leaving a tool inside. Chick Perrow, as you might guess, loves the ASRS. "For designers," he writes, "it offers a database that often generates counterintuitive findings about system flaws; for the organization, it reinforces the notion that someone is, indeed, trying."

A fundamental feature of complex systems is that we can't find all the problems by simply thinking about them. Complexity can cause such strange and rare interactions that it's impossible to predict most of the error chains that will emerge. But before they fall apart, complex systems give off warning signs that reveal these interactions. The systems themselves give us clues as to how they might unravel.

But we often fail to pay attention to those clues. As long as things turn out OK, we tend to assume that our system is working well—even if our success is due to dumb luck. This is called outcome bias. Take the example of Stefan Fischer, a fictional project manager working on the launch of a tech company's new tablet. A few months before the launch, the engineer in charge of the tablet's camera took a job at another firm. As a result, the team fell behind schedule. To save time, Stefan decided to skip an evaluation of alternative camera designs.

In an experiment, we asked eighty business school students to evaluate Stefan's performance after reading about the project and seeing one of three outcomes. In the *success case*, the tablet sold well, and there were no problems. In the *close call case*, the project succeeded only because of blind luck: the camera's design caused the tablet to overheat, but by pure chance, the processor could be updated to control the heat, and the tablet still sold and performed well. In the *failure case*, too, the camera caused the tablet to overheat—but in this case, the processor couldn't be updated, the overheating became a big problem, and the tablet didn't sell well.

For the students who evaluated Stefan (and for a group of NASA engineers who participated in a similar study of an unmanned spacecraft), *the outcome* determined their assessment. When the tablet was successful, Stefan got good marks. Even when he succeeded because of blind luck, people saw him as highly competent, intelligent, and worthy of a big promotion. They questioned the quality of his decisions only when the tablet failed. As long as the project wasn't a disaster, they didn't care that Stefan had just been lucky. They saw no difference between good luck and good performance.

Remember Knight Capital's $500 million trading loss? It stemmed from a simple mistake by an IT worker who forgot to copy new computer code to all eight of Knight's servers. At some point in the past, IT workers had almost certainly made the same sort of mistake, gotten lucky, and fixed the problem without anything bad happening. They concluded that the system was working just fine; after all, disaster was avoided. But in reality, every software rollout was a roll of the dice.

Many of us do this in our everyday lives, too. We treat a toilet that occasionally clogs as a minor inconvenience rather than a warning sign—until it overflows. Or we ignore subtle warning signs about our cars—like rough gear shifting or a tire that slowly loses air—rather than taking the car into the shop.

To manage complexity, we need to learn from the information our systems throw at us in the form of small errors, close calls, and other warning signs. In this chapter, we have seen three organizations struggle with this problem in different ways. In Flint, officials downplayed a series of warning signs and insisted that the water was safe to drink. They didn't even acknowledge they had a problem. Engineers at the Washington Metro did better. They knew what the issue was and created testing procedures and a monitoring program to keep an eye on it. But these safeguards got lost in the morass of daily operations. Though there was a solution, it wasn't put into practice. Finally, managers at United Airlines went even further. They knew about the problem and warned every pilot in their organization about it. But that warning didn't reach people beyond United—it never got to TWA pilots, including those in charge of Flight 514.

Each of these stories takes us one step closer to a solution that works. And it turns out that some organizations have figured out how to learn from small lapses and near misses. Researchers call this learning process *anomalizing*, and it looks something like this:

The first step is to gather data—by collecting close call reports and measuring things that go wrong. For example, airlines gather not only near-miss reports but also data directly from flights.

Next, the issues raised need to be fixed—close call reports shouldn't gather dust in a suggestion box. At an Illinois hospital, for example, a nurse almost mixed up the medication for two patients in the same room. The patients had similar last names and were prescribed drugs with similar names—Cytotec and Cytoxan. She caught her mistake and submitted a close call report. In response, the patients were separated to help the *next* nurse avoid making the same mistake.

The third step is to dig deeper to understand and address the root causes. A quality manager at a community hospital noticed repeated medication errors in one unit. Rather than seeing these mistakes as a series of isolated incidents, the quality team dug deeper to understand the underlying problem. The nurses, it turned out, were constantly interrupted as they stood in the hallway preparing meds.

In response, managers created a dedicated, distraction-free medication prep room.

Once we understand a problem, we need to realize that close calls are not secrets. They should be shared—either throughout an organization or, as with *Callback*, across an entire industry. Sharing missteps makes it clear that mistakes are a normal part of the system and helps us anticipate issues that we ourselves may one day face.

As the final step, we need to make sure that the solutions we create in response to warning signs actually work. On some flights, for example, an extra pilot rides in the cockpit to observe the crew at work, looking for things like missed checklist items or confusing procedures. This approach lets airlines audit their own solutions. Otherwise things can get lost in the shuffle. As happened at Metro, sometimes the very people who are supposed to use a solution may not even know that it exists. Auditing also helps ensure that the cure isn't worse than the disease. This might be the case if, for example, a fix introduces too much complexity or additional monitoring creates too many false positives.

An organization's culture sits at the center of all this. As Ben Berman, the airline captain and accident investigator, told us, "If you're going to shoot the messenger, no one will tell you about the mistakes and incidents that happen in your system." By openly sharing stories of failures and near failures—without blame or revenge—we can create a culture in which people view errors as an opportunity to learn rather than as the impetus for a witch hunt. "The measure of a safe organization is not whether a person who makes a great catch gets a thank-you note from the CEO," wrote Bob Wachter, the UCSF physician who examined Pablo Garcia's overdose. It's whether someone who raises an issue but *turns out to be wrong* also gets a thank-you note.

You might be reading this and thinking, *Well, that's great for airlines and hospitals. But what do I do if my organization doesn't have errors tied to specific operational incidents?* What do you even track then? And what about issues that aren't related to safety, things that you don't want to share with your competitors?

The answer comes from Danish organizational researcher Claus Rerup. Using data from a bunch of interesting settings—including rock concerts, ferry accidents, and big multinational companies— Rerup studies how organizations pay attention to weak signals of failure to prevent disaster.

Over the course of several years, Rerup conducted an in-depth study of global pharmaceutical powerhouse Novo Nordisk, one of the world's biggest insulin producers. In the early 1990s, Rerup found, it was difficult for anyone at Novo Nordisk to draw attention to even serious threats. "You had to convince your own boss, his boss, and his boss that this was an issue," one senior vice president explained. "Then he had to convince his boss that it was a good idea to do things in a different way." But, as in the childhood game of telephone—where a message gets more and more garbled as it passes between people—the issues became oversimplified as they worked their way up the chain of command. "What was written in the original version of the report . . . and which was an alarm bell for the specialist," the CEO told Rerup, "was likely to be deleted in the version that senior management read."

At the time, Novo Nordisk employees who worked in manufacturing knew that the company might fail to meet the increasingly strict standards of the U.S. Food and Drug Administration (FDA). But senior managers had no idea that a crisis was on the way. In 1993, the company hired a group of retired FDA inspectors to run a mock audit. The inspectors found a shocking number of problems. It looked like Novo Nordisk might lose its license to sell insulin in the United States. The firm discarded six months of supplies and asked Eli Lilly, one of its main competitors, to take over its customer base in the

United States. In the end, the failure to meet FDA standards rocked the company's reputation and cost it over $100 million.

In the wake of the failure, Novo Nordisk didn't blame individuals. Nor did it simply encourage managers to be more mindful. Instead, it implemented organization-wide changes that bolstered its ability to notice and learn from warning signs.

To identify emerging problems, Novo Nordisk created a department of about twenty people who scan for new challenges coming from outside the company. Part of what they do is talk with non-profits, environmental groups, and government officials about big issues, like genetic modification and changing regulations, that managers might ignore or simply not have the time to think about. Once an issue has been identified, the group brings together ad hoc teams from different departments and levels of seniority to dig into how it might affect their business and to figure out what they can do to prevent problems. The goal is to make sure that the company doesn't ignore weak signs of brewing trouble.

Novo Nordisk also conducts audits to look for problems *inside* the company. It uses facilitators to make sure important issues don't get stuck at the bottom of the hierarchy (as they did before the insulin manufacturing crisis). The facilitators—around two dozen people recruited from among the company's most respected managers—work with every unit at least once every few years. Two facilitators interview about 40 percent of a unit's employees to uncover concerns. As one facilitator put it, we "talk about the issues that are normally not being discussed. Nothing is taboo."

The facilitators then analyze the data they've collected and evaluate whether there are concerns unit managers may be ignoring. "We go around and find a number of small issues," a facilitator explained. "We don't know if they would develop into something bigger if we ignored them. But we don't run the risk. We follow up on the small stuff."

When the facilitators highlight a problem, unit managers pay attention. Concerns are no longer filtered up through layers of hierarchy. And it's not just about raising awareness. Facilitators come up with a list of actions that managers need to take to improve their units. Each of those actions is assigned to a person and tracked to make sure it is fixed—in a recent year, 95 percent of corrective actions were completed on time.

Novo Nordisk's program may seem like a big undertaking, but Novo Nordisk is a big company. The program costs just a fraction of 1 percent of its annual revenue. And these principles can be applied on a smaller scale, too—even in a team or a division within a larger organization. In fact, Rerup and a colleague also studied how family firms use a version of these interventions by relying on just one person: a trusted advisor. These advisors hovered in the background and helped business owners notice threats from competitors, technological disruptions, and regulatory changes. They'd even anticipate discord within the family and remind owners to talk to their siblings before making a big decision. Like the dedicated groups at Novo Nordisk, these advisors combed the whole business for emerging problems, spotted warning signs, and got decision makers to pay attention.

In the danger zone, our systems are so complex that it's hard to predict exactly what will go wrong ahead of time. But there *are* warning signs—the writing is often on the wall. We just need to read it.

## Chapter Seven

# THE ANATOMY OF DISSENT

### "You kept your head down, you did your job, or you lost both."

## I.

In the fall of 1846, a young woman in the final days of her pregnancy knocked on the massive oak door of the maternity unit of Vienna's sprawling General Hospital. Two nurses came out, took her by the arms, and guided her up a long staircase. A medical student, who sat at a small table at the top, assigned her to the hospital's First Obstetrical Clinic.

When the woman realized that the First Clinic was the unit staffed by doctors, rather than by midwives, she was aghast. She begged the student to send her instead to the Second Clinic, the midwives' unit. She knelt down and wrung her hands, pleading with him, but he didn't listen. Rules were rules. Patients were assigned to one of the two clinics based on the day of the week they arrived, and the calendar said she must go to the First Clinic.

The next day, she gave birth to a boy in a small room of the First Clinic. Three days later, she died.

Her story was typical. Many expectant women who came to the hospital had heard about the First Clinic and were desperate to avoid it. And many of those who ended up there died within days of giving birth. The symptoms were always the same: terrible fever, shivers, and abdominal pain that was mild at first but soon became excruciating. The babies often died, too. The cause was childbed fever, a dreaded disease of the time.

Shortly before the young woman had died, a priest and his assistant had come to the clinic to deliver the last rites. As the two walked through the wards, the assistant waved a small bell to signal the priest's arrival. This was an all-too-familiar sound. On most days, and sometimes more than once a day, a priest made the rounds to deliver spiritual relief.

As the priest and his helper made their way to the room where the young woman lay dying, they walked by a young doctor, a stout man with gray-blue eyes, big shoulders, and thinning blond hair. It was Ignác Semmelweis, a twenty-eight-year-old medical school graduate from Hungary and the clinic's recently appointed chief resident.

Semmelweis heard the ominous tolling of the bell nearly every day, but it still got to him. "When I heard the bell hurried past my door, a sigh would escape my heart for the victim that once more was claimed by an unknown power," he later wrote. "This bell was a painful exhortation to me to search for this unknown cause."

What exactly killed these women was indeed unknown. Most of Semmelweis's contemporaries, including his domineering boss, Professor Johann Klein, thought that childbed fever was the result of a kind of noxious atmosphere that hung over the city. But Semmelweis just didn't buy it. Take a look at this graph comparing the two clinics:

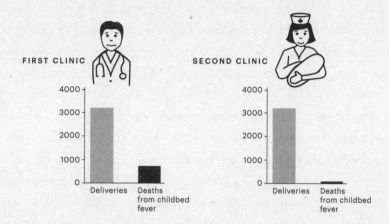

Unless this harmful air somehow hovered only around the First Clinic, the theory couldn't explain why childbed fever was so much more common there. In the Second Clinic, sixty women died from childbed fever in an average year. In the First Clinic, *six hundred to eight hundred* mothers died.

It was a stunning difference considering that the number of births was similar in both clinics and that their wards were nearly identical, except for one thing. The First Clinic was staffed by doctors and medical students, and the Second Clinic by midwives and their students.

And the disease wasn't raging in the city beyond the hospital's walls. It rarely occurred with home births, regardless of whether a private physician or a midwife carried out the delivery. Even women who delivered on the street contracted the disease much less often than did the women who gave birth in the First Clinic. *It was safer to give birth in an alleyway than in the hospital.* Clearly, there was something strange about the First Clinic—and the First Clinic only.

One difference between the practices of doctors and midwives was that women gave birth on their backs in the doctors' clinic and on their sides in the midwives' clinic. To test if this mattered, Semmelweis had women in the First Clinic deliver on their sides. But it made no difference. He also changed the way drugs were administered and improved the ventilation of the First Clinic's wards, but to no avail.

Frustrated with his lack of progress, Semmelweis went on a short vacation to Venice in the spring of 1847. He hoped the beauty of the city would help clear his head. But when he returned to the hospital, he received devastating news. One of his most admired colleagues, the forensic pathologist Jakob Kolletschka, was dead. While he was performing an autopsy alongside Kolletschka, a student had accidentally pricked Kolletschka's finger with a scalpel. Within days, Kolletschka had fallen ill and died.

When Semmelweis read the postmortem report, he was shocked. What had killed Kolletschka was eerily similar to the disease Semmelweis had seen time and time again at the First Clinic.

This was a crucial clue. Semmelweis suspected that Kolletschka had died from invisibly small infectious particles—what we'd call bacteria today—that had entered his body when his finger was pricked. And if his disease and childbed fever were indeed one and the same, then it must be those same particles that were killing women in the First Clinic. With this insight, the solution clicked into place. The midwives in the Second Clinic didn't do autopsies. But the doctors and medical students often came to the First Clinic *directly* from the autopsy rooms, and they had been infecting the women at the clinic with the invisible, lethal matter.

We now know that childbed fever can be caused by a variety of bacteria, some of which are present in cadavers regardless of the cause of death. But in Semmelweis's time, decades before the germ theory of disease gained acceptance, there seemed to be absolutely no reason for a doctor to change clothes or thoroughly wash hands after dissecting a cadaver. Doctors might have quickly rinsed their hands with soap and water, but it was far from a thorough scrub. In fact, when they came to the clinic from the autopsy rooms, their hands often gave off what Semmelweis called a "cadaverous smell."

Semmelweis didn't know about germs, but he reasoned that destroying the odor would destroy the lethal material. He placed a bowl of chlorine solution at the First Clinic's entrance and ordered his staff to wash their hands in it when entering the unit.

The results were astonishing. Within weeks, the clinic's death rate fell sharply. In the first full year of the intervention, the mortality rate due to childbed fever dropped to just above 1 percent. In a place where death used to be a daily occurrence, entire months would pass without a single fatal case of childbed fever.

By this time, Semmelweis knew beyond doubt that he was right. He also knew that his discovery had a horrific implication. "I have handled cadavers extensively," he wrote. "I must here confess that God only knows the number of patients who have gone to their graves prematurely by my fault."

It was one thing for Semmelweis to accept this painful truth. It was quite another to try to convince the medical establishment of his theory. After all, his findings implied that, for decades, doctors in Vienna, and indeed all over Europe, had killed mothers and babies, quite literally, with their bare hands. He had to persuade his colleagues that they had been wrong and that their false beliefs had caused innocent people to die.

It was a daunting challenge, but Semmelweis spoke up. "The remedy does not lie in concealment," he wrote. "This misfortune should not persist forever, for the truth must be made known to all concerned."

But how could he convince a complacent old guard, one that resented younger physicians? How could he convince people like Professor Klein, who had led the maternity hospital for twenty-five years, that he was so wrong about something so important?

———————

IT'S DIFFICULT to be a dissenter. We often feel the need to go along with what others in our group think, and neuroscience shows that this desire for conformity isn't just the result of peer pressure. It is wired into our brains.

In one experiment, scientists used functional magnetic resonance imaging (fMRI) to see how our brains react when we hold an opinion that deviates from our group's consensus. It turns out that two things happen when we go against the grain. First, a brain region involved in error detection becomes very active. The nervous system notices a mistake and triggers an error message. It's as though your brain is saying: *Hey, you're doing something wrong! You need to make changes!* At the same time, an area of the brain that anticipates rewards slows down. Your brain says: *Don't expect that you'll be rewarded! This won't work out well for you!*

"We show that a deviation from the group opinion is regarded by the brain as a punishment," said the study's lead author, Vasily Klucharev. And the error message combined with a dampened reward signal produces a brain impulse indicating that we should adjust our opinion to match the consensus. Interestingly, this process occurs even if there is no reason for us to expect any punishment from the group. As Klucharev put it, "This is likely an automatic process in which people form their own opinion, hear the group view, and then quickly shift their opinion to make it more compliant with the group view."

This played out in a fascinating study led by Emory University neuroscientist Greg Berns. Participants looked at pairs of three-dimensional objects, each shown from a different angle, and had to tell if the objects in each pair were identical or different. Each participant was put in a group of five volunteers, but the other four people in the group were actually actors who worked for the researchers.

Sometimes the actors answered correctly, but sometimes they all gave the wrong answer. Then it was the real participant's turn to answer, and the researchers used a brain scanner to capture the moment.

People went along with the group on the wrong answer more than 40 percent of the time. That's not too surprising—many experiments demonstrate people's willingness to conform. What is interesting is what the brain scanner showed. When people agreed with their peers' incorrect answers, there was little change in activity in the areas associated with conscious decision-making. Instead, the regions devoted to vision and spatial perception lit up. It's not that people were consciously lying to fit in. It seems that the prevailing opinion actually *changed their perceptions*. If everyone else said the two objects were different, a participant might have started to notice differences even if the objects were identical. Our tendency for conformity can literally change what we see.

And when people went against the group, there was a surge in activity in brain regions involved in the processing of emotionally charged events. This was the emotional cost of standing up for one's beliefs; the researchers called it "the pain of independence."

When we shift our opinions to conform, we're not lying. We may not even be conscious that we're giving in to others. What's happening is something much deeper, something unconscious and uncalculated: our brain lets us avoid the pain of standing alone.

These results are alarming because dissent is a precious commodity in modern organizations. In a complex, tightly coupled system, it's easy for people to miss important threats, and even seemingly small mistakes can have huge consequences. So speaking up when we notice a problem can make a big difference.

But it seems we just aren't wired for dissent. "Our brains are exquisitely tuned to what other people think about us, aligning our judgments to fit in with the group," says Professor Berns. "One

reason behind conformity is that, in terms of human evolution, going against the group is not beneficial to survival."

## II.

At a railway station outside Hanover, Germany, an elegant fifty-
year-old man stepped out of the crowd, walked up to the tracks, and
threw himself before an oncoming train. He was crushed to death.
The man was Gustav Adolf Michaelis, a distinguished German physician who had helped found scientific obstetrics.

Michaelis was one of the few people who had embraced Semmelweis's message when it first reached the maternity hospitals of
Europe. Soon after hearing about the discovery in Vienna, Michaelis introduced a requirement to use chlorinated water at his own
clinic in Kiel, Germany. The intervention worked. But as the death
rate plummeted, Michaelis grew distraught. He saw the accumulating evidence for Semmelweis's thesis as proof of his own guilt. He
was horrified when he realized how many women his past practices
might have killed. His beloved niece, whose baby he had helped
deliver at his clinic just weeks before introducing chlorinated hand
washing, had died of childbed fever. He just couldn't go on.

Most other physicians didn't recognize their culpability. Some
maintained that the periodic nature of childbed fever outbreaks
meant that the cause had to be some sort of atmospheric influence.
Doctors whose research was directly contradicted by the theory saw
it as a personal attack. Many found the idea that doctors' hands
could transmit a disease absurd. Others just ignored the discovery
and saw no reason to change their practices.

Semmelweis's boss, Professor Klein, resented him. "From the

beginning, he had viewed with alarm the increasing influence of the younger physicians at the medical school," writes the medical historian Sherwin Nuland. "And being human, he was having difficulty facing the increasing evidence that Semmelweis had discovered something truly valuable that might save many lives, something that his own refusal to change an outmoded viewpoint had prevented him from seeing."

When Semmelweis's two-year term as chief resident ended, he applied for renewal. Klein said no. Semmelweis appealed to the dean's office, but the old guard closed ranks. A senior professor argued that it was important to remove Semmelweis because the tension between him and Klein was hurting the clinic. Having Semmelweis around was just too much trouble. Semmelweis was dismissed, and one of Klein's protégés replaced him.

Semmelweis then applied for a teaching appointment that would give him access to some of the hospital facilities, including the autopsy rooms. But his application was denied. He applied again, and this time he was successful. But his appointment wasn't approved until eighteen months after his initial application. And, at the last moment, the terms of the position changed. Despite his expectations, Semmelweis wasn't allowed to teach using cadavers. The contract said he had to teach using a wooden anatomical model.

This was the final straw. Though the influence of the old guard was slowly fading, and Semmelweis had the support of a handful of rising stars in the medical profession, he couldn't even get a teaching position without restrictions. He was tired of the petty hostility from Klein's circle and frustrated with the challenges to his theory. He saw himself as a pioneer; others treated him like a pariah.

Five days after he received the new terms of his teaching arrangement, Semmelweis hastily left Vienna. He told no one, not even his closest associates, where he was going.

———

AS SEMMELWEIS LEARNED, speaking up is just one side of the equation. Dissent makes no difference if no one listens. And listening to a dissenting voice can be as hard as speaking up.

It turns out that the effect of being challenged—of having your opinions rejected or questioned—isn't just psychological. Research shows that there is a real, physical impact on the body. Your heart beats faster and your blood pressure rises. Your blood vessels narrow as if to limit the bleeding that might result from an injury in an impending fight. Your skin turns pale, and your stress level skyrockets. It's the same reaction you would have if you were walking in the jungle and suddenly spotted a tiger.

This primal fight-or-flight response makes it hard to listen. And, according to an experiment conducted at the University of Wisconsin–Madison, things get even worse when we are in a position of authority—when we are in Professor Klein's shoes.

In the study, three strangers had to sit around a table in a lab and discuss a long list of issues, like an alcohol ban on campus or the need for mandatory graduation exams. It got boring quickly. Luckily, after thirty minutes, a research assistant came in with a plate of chocolate chip cookies, a nice relief from the task. What participants didn't know is that the plate of cookies was part of the experiment. In fact, it was the most crucial part.

Half an hour earlier, just before the session started, the researchers had randomly picked one of the three strangers and told the group that that person would serve as an evaluator of sorts. The role came with no real power; it just involved assigning "experimental points" to the other two people in the group based on their contributions to the discussion. These points had no substantive meaning at all. They didn't affect participants' compensation or their chances of being invited back for future studies. And because the study results were anonymous, no one outside the lab would even know how many points anybody received.

It was a fleeting, trivial sense of power. The evaluators knew they were chosen by sheer luck and not because of their skills or experience. They knew their evaluations had no real power.

Yet, when the plate of cookies arrived, they behaved very differently from the others. The plate didn't have enough seconds for everyone, and the evaluators were more likely than their peers to take an extra cookie. It took just a little taste of being the boss to make people feel entitled to a scarce resource.

"Everybody takes one cookie," explained Dacher Keltner, one of the researchers who ran the study. But who takes the first *extra* cookie? "It's our person in the position of power who reaches out, grabs the cookie, and says, 'that's mine.'"

When the researchers later watched the videotapes of the study, they were struck not only by how much the evaluators ate but also *how* they ate. They displayed signs of "disinhibited eating," psychology-speak for eating like an animal. They were much more likely to chew with their mouths open and scattered more crumbs, both on their faces and on the table, than the other participants.

The cookie study is a simple experiment, but it has big implications. It suggests that even the faintest sense of power—being in charge of something clearly inconsequential—can corrupt. And it's just one of many studies drawing the same conclusion. Research shows that when people are in a position of power, or even just have a sense of power, they are more likely to misunderstand and dismiss others' opinions, more likely to interrupt others and speak out of turn during discussions, and less willing to accept advice—even from experts.

In fact, having power is a bit like having brain damage. As Keltner put it, "people with power tend to behave like patients who have damaged their brain's orbitofrontal lobes," a condition that can cause insensitive and overly impulsive behavior.

When we are in charge, we ignore the perspectives of others. This is a dangerous tendency because more authority does not necessarily equal better insights. A complex system might reveal clues that a failure looms, but those warning signs don't respect hierarchy. They often reveal themselves to folks on the ground rather than to higher-ups in the corner office.

Yet because people don't expect their boss to listen, they don't speak up. This is especially true if the boss is an autocratic figure like Professor Klein. But it doesn't take a tyrant to suppress dissent. Even the best-intentioned bosses can cause employees to clam up. That's the conclusion from years of research by Jim Detert, one of the world's leading experts on the issue.

"Whether you realize it or not, you're probably conveying your power through subtle cues," write Detert and his coauthor Ethan Burris. "When someone ventures into your office, do you lean back in your chair with your arms clasped behind your head? You may think you're setting a relaxed tone, but you're really displaying dominance."

When Detert and his colleagues studied how companies try to get employees to speak up, they found that the "best practices" were anything but. Whether they ran a restaurant chain, a hospital, or a financial institution, most leaders had the same response when the researchers asked them what they did to help their employees speak up. "I have an open-door policy," they said. But when Detert and his colleagues talked to employees, they learned that open-door policies had little effect. The onus of starting a conversation with the boss and bringing up problems was still on the subordinates, and that's a daunting hurdle. And sometimes the boss with an open-door policy actually sat in an office behind several closed doors and a robust defensive line of assistants.

Other leaders solicit input proactively, but their attempts often fall flat. A popular practice is to collect anonymous feedback.

Anonymous surveys, suggestion boxes, and hotlines with caller-ID blocking are everywhere, and the assumption is that the promise of anonymity will help people speak up and guarantee candid responses. But the emphasis on anonymity actually highlights the dangers of speaking up. As Detert and Burris put it, "The subtext is 'It's not safe to share your views openly in this organization.'"

# III.

Nearly two decades after his discovery, a forty-eight-year-old Ignác Semmelweis, balding, corpulent, and a shadow of his former self, found himself committed to a state-run mental asylum in Vienna. He tried to leave, but the guards overpowered him. One rushed up and punched him in the stomach. Another knocked him to the ground. They hit and kicked him as he lay there. They stomped on him. Once he was restrained, they left him in a darkened cell. Two weeks later, he died from his injuries. His body was transferred to the nearby General Hospital and autopsied on one of the very tables he had used so often during his work there.

After his departure from Vienna in 1850, Semmelweis had lived in Hungary. Though he replicated his handwashing program with impressive results in a local hospital, most obstetricians continued to reject his doctrine. His sudden and unexplained escape from Vienna, which had alienated even his closest supporters, didn't help his case. Neither did his growing tendency to berate his critics. In 1860, he published a book in which he laid out his theory and lashed out against his detractors. When the book was met with criticism, he wrote a series of fuming open letters to his critics: "Your teaching," he wrote to one professor, "is founded upon the dead bodies of lying-in women murdered through ignorance." These bitter screeds marked the beginning of a drift toward madness. Semmel-weis's behavior became increasingly erratic, and by 1865, his family and friends saw but one option: committing him to a mental asylum.

The medical establishment didn't accept Semmelweis's ideas un-til years later, when advances in microbiology finally gave rise to germ theory—the idea that microorganisms can cause disease. Un-til then, handwashing didn't catch on, and women and babies con-tinued to die from childbed fever.

It's tempting to think that things would be different today—that we wouldn't miss something so obvious. After all, we are modern people who believe in science. But that's exactly what Semmelweis's contemporaries were thinking, too. They were smart people work-ing in some of the world's best hospitals and universities. They be-lieved in science. They just thought Semmelweis's idea missed the mark. His dissent, no matter how much evidence he marshaled, didn't convince them.

The unrivaled complexity of today's systems means that we are probably missing some risks that are just as obvious as the one Sem-melweis discovered. In a few decades, people might look back and think of us the way we think of Professor Klein and his friends: *How could they have been so blind?*

People in our organizations often know something about hidden risks or have a nagging suspicion that something isn't quite right. There are Semmelweises out there—someone we manage or per-haps one of our peers. How can we get them to speak up?

## Lesson 1: Charm School

Robert, a large, muscular man in his sixties, arrived for a routine checkup at his dentist's office in downtown Toronto. Robert had al-ways preferred an 8:00 a.m. appointment and was never late. And he always looked healthy and full of energy when he walked into the waiting room and greeted Donna, the office's longtime receptionist.

But when Donna saw him that morning, something didn't feel right to her. His face was red, and he was sweating. She sat him down and asked if he was OK. "Yeah, I'm fine," he told her. "I just didn't sleep well. I had indigestion. And my back hurts a little." He had looked up his symptoms online, but he didn't want to bother his doctor.

It sounded innocent enough, but Donna had a strange feeling that something was amiss. Though the dentist, Dr. Richard Speers, was in the middle of performing a procedure on another patient, she went in to see him. "Dick, Robert is here, and something just doesn't feel right to me. Can you come out and take a look at him?"

"I'm really busy right now," Speers replied.

"I really think you should see him," Donna insisted. "Something isn't right."

"But I'm in the middle of this," said Speers.

"Dick, I *want* you to see him."

Speers gave in. He had always trained his staff—his dental assistant, his hygienist, and even his receptionist—to speak up when something didn't feel right. He thought they might catch something he would miss.

He took off his gloves and went to the waiting room. He asked Robert a few questions: Had he taken any Tums for his indigestion? Did it help? Was there any pain in his left arm? Any discomfort between his shoulder blades? Robert had taken Tums, but that didn't help. He did feel some pain in his left arm, around his wrist. And, yes, he had upper back pain.

"Is there a history of heart disease in your family?" Speers asked.

"Yes, my father and brother both died of a heart attack," Robert replied.

"How old were they?"

"They were both my age."

Without delay, Speers sent him to the cardiac center of Toronto General Hospital, just down the street. Robert was eighteen hours into a heart attack. Triple bypass surgery saved his life.

In his free time, Dr. Speers is a pilot and aviation enthusiast, and he's been on a mission to teach dentists safety lessons from the airline industry. The biggest lesson he learned from pilots was to get people lower down in the hierarchy to speak up and to get higher-ups to listen.

Since the 1970s, a series of fatal accidents have forced changes in the airline industry. In the bad old days, the captain was the infallible king of the cockpit, not to be challenged by anyone. First officers usually kept their concerns to themselves, and even when they did speak, they would only hint at problems. Organizational researcher Karl Weick described their attitude like this: "I am puzzled by what is going on, but I assume that no one else is, especially because they have more experience, more seniority, higher rank."

But as the industry grew, aircraft, air traffic control, and airport operations became too complex for this approach to work. The captain was king, but the king was often wrong. There were too many moving parts and they were too intricately connected for one person to notice and understand everything.

Captains and first officers usually alternate flying the airplane. The flying pilot manipulates the primary controls. The nonflying pilot talks on the radio, runs through checklists, and is expected to challenge the flying pilot's mistakes. About half of the time, the captain is the flying pilot, and the first officer is the nonflying pilot. In the other half, the roles are switched. So, statistically, roughly 50 percent of accidents should happen when the captain is flying the plane, and 50 percent when the first officer is in charge of the controls. Right?

In 1994, the NTSB published a study of accidents due to flight crew mistakes between 1978 and 1990. The study reported a staggering finding. Nearly three-quarters of major accidents occurred during the captain's turn to fly. *Passengers were safer when the less experienced pilot was flying the plane.*

Of course, it's not that captains were poor pilots. But when the captain was the flying pilot, he (and most often it was a "he") was harder to challenge. His mistakes went unchecked. In fact, the report found that the most common error during major accidents was the failure of first officers to question the captain's poor decisions. In the reverse situation, when the first officer was flying the plane, the system worked well. The captain raised concerns and pointed out mistakes and helped the flying pilot understand complex situations. But this dynamic worked only in one direction.

All this changed with a training program known as Crew Resource Management, or CRM. The program revolutionized the culture not just of the cockpit but also of the whole industry. It reframed safety as a team issue and put all crew members—from the captain to the first officer to the cabin crew—on more equal footing. It was no longer disrespectful to question the decisions of a superior—it was required. CRM taught crew members the language of dissent.

Parts of CRM sound obvious, even outright silly. An important part of the training, for example, focuses on a five-step process that first officers can use to raise a concern:

1. Start by getting the captain's attention. ("Hey, Mike.")
2. Express your concern. ("I'm worried that the thunderstorm has moved over the airport.")
3. State the problem as you see it. ("We might get some dangerous wind shear.")
4. Propose a solution. ("Let's hold until the storm is clear of the airport.")
5. Get an explicit agreement. ("Does that sound good to you, Mike?")

These steps sound barely more sophisticated than what we might teach a child about how to ask for help. Yet they were rarely followed before CRM came along. First officers would state a fact ("the thunderstorm has moved over the airport") but would hesitate to get the captain's attention and express how concerned they were, let alone propose a solution. So even when they tried to express a grave concern, it often sounded more like a casual observation.

CRM was a huge success. Since it took hold in U.S. commercial aviation, the overall rate of accidents involving flight crew mistakes has declined sharply. And whether the flying pilot is the captain or the first officer no longer matters. In the 1990s, just half of the accidents—rather than three-quarters—happened when it was the captain's turn to fly.

The program works because it gives everyone, from baggage handlers to pilots, a sense of purpose. The message is that every single person can make an important contribution to safety, and everyone's views are important. And, as Daniel Pink explains in his book *Drive*, this approach—giving people a sense of purpose and autonomy—is often the most effective way to motivate them.

The ideas behind CRM have also spread to other fields struggling with increasingly complex operations, like firefighting and medicine. In a 2014 article in the *Journal of the Canadian Dental Association*, Dr. Speers and his coauthor, dentistry professor Chris McCulloch, described what Crew Resource Management would look like in the dental office.

"Dentists need to minimize hierarchy in their operatories by creating an atmosphere in which all personnel feel comfortable speaking up when they suspect a problem," they wrote. "A team member may see something the dentist is oblivious to, such as undetected caries [cavities] or a tooth that is about to receive inappropriate treatment. Dental team members should be encouraged to cross-check each other's actions, offer assistance when needed, and address errors in a non-judgmental fashion."

And it turns out that speaking up is helpful not only when others are unaware of a problem but also even when everyone else has also noticed the very same issue. In a painstaking study of dozens of wildfires, organizational researchers Michelle Barton and Kathleen Sutcliffe discovered the core factor distinguishing wildfire incidents that ended badly from those that didn't. The main difference wasn't whether firefighters noticed emerging signs of trouble. In fact, during both kinds of incidents—including many that ended disastrously—the crews did recognize early warning signs. Instead, the difference was whether crew members had *voiced* their concerns about the problems that everyone else had also noticed. If they had, their private concerns became public knowledge and triggered a discussion. As the researchers put it, speaking up allowed crew members to "create a kind of artifact—a statement that now hangs in the air between group members and must be acknowledged or denied, but in any case, responded to."

It's not only pilots, doctors, and firefighters who benefit from this approach. Google, for example, ran a large experiment among its engineers called Project Aristotle that showed that a team's willingness to share concerns contributed to how well it performed. Other research shows that a bank's best-performing branches were the ones where employees spoke up the most.

But learning to embrace dissent is hard. When Crew Resource Management was introduced, many pilots thought it was useless psychobabble. They called it "charm school" and felt it was an absurd attempt to teach them how to be warm and fuzzy. But as more and more accident investigations revealed how failures to speak up and listen led to disasters, attitudes began to shift. Charm school for pilots has become one of the most powerful safety interventions ever designed.

## Lesson 2: Soften Power Cues

In a large hospital in Texas, a highly skilled ER doctor struggled to make his patients feel comfortable. Though he had an excellent safety record and his colleagues respected him, he received low scores from his patients, who never quite felt at ease with him. When nurses pointed out that some patients even withheld important information from him, he knew he needed to do something different.

At the advice of the hospital's COO, he decided to make one small change: when talking with patients during his rounds, he would no longer stand by the bed. Instead, he'd grab a chair and sit down so he and the patient could talk face-to-face. He changed nothing else, and his interactions with patients were still short. But his patient satisfaction scores shot up, and patients began to open up to him.

Ben Berman, the airline captain and former accident investigator, uses a similar small trick. "I've never done a perfect flight," he says every time he meets a new first officer before a flight. This open declaration makes it easier for the more junior pilot to challenge him, despite his intimidating credentials as an experienced captain, top accident investigator, and author of a book on pilot error.

In the summer of 2011, Ken Freeman, the dean of Boston University's business school, took a radical step to soften power cues. Freeman became dean in 2010 after decades as a powerful executive in the corporate world. When he arrived at the school, his office was a stately, wood-paneled room on a high floor, far from the hustle and bustle of classrooms and student life. It was "bigger than any that I ever had in the corporate world," he said. An assistant, stationed outside, acted as a gatekeeper. Few people ever ventured up there.

After a year in the fancy office, Freeman decided to move. He picked a simple, small room with a clear-glass exterior wall in the middle of the building's busy second floor. "My office on the second floor is smaller than the vast majority of offices occupied by our faculty," he said. There is no assistant outside the door, and people can see Freeman through the glass wall. And the room is just down the hall from classrooms and a coffee shop popular with faculty and staff. "This enables me to have daily access to our students, faculty, and staff in a way that just wasn't possible when I was in a more formal office setting. I have drop-ins that start as early as 7:00. In a typical day, I'd say it's probably in the range of ten people."

At the other end of the spectrum from Freeman's tiny fishbowl is the private elevator of Richard Fuld, the disgraced CEO who ran Lehman Brothers as the investment bank collapsed into the largest bankruptcy in U.S. history. Former Lehman vice president Lawrence McDonald described Fuld's morning ritual: "His driver would call Lehman Brothers at the front desk, and the front desk attendant would press a button, and one of the elevators in the southeast corner of the building would become frozen. A security guard would come over and hold it until Mr. Fuld arrived in the back door. He comes in through the back door, so there's only like fifteen feet where King Richard Fuld is exposed to the rabble, I guess you'd call us."

The elevator ritual became a symbol of Fuld's leadership style. As McDonald put it, "At Lehman Brothers, you kept your head down, you did your job, or you lost both."

## Lesson 3: Leaders Speak Last

Eastern High School is in trouble. Something needs to be done quickly, and you're on the team that's supposed to find a solution. The local school system suffers from financial problems, falling tax revenues, and conflicts with the teachers' union. Though Eastern has always been an elite public school, it now faces an influx of less-well-prepared students because of redistricting. And some teachers just can't keep up. Ms. Simpson, an aging algebra teacher, for example, can no longer maintain order in the classroom. The president of the school board, whose son is in Ms. Simpson's class, fumes with anger. He calls on the superintendent of schools to improve the situation immediately, but without spending any extra money.

The superintendent puts together a team to deal with the crisis. The team includes four people: the superintendent himself, the principal of Eastern High, the school counselor, and you. As a member of the school board, you attend as a spokesperson for the parents.

Each of you brings different pieces of information to the table. The superintendent, for example, knows that other principals in the system were asked to allow Ms. Simpson to be transferred to their schools and refused. The principal knows that Ms. Simpson had a mild stroke two years earlier and that other faculty members are very fond of her. The counselor knows that students usually get easy As from Ms. Simpson and that they don't think she is a good math teacher. And you know that parents are opposed to increased taxes. What solutions will you come up with as a group?

This scenario was the setup of a simple but very important experiment that psychologist Matie Flowers conducted in the 1970s. Flowers created forty teams and assigned people to one of four roles in each team: superintendent, principal, school counselor, or school board member. Each person received an information sheet describing six or seven facts that were relevant to the situation but were unavailable to other team members. The idea was to simulate a complex situation where different people have access to different information. The teams then got to work and tried to come up with solutions.

The twist in the experiment was that Flowers randomly divided the participants playing the superintendent role into two groups: directive leaders and open leaders. Directive leaders were trained to state their own suggested solution at the beginning of the discussion and to emphasize that the most important thing was for the team to agree on its decision. Open leaders, in contrast, did not state their own preferred solution until all other members had the opportunity to offer their ideas. And open leaders emphasized that the most important thing was to discuss all possible viewpoints.

Flowers tape-recorded the sessions, and two independent judges analyzed the recordings. They counted the number of different solutions that team members proposed, and the number of facts from the information sheets that came up during the discussion. Take a look at the results:

| | TEAMS WITH A DIRECTIVE LEADER | TEAMS WITH AN OPEN LEADER |
|---|---|---|
| Number of solutions proposed | 5.2 | 6.5 |
| Number of facts mentioned | | |
| Total | 11.8 | 16.4 |
| Before reaching consensus | 8.2 | 15.5 |
| After reaching consensus | 3.6 | 0.9 |

Teams with open leaders offered more solutions. They also shared more facts during their discussion. The most striking pattern emerged when the judges separately counted the facts that had come up before and after the group agreed on a solution. Before reaching a decision, teams with open leaders shared almost twice as many facts as teams with directive leaders. So an open leadership style didn't just produce more solutions but also a better-informed discussion leading up to a decision. Under directive leaders, in contrast, nearly one-third of the shared facts came up only *after* consensus had been reached. At that point, of course, new facts made little difference and could only be used to justify a decision that had already been made.

Flowers's study showed just how little it took to gather more facts and elicit more solutions. It didn't take a born leader with exceptional charisma and skill. In fact, open leaders in the experiment were picked randomly and were given only a brief training. Yet their teams consistently did better than the other groups.

A few words can make a big difference. You can start a meeting like this: *The most important thing, I think, is that we all agree on our decision. Now, here is what I think could be done.* Or you can say: *The most important thing is that we air all possible viewpoints to reach a good decision. Now, what does each of you think should be done?*

Most of us aren't superintendents or CEOs, but open leadership works in all sorts of situations. Parenting expert Jane Nelsen describes a problem-solving session with her two youngest kids. Every week, Nelsen randomly assigned her kids two big chores each. After a few months, both kids started to complain that the *other* was getting the easier chores. So the family decided to discuss the issue at their weekly meeting.

Nelsen was convinced that random chore selection was fair, but she opened the discussion without sharing her view. "I simply put the problem on the agenda. Their solution was so simple and so profound, I don't know why I didn't think of it sooner." The kids' idea: list the chores on a board in the morning and let whoever wakes up first choose which two to do. "Once again," she writes, "I was reminded of what great solutions they can come up with when we give them a chance."

Just because parents have more experience in life doesn't mean that they'll have a better idea of what will actually work with their kids. But if Nelsen had spoken first, her kids might never have shared their idea.*

---

* Chris (one of the authors of this book) recently validated the effectiveness of this approach during a discussion that he and his four-year-old son had about appropriate ways to play with foam swords. Open leadership really works.

"It all goes back to the need for us to have a more sophisticated appreciation of how much humans are attuned to hierarchy," Jim Detert told us. He went on:

> You need to realize that most people are really concerned—consciously or not—of offending authority and ruining social relationships. So, as a boss, it's not enough for you to create a generally pleasant environment and have an open-door policy. You need to be much more active than that. Don't wait for people to come to your office to speak up—go to theirs. If no one speaks up in a meeting, don't assume they all agree—actively ask for divergent viewpoints. And schedule frequent conversations when people can share ideas with you. That way speaking up isn't extraordinary but a casual, routine thing.

Most of all, Detert warns that it's not enough just to avoid doing things that stifle skeptical voices. "You need to realize that if you are not encouraging people to speak up, you're discouraging them. Not doing anything negative just isn't enough."

But what if all these steps trigger an avalanche of unfounded concerns and off-base comments? Is there such a thing as *too much* speaking up? No doubt, some ideas you hear will be bad. A few might come from disgruntled employees inclined to complain for complaining's sake. "When you encourage people to speak up, you shouldn't expect that they'll only bring good ideas to you," says Detert. "But you need to weigh the costs of wasting time on some useless ideas against the costs of missing something very important. You need to decide what matters more."

In a simple system, encouraging people to speak up may not be so important. Failures are more obvious and easier for everyone to notice, and small errors don't usually cause big meltdowns. But in a complex system, the ability of any one individual to know what's going on is limited. And if the system is also tightly coupled, skeptical voices are crucial because the cost of being wrong is just too high. In the danger zone, dissent is indispensable.

## Chapter Eight

# THE SPEED BUMP EFFECT

"He's a black guy. I wanted him to
succeed, but didn't get there."

## I.

When Sallie Krawcheck, the former chief financial officer of Citigroup, sat down for an interview with PBS correspondent Paul Solman, they talked about the 2007–2008 financial crisis that had shaken the world economy a few years earlier.

> KRAWCHECK: I think about my old industry—financial services, where my experience watching those companies go into the downturn was not, "it's a bunch of evil geniuses who perfectly foresee the downturn." Quite the opposite. It was a group of hard-working individuals who miscalled the downturn. And as I think back to those teams, which are pretty non-diverse, they were people who had grown up together, gone to the same schools, looked at the same data over years and years, and came to the wrong conclusions.
>
> SOLMAN: Peas in a pod.

KRAWCHECK: Peas in a pod, so to speak. I'm not sure they'd love it if you called them that, but peas in a pod. And I remember clear as a bell one day where a senior investment banker was describing a complex security, and a woman who was in a consumer banking role stopped and said, "What the heck is that? And why are we doing it?" And there wasn't, going into the financial crisis, enough of "What the heck is that?"

SOLMAN: But are women actually more likely to say, "I don't get it"?

KRAWCHECK: I think when you get diverse groups together who've got these different backgrounds, there's more permission in the room—as opposed to, "I can't believe I don't understand this and I'd better not ask because I might lose my job." There's permission to say, "I come from someplace else, can you run that by me one more time?" And I definitely saw that happen. But as time went on, the management teams became less diverse. And in fact, the financial services industry went into the downturn white, male and middle aged. And it came out whiter, maler and middle-aged-er.

In the interview, Krawcheck argued passionately for diversity. But is she right? Can diversity help us avoid failure in a complex world?

HALF A DOZEN PEOPLE sat in the waiting room of a behavioral research lab in Singapore. All of them were ethnic Chinese who lived in the city-state and had come to the lab to compete in a stock-trading simulation. What they didn't know was that they were about to participate in an experiment that would upend much of the conventional wisdom about diversity. In fact, they had no idea that the study had to do with diversity at all.

A research assistant came in and escorted each person from the waiting room to an individual cubicle with a computer and a trading screen. The participants then received instructions on how to calculate the value of the stocks.

The simulation was a simple version of a real stock market. The six participants were free to buy and sell the stocks among one another using their computers, and they could see all completed transactions, bids, and offers on their screens. After a practice round, they began trading for real money.

The researchers ran this simulation with dozens of groups. Some groups were homogeneous—all Chinese, the majority ethnic group in Singapore. Other markets were more diverse: they included at least one member of an ethnic minority, Malays or Indians. The researchers monitored the accuracy of trades in these different markets. How close were the prices to the correct values of the stocks, based on the information available to the traders?

"The diverse markets were much more accurate than the homogeneous markets," said Evan Apfelbaum, an MIT professor and one of the study's authors. "In homogeneous markets, if someone made a mistake, then others were more likely to copy it," Apfelbaum told us. "In diverse groups, mistakes were much less likely to spread."

These results held up even when the researchers took the experiment to a very different part of the world: Texas, where the diverse markets included a mix of whites, Latinos, and African Americans. Just like their counterparts in Singapore, the Texas participants priced stocks more accurately when they were in diverse company.

And homogeneous markets led to more price bubbles—and crashed more severely when those bubbles burst. *Diversity deflated the bubbles.*

What made the diverse groups different?

Before the participants started trading, they individually answered questions about a few pricing scenarios. The researchers then used these answers to see if diverse groups had come to the lab already equipped with better pricing skills. But that wasn't the case.

The answer lay in the trading data. In homogeneous markets, traders seem to have put a lot of confidence in their peers' decisions. Even if someone made a mistake, people often assumed it was a reasonable choice. They trusted one another's judgments—even bad judgments. In diverse markets, people scrutinized mistakes more intensely and copied them less often. They saw errors for what they were. They distrusted each other's views.

Having minority traders wasn't valuable because they contributed unique perspectives. Minority traders helped markets because, as the researchers put it, "their mere presence changed the tenor of decision making among all traders." In diverse markets, *everyone* was more skeptical.

We tend to trust the judgment of people who look similar to us, so homogeneous groups reduce tension and make for smooth, effortless interactions. Of course, that's not always a bad thing. It can be easier to get things done when we are confident that we can rely on our peers' judgment. But it seems that homogeneity makes things *too* easy. It leads to too much conformity and not enough skepticism. It makes it easier for us to fall for bad ideas.

Diversity, in contrast, is less familiar and feels less comfortable. It threatens to be a source of friction. And that makes us more skeptical, more critical, and more vigilant, all of which make us more likely to catch errors. "We tend to think that if someone looks different, they also think different—that they have different views, different assumptions," Apfelbaum told us. "That leads to healthy decision making. There might be some discomfort, but it makes us more objective."

Apfelbaum and his colleagues dug further with another experiment. In that study, they put together groups of four participants and asked each person to evaluate the profiles of high school students who had applied to a top university. Here's an example:

| | STUDENT A | STUDENT B |
| --- | --- | --- |
| Grade Point Average (out of 4.0) | 3.94 | 3.41 |
| SAT (Standardized Test) scores | | |
| Critical Reading (out of 800) | 750 | 630 |
| Math (out of 800) | 730 | 620 |
| Advanced Placement Classes | 2 | 3 |
| Extracurricular Activities | Environmental Club<br>National Honor Society<br>Writing Tutor | Drama Club<br>Ballroom Dancing<br>Students Against Drunk Driving |

Which student do you think would be a better candidate for admission to an elite school?

If you are like most people, you answered A. It seems like an easy decision. Student A had nearly perfect grades and better test scores on both critical reading and math. Though B took one more Advanced Placement course, A is clearly stronger academically. And A's extracurricular record doesn't seem any worse than B's. When you ask people individually rather than in a group, most respondents pick Student A.

But the experiment had a twist. In each group of four, only one person was an actual participant. The other three were actors, instructed to give the wrong answer when it was time to share their choices. The real participants didn't know the others were in on the experiment.

The three actors went first. "Student B," said the first person. "Student B," said the second. "Student B," echoed the third. Then it was the real participant's turn. Some people resisted conformity and, after some hesitation, picked Student A. But many went along with the rest of the group even though Student B was by most criteria an inferior applicant.

You might recognize this setup from the famous Asch conformity experiments, where many people in a similar situation yielded to the group and declared that two lines were of the same length even when one was clearly longer than the other. But Apfelbaum and his colleagues added a new dimension to the experiment. In some of the groups, both the real participant and the three actors were white. In other groups, the actual participant was white, but two or three of the actors were racial minorities. This made a big difference. In racially similar groups, participants often conformed to the group and endorsed Student B. In diverse groups, people were much less likely to accept the wrong answer.

Why does this happen? As in the trading experiment, participants in homogeneous groups were more likely to second-guess themselves when their peers made questionable choices. "It appears to be a 'benefit of the doubt effect,'" Apfelbaum explained. "In homogeneous groups, people seem to rationalize their peers' mistaken views. They try to think of reasons the others might actually be right—why the weaker applicant might actually be better. In diverse groups, this happens less."

In diverse groups, we don't trust each other's judgment quite as much, and we call out the naked emperor. And that's very valuable when dealing with a complex system. If small errors can be fatal, then giving others the benefit of the doubt when we think they are wrong is a recipe for disaster. Instead, we need to dig deeper and stay critical. Diversity helps us do that.

Other studies have come to the same conclusion. In a fascinating experiment in 2006, researchers created teams of three—some all-white, some racially diverse—and gave them a murder mystery to solve. It was a complicated case. A businessman had been murdered, and there were several suspects and lots of information to sort through: witness statements, transcripts of interrogations, detectives' reports, maps of the crime scene, newspaper clippings, and a personal note written by the victim. These materials contained dozens of clues to the mystery, and the researchers made sure that all team members had access to many of the same clues. But the researchers also gave each person a few unique clues that only he or she knew; the team needed all these clues to find the murderer. This setup captured two important features of complex systems: the truth wasn't directly observable, and no one person knew all the relevant facts.

Diversity helped solve the mystery. Diverse teams were more likely to recognize that different team members knew different things. These teams also spent much more time sharing and discussing the clues. "The groups with racial diversity significantly outperformed the groups with no racial diversity," writes the lead author of the study, Columbia professor Katherine Phillips. "Being with similar others leads us to think we all hold the same information and share the same perspective. This perspective . . . stopped the all-white groups from effectively processing the information."

And researchers found similar results during mock trials with real jurors: racially mixed juries shared more information, discussed a wider range of relevant factors, and even made fewer mistakes when recalling case facts. Again, it's not that minority jurors performed better than white jurors. When the jury was diverse, *everyone* did better.

Gender diversity has similar effects. Accounting professors Larry Abbott, Susan Parker, and Theresa Presley, for example, have found that companies that lack gender diversity on their board of directors are more likely to issue financial restatements—revisions of their previous statements due to error or fraud. A financial restatement is an embarrassing failure and can shake investors' confidence in a company, but it seems that even a small increase in gender diversity makes it less likely that a restatement will be needed. "A more diverse, less cohesive board may be more likely to question assumptions and inquire as to the comparability of accounting with industry practice, resulting in more in-depth discussion and slower decision-making," the researchers wrote. "These actions are consistent with board gender diversity reducing groupthink and leading to an improved monitoring process."

Ironically, lab experiments show that while homogeneous groups do less well on complex tasks, they report *feeling* more confident about their decisions. They enjoy the tasks they do as a group and think they are doing well. Being around similar people feels good. It's comfortable. There is no friction, and everything is familiar and flows smoothly. Diversity, in contrast, feels strange. It's inconvenient. But it makes us work harder and ask tougher questions.

# II.

The following conversation took place at a prestigious American consulting firm a few years ago. It's the transcript of an actual discussion between two consultants who were evaluating Henry, a job candidate they had both interviewed.

> INTERVIEWER 1: He's a black guy. I wanted him to
> succeed, but didn't get there.
> INTERVIEWER 2: He's very polished and presents well
> but is not structured in his approach. He couldn't

even say, "These are the three points I'd like to talk about."

INTERVIEWER 1: It took a lot of prompting. *(Sighs.)*

INTERVIEWER 2: He is a diversity candidate.

INTERVIEWER 1: He's not a disaster, but definitely not a bring back.

*Henry was very polished, he's a good presenter, he would add diversity to the firm, and they wanted him to succeed. But his responses lacked structure.*

This same pair of interviewers also considered Will, a white guy. "He's super polished, confident, and easy to put in front of the client," one of the interviewers noted. "But he has no business intuition." The other interviewer agreed: Will's approach lacked structure. But *that* was OK. Will was new to consulting case interviews; he just needed some more practice. So they called him back for the next round of interviews. They even gave him some feedback before his next interview: he needed to "work on his structure." Henry didn't get a second chance.

These consultants didn't think they had a bias problem. Even as bias crept in, they thought they were evaluating candidates based on merit. For years, orchestras faced the same issue. They viewed themselves as meritocracies, hiring only the best musicians. But they tended to hire many more men than women, despite the gender diversity of candidates and the perceived fairness of auditions.

When orchestras started using a curtain to shield candidates' gender from judges, their hiring bias went away, and diversity spiked. Many of the best orchestras now have an equal number of men and women.

But in most hiring and promotion decisions, we can't just add a curtain. So companies have adopted a huge number of diversity programs over the past three decades. Most of these, however, didn't move the needle. In the United States, in firms with more than one hundred employees, the proportion of black men in management stayed steady at around 3 percent between 1985 and 2014. The proportion of white female managers has been stuck at around 30 percent since 2000. In some fields, such as financial services, the numbers are even worse. It turns out that most attempts to increase racial and gender diversity in leadership roles fail.

It's a paradox: diversity programs are everywhere, and firms are putting more and more money and effort into them, but we're not seeing results. Why?

Harvard sociologist Frank Dobbin and his colleagues pored over thirty years of data from more than eight hundred firms to answer this question. They discovered something stunning: the most frequently used diversity programs didn't increase diversity. In fact, they made firms *less diverse*.

Take mandatory diversity training. It's a very popular program—most Fortune ˙500 firms and nearly half of midsize companies use it—but it just doesn't work. Companies introducing it saw the proportion of Asian American managers fall by 5 percent and the share of black female managers shrink by nearly 10 percent within five years. And there was no improvement at all in the representation of white women, black men, and Hispanics.

The results were similar for other popular programs, such as mandatory job tests (which aim to ensure a fair hiring process) and formal grievance procedures (which employees can use to challenge pay, promotion, and termination decisions). It seems these programs should reduce bias against minorities and women, but they actually make things worse.

Dobbin and his colleagues interviewed hundreds of managers to find out why. It turns out that these programs fail to work because they focus on *policing* managers' actions—they try to strong-arm managers and limit their discretion in hiring and promotion decisions. But managers resist this approach. "You won't get managers on board by blaming and shaming them with rules and reeducation," the researchers wrote. "As social scientists have found, people often rebel against rules to assert their autonomy. Try to coerce me to do X, Y, or Z, and I'll do the opposite just to prove that I'm my own person."

In a recent lab experiment, for example, when people felt pressure to agree with a brochure that condemned racial prejudice, they showed *more* racial bias after reading it. The brochure reduced prejudice only when people felt that they were free to agree or disagree— when the choice was theirs. Dobbin and his colleagues saw the same kind of thing with job tests, too. At a West Coast food company, for example, managers made only strangers—mostly minorities—take the test but hired their white friends without testing them.

What can leaders do? Here are a few solutions that three decades of data have shown to work.

One tool that works is *voluntary* diversity training. Though people grumble about mandatory programs, they are often happy to participate in voluntary ones. And they are much more receptive to new ideas if they see the training as an optional learning opportunity rather than a forced ritual.

Targeted recruitment is another good approach. The idea is to seek out candidates from underrepresented groups, either within the organization or through existing recruitment programs at universities or minority professional organizations. As with diversity training, it should be up to managers to decide if they want to participate. That way, they will see the program as a way to access a larger talent pool rather than a heavy-handed mandate that limits their authority. "Our interviews suggest that managers willingly participate when invited," the researchers wrote. "That's partly because the message is positive: 'Help us find a greater variety of promising employees!'"

Formal mentoring programs for junior employees (regardless of race and gender) and cross-training programs (where management trainees are rotated through different roles) also help. That's because these measures don't *impose* rules about diversity. They often aren't even designed with diversity in mind. Instead, they expose managers to different groups, and that alone reduces bias. A male senior manager, assigned to mentor a young woman from a minority group, may get to know her work quite well. When a management role opens up, he might be more likely to suggest her as a candidate for promotion.

Of course, many organizations have informal mentoring arrangements. But formal programs that assign mentors to mentees work much better. Here's Dobbin and his colleagues:

> While white men tend to find mentors on their own, women and minorities more often need help from formal programs. One reason . . . is that white male executives don't feel comfortable reaching out informally to young women and minority men. Yet they are eager to mentor assigned protégés, and women and minorities are often first to sign up for mentors [in a formal program].

It also turns out that just having someone track diversity can help. For a business unit, that might mean having someone whose job it is to promote diversity—even if they don't have much power beyond collecting and reporting data. Diversity task forces, for example, periodically look at diversity numbers for different units and figure out opportunities to increase diversity: Is a particular department not getting a diverse enough applicant pool? Are women and minorities who have been at the firm for years not being promoted? Are they not even applying for promotions in certain areas? Once they have answers, task force members can bring up these issues in their own departments.

Tracking diversity in this way works because people want to appear fair-minded. When managers know that someone keeps an eye on the numbers, it makes them ask themselves: Should I take a step back? Do I need to think about a broader set of people who are qualified? Am I just considering the first people who came to my mind?

Many well-meaning leaders who are committed to promoting diversity are frustrated because their efforts have made little difference. The most common strategies, which are all about rules and control, have failed. But the approaches outlined here—voluntary diversity training, targeted recruitment, formal mentoring and cross-training programs, and diversity task forces—work. In Dobbin's sample of firms, these programs boosted the number of female and minority managers in just five years, often by double-digit percentages.

These things work because they're soft tools. They don't try to strong-arm people into giving up control. Instead of enforcing a list of dos and don'ts, they engage managers. They expose them to a wider variety of people. And they appeal to their desire to look good in the eyes of others.

In the age of complex systems, diversity is a great risk management tool. But we can't force-feed it to an organization. Things get worse, not better, when we use the usual bureaucratic procedures. We need to ease up on the control tactics. Building a diverse organization is a hard problem with a soft solution.

## III.

The blood-testing company Theranos was once one of the hottest healthcare ventures in the United States. In October 2015, the *New York Times* named its founder, Elizabeth Holmes, who'd started the company as a nineteen-year-old Stanford dropout, one of "five visionary tech entrepreneurs who are changing the world." Right around the same time, she appeared on the cover of *Inc.* magazine. The headline: "The Next Steve Jobs." Theranos was valued at $9 billion, and Holmes, at only thirty-one, had already amassed a net worth of $4.5 billion. A few months earlier, *Time* magazine named her one of its one hundred most influential people. Investors poured hundreds of millions of dollars into the company.

It seemed that Theranos had invented a way to run dozens of medical tests using just a drop of blood. With a prick on your finger, you could get tested for hundreds of conditions. No need to draw blood intravenously. No need for big needles. And all this at a fraction of the cost of existing tests.

It seemed like an incredible technology that would disrupt the entire healthcare establishment. "Turning a blood test into an inexpensive, accessible and even (almost) pleasant experience—rather than an expensive, dreaded and time-consuming procedure—makes people more likely to get tested," noted the *New York Times.* "As a result, medical problems can be identified earlier, enabling the prevention or effective treatment of diseases ranging from diabetes and heart ailments to cancer."

Theranos was going to be the next big thing in Silicon Valley. But John Carreyrou, a Pulitzer Prize–winning investigative reporter with the *Wall Street Journal*, didn't buy the hype. He'd read a magazine profile of Holmes and was surprised by how vaguely she talked about the company's technology. "There were some brief critical sections in there that raised questions for me, but I didn't think all that much more of it," says Carreyrou. Then he got a tip that "things might not be exactly as they seem at this company."

Carreyrou began to investigate Theranos, and on October 15, 2015, the *Wall Street Journal* ran his story. It was a devastating report, raising questions about the accuracy of the company's testing device and revealing that Theranos didn't even use its own technology for most of its tests. Employees admitted that they'd run the vast majority of tests on traditional blood-testing machines bought from other companies. "The 31-year-old Ms. Holmes's bold talk and black turtlenecks draw comparisons to Apple Inc. cofounder Steve Jobs," Carreyrou wrote. "But Theranos has struggled behind the scenes to turn the excitement over its technology into reality."

After this initial blow, the house of cards began to wobble. Journalists and regulators continued to investigate the company. And Theranos was soon under legal siege. Its partner, the drugstore chain Walgreens, filed a lawsuit for breach of contract. Some of Theranos's biggest financial backers also sued, alleging that the company and its founder had lied to them about the technology. Tens of thousands of blood test results were voided, and lawsuits began to pile up from patients who'd received false results. In 2016, *Fortune* named Holmes one of the "world's most disappointing leaders." *Forbes* revised her estimated net worth: zero.

Months before the meltdown, Dr. David Koch, the president of the American Association for Clinical Chemistry, had been asked to comment on Theranos's promise. Koch is a leading expert in the field, but he had little to say. "It's impossible to comment on how good this is going to be," he said. "I really can't be more definitive because there's nothing to really look at, to read, to react to."

Theranos was famously secretive. Holmes insisted that the company had to operate in "stealth mode" to protect its technology. Few had seen its data. No peer-reviewed studies examined its devices. And when journalist Ken Auletta asked Holmes to explain how the technology worked, her response was: "A chemistry is performed so that a chemical reaction occurs and generates a signal from the chemical interaction with the sample, which is translated into a result, which is then reviewed by certified laboratory personnel." Auletta called this answer "comically vague."

Several investment firms passed on Theranos because of this vagueness. "The more we tried to drill down, the more uncomfortable she got," one potential investor told the *Wall Street Journal*. Google Ventures also considered an investment: "We just had someone from our life-science investment team go into Walgreens and take the [Theranos] test. And it wasn't that difficult for anyone to determine that things may not be what they seem here"—because Walgreens wanted to do a full blood draw instead of using Theranos's "revolutionary" finger prick.

Some outsiders figured out that something was amiss. But what about insiders? What about the board of directors, whose job it is to make sure that a company is on the right track?

Well, here is a list of Theranos's board members in the fall of 2015:

| NAME | CLAIM TO FAME | BIRTH YEAR | SEX |
|------|---------------|------------|-----|
| Henry Kissinger | Former U.S. Secretary of State | 1923 | Male |
| Bill Perry | Former U.S. Secretary of Defense | 1927 | Male |
| George Shultz | Former U.S. Secretary of State | 1920 | Male |
| Sam Nunn | Former U.S. Senator | 1938 | Male |
| Bill Frist | Former U.S. Senator | 1952 | Male |
| Gary Roughead | Former Navy Admiral | 1951 | Male |
| James Mattis | Former Marine Corps General | 1950 | Male |
| Dick Kovacevich | Former CEO of Wells Fargo | 1943 | Male |
| Riley Bechtel | Former CEO of Bechtel | 1952 | Male |
| William Foege | Former epidemiologist | 1936 | Male |
| Sunny Balwani | Theranos executive (President and COO) | 1965 | Male |
| Elizabeth Holmes | Theranos executive (Founder and CEO) | 1984 | Female |

"It's a board like no other," declared *Fortune* magazine. "Theranos has assembled what may be, in terms of public service, the most illustrious board in U.S. corporate history."

It was indeed an exceptional group. You rarely see a board with so many former cabinet secretaries, senators, and high-ranking military officials. But the group was also remarkable for its lack of diversity. Other than the two Theranos executives, every single board member—ten out of ten—was a white man. And every one of those directors was born before 1953. Their average age: seventy-six years old.

Not only did Theranos's board lack the sort of surface-level diversity that Apfelbaum's research identified as important, but it also lacked medical or biotechnology expertise. The only still-licensed medical expert in the group was former senator Bill Frist, who'd begun his career as a surgeon. William Foege, age seventy-nine, had once been a leading epidemiologist, but had retired from medicine many years earlier. As a group, Theranos's directors would have been more at home at a public policy think tank than at a cutting-edge medical technology firm.

Just after the *Wall Street Journal* published its first critical examination of Theranos, *Fortune* editor Jennifer Reingold called out the board for its lack of expertise. She wondered if a group with so little collective experience in Theranos's core field could oversee the company effectively. "While it's probably useful to have a retired government official or two to teach and offer good leadership skills, when there are six with no medical or technology experience . . . one wonders just how plugged in they are to Theranos' day-to-day activities." A mix of backgrounds, Reingold suggested, would have been better.

She was right. To understand why, we have to shift gears and industries. We have to learn why directors who were public servants, military leaders, and retired doctors—the same backgrounds that damned the Theranos board—helped hundreds of small banks weather the financial crisis.

Here is a list of a few community banks founded in the United

States in the late 1990s. It's just a tiny sample from a much longer list, but it captures the basic pattern quite well. Can you spot what it is?

| NAME | LOCATION | BANKERS ON THE BOARD | FAILED? | YEAR CLOSED |
|---|---|---|---|---|
| Florida Business Bank | Melbourne, FL | 36% | No | |
| Kentucky Neighborhood Bank | Elizabethtown, KY | 20% | No | |
| Michigan Heritage Bank | Farmington Hills, MI | 56% | Yes | 2009 |
| New Century Bank | Chicago, IL | 60% | Yes | 2010 |
| Paragon Commercial Bank | Raleigh, NC | 33% | No | |
| Pierce Commercial Bank | Tacoma, WA | 63% | Yes | 2010 |

You probably noticed that all the bank failures occurred in 2009 and 2010. That pattern makes sense. The Great Recession wasn't kind to small banks.

But there is something else about the list, something more peculiar. You might have spotted that the banks that failed had *more* bankers on their boards of directors than did the banks that survived. If you noticed that, you're on to something. A recent study that tracked more than thirteen hundred community banks over nearly two decades across the United States revealed a similar pattern. Banks with many bankers on the board were more likely to fail than banks whose directors had come from a wider range of backgrounds: not only bankers but also nonprofit folks, lawyers, doctors, government people, military officers, and others. Though many of these backgrounds have nothing to do with banking, this kind of diversity—diversity in expertise—saved the banks.

This effect was strongest for banks in complex, uncertain markets. And it's not that banks with riskier profiles appointed more bankers as directors. Nor did banker-dominated boards accept more risk to achieve higher returns. The study ruled out these explanations. To figure out what was going on, the study's lead author—John Almandoz, a professor at Spain's IESE business school—interviewed dozens of board members, bank CEOs, and bank founders. He found three things.

The first is that directors with a banking background often relied too much on their experience. Over and over again, interviewees used the word "baggage" to describe what bankers brought to the board. As one director put it, "The benefits of not having prior bankers is that there is no baggage to speak of in terms of, 'With this other bank, we did it this way.'"

Then there was overconfidence. "If I got a board which has got a lot of bankers on it, they are going to tend to reach for loans a little bit more because they believe that they have got a little bit more background and experience," a board member explained. "Whereas other people who aren't bankers tend to be a little more cautious."

The third issue was the lack of productive conflict. When amateur directors were just a small minority on a board, it was hard for them to challenge the experts. On a board with many bankers, one CEO told the researchers, "Everybody respects each other's ego at that table, and at the end of the day, they won't really call each other out." But on a board with more nonbankers, "when we see something we don't like, no one is afraid to bring it up."

Boards that weren't dominated by experts behaved like racially diverse teams. The directors argued and questioned each other's judgment. They took nothing for granted. Bankers didn't speak the same language as doctors and lawyers, so even "obvious" things had to be spelled out and debated. There was friction, and toes were stepped on. It wasn't easy. But still, these boards had the best of both worlds. Unlike Theranos, they had a handful of true experts, bankers with deep industry expertise. But—thanks to the amateurs—the weight of that expertise didn't quash debate and dissent. "Amateurs," Almandoz told us, "have the naiveté to ask questions about things the experts take for granted."

It's a familiar conclusion. Remember what Sallie Krawcheck said about diversity? Diversity works because it makes us question the consensus. *What the heck is that? Why are we doing it? Can you run that by me one more time?*

Surface-level diversity and diversity in expertise work in remarkably similar ways. In both cases, diversity is helpful not so much because of a unique perspective that minorities or amateurs bring to the table but because diversity makes the whole group more skeptical. It ensures that a team doesn't work together too smoothly and agree too easily. And that's a big deal in complex, tightly coupled systems, where it's easy to miss big threats and make mistakes that will spiral out of control.

Diversity is like a speed bump. It's a nuisance, but it snaps us out of our comfort zone and makes it hard to barrel ahead without thinking. It saves us from ourselves.

## Chapter Nine

# STRANGERS IN A STRANGE LAND

### "Are they magicians or something?"

## I.

Dan Pacholke took a deep breath as he stared at the phone. He had to call Veronica Medina-Gonzalez about her son, Ceasar. Pacholke, a former corrections officer who now headed the Washington State Department of Corrections, oversaw an $850 million budget, eight thousand employees, and nearly seventeen thousand inmates. He didn't usually have to call victims' families. But, then again, the Department of Corrections didn't usually kill people.

Seven months earlier, on a cloudy May evening in 2015, Ceasar Medina and a few friends had been hanging out after hours in a tattoo parlor, eating pizza and drinking beer, when two gunmen forced their way through the back door of the shop. A tattooed man wearing Air Jordans and a light gray hoodie charged into the lobby with his pistol at the ready. He forced Medina to the floor next to the front counter and shoved his gun into the back of his head. Suddenly the gunman leaped up, raised his pistol, and fired a shot. Medina heaved himself off the ground and ran. The gunman fired again, this time hitting Medina.

Their robbery botched, the gunmen fled. Medina's friends half carried, half dragged his body to the backseat of their car to take him to the hospital, but he died at the scene.

Detectives got to work right away. Surveillance cameras had captured the scene, and police circulated an alert with the shooter's photo. An officer in the Washington State Department of Corrections saw the alert and recognized the shooter: a man named Jeremiah Smith.

The officer knew Smith because Washington State had released him from prison just two weeks earlier, on May 14, after he had served time for robbery and assault. According to the Department of Corrections (DOC) prisoner management system, that was the last day of Smith's sentence. But the system was wrong. When Smith left prison, he still had more than three months left of his sentence. When Smith shot Ceasar Medina, he should have still been behind bars.

Smith's early release was caused by a coding error—a bug—in the DOC's prisoner management system. Dan Pacholke only found out about the problem at the end of 2015. But others in the DOC had learned about it years earlier. In 2012, Matthew Mirante, the father of a stabbing victim, contacted the Department's victim services unit. A truck driver for Boeing, Mirante suspected that the DOC had miscalculated the release date of his son's assailant. Using pencil and paper, it took him five minutes to calculate the sentence and confirm his suspicions: the assailant's release came forty-five days too early. At first, corrections employees thought that Mirante had gotten the math wrong. But then they ran his conclusions by a lawyer in the state's attorney general's office. The calculations were correct.

Mirante's discovery was just the tip of the iceberg. For more than a decade, errors in the prisoner management system, a byzantine piece of custom-built software, had led to the early release of thousands of felons. The whole system was a hodgepodge of what one manager called "complex interdependencies." This complexity both caused the sentencing error and hid it from DOC officials. Until Mirante ran his own calculation, *no one at the DOC even knew that there had been a mistake.* Trust in the system also created tight coupling. No one checked the calculations; everyone just did what the computer said. The computer might as well have opened the bars automatically.

How does that happen? How did a truck driver clue the Department of Corrections into a problem in a prisoner sentencing system that programmers, lawyers, and department officials had missed for years? The answer lies not in Mirante himself or in his profession. Many in the DOC could have made the same simple calculation. Mirante saw the error precisely because he *wasn't* in the Department. He was an outsider, not bound by the organization's rules, assumptions, or politics.

Once managers realized that Mirante was right, they submitted a request for programmers to fix the software. But the fix, which was initially expected to take three months, was pushed back more than a dozen times. In the meantime, no one understood the startling implications of Mirante's discovery.

Three years after Mirante's original inquiry, programmers finally made the changes and started testing their fix to see how current prisoners' sentences would be affected. When they had fixed sentencing issues in the past, they usually saw just a few issues—unusual cases when a release date would be shifted by a few days. But fixing the problem that Mirante raised shifted three thousand release dates by an average of two months. It was, as the DOC's chief information officer put it, an "'oh shit' moment."

When we talked with State Senator Mike Padden, who chairs the State Senate's Law and Justice Committee, he was aghast that officials had ignored the issue for so long. Contrast that, he told us, with what happens when a prisoner escapes: "They pull out all the stops to get that person back!" But in this case, they let thousands of prisoners go early.

On the call to Medina's mother, Pacholke offered his condolences and apologized for the mistake. A few weeks later, he resigned. Medina's mother filed a $5 million claim against the DOC. Though Jeremiah Smith had pulled the trigger and shot Ceasar Medina, she argued, the DOC bore responsibility. For three years, they ignored a valuable contribution from an outsider, and as a result, her son was dead.

# II.

If Georg Simmel were alive today, he'd be a superstar public intellectual with gobs of Twitter followers, a viral TED Talk, and a *New York Times* bestseller. Or at least that's the kind of status he enjoyed in late-nineteenth-century Berlin. A brilliant social theorist and a bit of a showman, Simmel dazzled audiences, and his lectures were wildly popular with both students and people outside the university. He was also a prolific writer who published articles not just in academic journals but also in newspapers and magazines. And his writings covered a fascinating array of topics, from urban life and the philosophy of money to flirtation and high fashion.

Despite all this, Simmel was an outsider in the German academic system. For much of his career, he was an unpaid lecturer, and he was passed over for professorships again and again. In 1901, he finally received the rank of *Ausserordentlicher Professor*, but that was, as one of his biographers noted, "a purely honorary title that still did

not allow him to take a part in the affairs of the academic community and failed to remove the stigma of an outsider."

One obstacle was Simmel's Jewish background. Another was his
popular appeal, which many academics resented. "He is, at any rate,
a dyed-in-the-wool Israelite, in his outward appearance, in his bearing, and in his manner of thinking," wrote a prominent historian in
a letter of evaluation when the University of Heidelberg considered
Simmel for a professorship. "He spices his words with clever say-
ings. And the audience he recruits is composed accordingly. The
ladies constitute a very large portion," and so do people "who are
still flooding in semester after semester from the countries to the
East." The verdict: "The worldview and philosophy of life which
Simmel represents . . . are only too obviously different from our
German Christian-classical education."

Simmel didn't get the job. But, in the same year, he published a
short piece that would later become one of his most influential
contributions—an essay that now appears on university syllabi
around the world and continues to inspire social scientists. It was
called "The Stranger."

A stranger is someone who is *in* a group but not *of* the group.
Simmel's archetypal stranger was the Jewish merchant in a medieval
European town—someone who lived in the community but was different from the insiders. Someone close enough to understand the
group, but at the same time, detached enough to have an outsider's
perspective.

Simmel argued that the power of strangers lay in their objectivity:

[The stranger] is not bound by roots to the particular constit-
uents and partisan dispositions of the group . . . [and] is
not bound by ties which could prejudice his perception, his

understanding, and his assessment of data . . . he examines conditions with less prejudice; he assesses them against standards that are more general and more objective; and his actions are not confined by custom, piety, or precedent.

And for these reasons, strangers can help uncover the truth. A classic example, Simmel argued, was the practice of medieval "Italian cities of recruiting their judges from outside, because no native was free from entanglement in family interests." This was the institution of the *podestà*, a chief magistrate brought in from another city to serve as an impartial arbitrator. These officials were usually appointed for a short term to make sure they wouldn't get too tangled up in local affairs. But while in office, a *podestà* had a great deal of power. "The citizens, seeing that there often arose among them quarrels and altercations," notes the Bolognese chronicler Leandro Alberti, "began to create a man of foreign birth their chief magistrate, giving him every power, authority, and jurisdiction over the city, as well over criminal as over civil causes." *All power to the strangers!*

We have already seen the power of strangers in this book. Matthew Mirante's calculation exposed problems at the Washington State Department of Corrections. Hackers Chris Valasek and Charlie Miller weren't engineers at Chrysler, yet they discovered big security flaws in Jeeps. In Flint, Michigan, LeeAnne Walters drew attention to the lead crisis that public health officials so studiously ignored. And in 2001, two outsiders—reporter Bethany McLean and short seller Jim Chanos—understood just enough to ask the right questions that unraveled Enron's fraud.

It's not that outsiders have a perfect, unbiased view of the world. Rather, as Simmel observed, their position lets them see *different* things than insiders do. In fact, the very same person might see things differently as an insider and as an outsider. What seems natural to us on the inside might seem strange or appalling when we're on the outside. Take Denny Gioia, a vehicle recall coordinator at Ford in the early 1970s. At the time, there was growing evidence of trouble with a popular model, the Ford Pinto. When the Pinto was struck from behind, its gas tank could rupture and burst into flames—even at fairly low speeds. But Gioia and his team chose not to recall the car. "It is difficult to convey the overwhelming complexity and pace of the job of keeping track of so many active or potential recall campaigns," writes Gioia, who is now a management professor. "I thought of myself as a fireman—a fireman who perfectly fit the description by one of my colleagues: 'In this office everything is a crisis. You only have time to put out the big fires and spit on the little ones.' By those standards the Pinto problem was distinctly a little one."

But Gioia the insider and Gioia the outsider saw the recall decision very differently. As he put it, "Before I went to Ford I would have argued strongly that Ford had an ethical obligation to recall. After I left Ford I now argue and teach that Ford had an ethical obligation to recall. But, *while I was there*, I perceived no strong obligation to recall."

But even when outsiders provide a useful perspective, there's a catch: insiders often ignore—or even fight against—their insights. At the DOC, managers downplayed Mirante's discovery. At Chrysler, officials published with little fanfare a manual fix to the problems that Valasek and Miller discovered—until *Wired* broke the story and forced Chrysler to issue a recall. In Flint, officials called LeeAnne Walters a liar until she managed to get a tenacious university professor on her side and show how widespread the issue was. And Enron executives pulled all the stops to discredit Chanos and McLean before the company finally collapsed.

The more complex and tightly coupled our systems become, the easier it is for insiders to miss something. But outsiders—thanks to the objectivity that Simmel described—show us how our systems might fail.

# III.

The whole thing stumped Bob Lutz. As vice chairman of General Motors, Lutz oversaw product development at the automaker. A longtime auto-industry executive who is obsessed with car design, he helped create the Chevy Volt, GM's innovative electric car. But under his watch, GM's engineers struggled to develop another environmentally friendly technology: clean-running diesel engines.

Lutz knew that diesel engines held promise. Widely used in Europe, they run on more energy-dense fuel than traditional gasoline-powered cars and can achieve nearly 30 percent higher fuel efficiency. "I and others were constantly arguing for some diesel cars," Lutz said. "I mean, we're meeting European emissions, we're one of the world's largest diesel engine producers. Why is it that we can't offer a diesel vehicle for the U.S.?"

But diesel is a tricky technology. Gasoline-powered engines run at close to the "ideal" ratio of fuel to air—the ratio at which fuel burns as completely as possible and minimizes harmful by-products. Diesel engines, though, are different. They don't operate near that ideal ratio, so they use other methods to contain harmful by-products. There are lots of ways manufacturers do this—by using other chemicals to break down by-products, trapping harmful particles, or simply using more fuel. But these methods add expensive components to diesel cars and reduce power and efficiency.

In Europe, diesel engines worked because fuel cost more, so diesel's efficiency meant savings for consumers. And European emission standards emphasized fuel efficiency over reducing harmful

by-products, so manufacturers didn't have to make as many performance or cost compromises. They could simply pollute more.

But automakers struggled to produce diesel cars that met strict
emissions standards in the United States—and in California in
particular—while remaining efficient and cheap. There was just one
exception: Volkswagen. Clean diesel technology was at the center of
Volkswagen's quest to become the world's largest auto manufacturer.
Lutz pushed his engineers to keep up: "What's wrong with you
guys? VW seems able to do it. *Are they magicians or something?*"

GM's engineers dug into the problem. They tested VW's diesel
cars on a dynamometer—basically a treadmill for cars—and they
passed all U.S. emissions standards. But they told Lutz, "We have no
idea how they get there. It's the same hardware that we tried by the
same suppliers . . . our engines are very similar. There's nothing we
can figure out why theirs would pass and ours won't."

GM did put a diesel engine in the Chevy Cruze, a compact car it
started producing in 2008. But the Cruze needed a lot of expensive
emissions-reducing technology to meet California's standards. "By
the time you got done," according to Lutz, "the car had to be sold at
a substantial loss. . . . You sacrifice so much in terms of money, and
performance, and even fuel economy, that at the end of the day you
ask yourself: Is it worth it?"

What did Volkswagen's engineers know that Lutz's team didn't?

Dan Carder found the first part of the answer. As the head of
West Virginia University's Center for Alternative Fuels, Engines,
and Emissions, Carder is an engine guy through and through. As an
undergraduate, he helped build some of the center's first engine-
testing labs. He wrote his master's thesis on particle emissions from
diesel engines, and he soon started developing new emissions tests.

In the late 1990s, the U.S. government discovered that heavy-
duty diesel engine manufacturers were cheating on their emissions.
They programmed the engine's software so that it would run

differently in the lab than during an actual long-distance drive. Manufacturers paid a huge fine and agreed to have their engines tested on the road rather than just in the lab.

That's when Carder's work shifted. He and his group designed portable equipment that they could hook up to trucks to measure emissions under actual driving conditions. After getting agreement from a truck's owner, Carder would head to a shipping yard after hours to hook up his test equipment—a complicated package of sensors measuring the gases and particles in the exhaust. The next morning, before dawn, he'd meet the drivers and spend the day with them, making measurements and troubleshooting his equipment. If he didn't get the data he needed, he'd have to go back the next day and do it all over again.

When the International Council on Clean Transportation, an environmental research group, floated the idea of testing passenger cars on the road, Carder and his group jumped at the chance. The researchers headed to Southern California, where the center had a long-standing mobile lab. As a bonus, the graduate students working on the project got to escape the West Virginia winter. In Los Angeles, they got their hands on three diesel cars: a Volkswagen Jetta, a Volkswagen Passat, and a BMW. The first thing they did was run the Environmental Protection Agency's standard procedures to make sure that they were dealing with normal cars, not ones that had been modified by previous owners. When they ran the tests in the lab, everything looked normal. Then it was time to measure the gases and particles that the cars emitted while driving on the road.

If you're imagining the testing equipment as a briefcase with a fancy computer screen in it, think again. To analyze the exhaust as they drove, the researchers stuffed so much testing equipment into the cars that it spilled out of the trunk, with connections welded to the exhaust pipe. The researchers had to install separate generators to avoid taxing the car's own electrical system. Once a cop pulled them over because he was suspicious of all the gear emerging from the back of the car.

"It was experimental," Carder told us. Wires and pipes broke, and generators failed because they weren't designed to deal with the car's vibration. "You had to fix it, you had to adapt it, you had to make patches, you had to find workarounds."

The data showed how efficiently the cars were running and how much pollution, such as nitrogen oxides, they emitted. Nitrogen oxides (NOx) lead to smog and acid rain, damage lung tissue, and cause respiratory problems.

The BMW's emissions matched the researchers' expectations. But the Volkswagen cars were a different story. During lab tests, the VWs had run cleanly. But on the road, they emitted between *five and thirty-five times* the allowed level of NOx.

That was a lot of NOx, but modern engines are opaque systems, and regulators sometimes allow manufacturers to exceed emission limits to prevent engine damage. For all Carder knew, there might have been a technical problem with the cars they had tested, or perhaps Volkswagen had a waiver that allowed it to exceed emission limits under certain conditions. He tried to engage Volkswagen on the issue but didn't make much progress. At the end of the day, though he wanted to know what had caused the odd results, he had to move on. "We're funded only through our research program," he told us. "Whether it was interesting or not interesting, whether we wanted to do more testing or wanted to do less testing, ultimately we have to pay the bills, so we moved on."

For Carder's team, the excessive NOx emissions were intriguing but not earth-shattering. The team had tested only three cars and didn't want to overgeneralize. Its report concluded with this dry note:

It is noted that only three vehicles were tested as part of this measurement campaign with each vehicle being a different after-treatment technology or vehicle manufacturer; conclusions drawn from the data presented herein are confined to these three vehicles. The limited data set does not necessarily permit drawing more generalized conclusions for a specific vehicle category or after-treatment technology.

Despite these understated conclusions, the results brought on one of the biggest scandals in corporate history.

Alberto Ayala was one of the first people to understand the implications of the discovery. Ayala ran a part of the California Air Resources Board (CARB), a powerful environmental regulator. The emissions testing world is close-knit, and as the West Virginia researchers started their testing, Ayala gave them access to CARB's facilities so they could measure the cars' performance in the lab. He followed their research, and when it became clear that the cars emitted so much more on the roads than in the lab, he decided that his group needed to look into things.

As a regulator, Ayala had a big advantage. He and his team could run a bunch of tests in their lab and then ask Volkswagen engineers to clarify the results. They also knew whether Volkswagen had any emissions waivers that would explain the deviations.

In regular lab tests, vehicles sit still on a treadmill even as their wheels move, and testers don't usually look at what happens when a driver turns the steering wheel. But CARB's engineers did look, and they found something very strange. Turning the steering wheel caused emissions to shoot up. The same thing happened when a person stood next to the car and rocked it back and forth. Under normal testing conditions—when the engine was running and the wheels were turning, but the steering wheel and the car itself weren't actually moving—emissions were in line with regulations. But when conditions resembled *real driving*, the car's software switched modes: though the engine performed better, emissions skyrocketed.

Slowly, systematically, Ayala and his team ruled out other explanations. "It took us another year and a half . . . we went beyond just the on-road testing. We did a lot of investigation, and that is what allowed us to really get to the bottom of what was happening, why it was happening, and how it was happening."

Ayala's team forced Volkswagen officials to admit the truth: they built their cars with a "defeat device"—regulatory-speak for any method that bypasses emissions controls. This was the final piece of the puzzle, the performance enhancement that GM's engineers couldn't figure out. Volkswagen cars ran differently on the road than on the treadmill. The "magic" Lutz had sought wasn't an engineering advancement. Volkswagen simply made the choice to cheat. Its diesel engines ran more efficiently but emitted more harmful by-products. And the company cut costs—saving around €300 per car—by not installing technologies that would have kept those by-products in check.

The word "device" evokes an image of a mechanical part attached to an engine. But when you opened the hood of a Volkswagen, there was no defeat device that you could see or touch. It was all software. And that software and its intricate source code were hidden from view. Volkswagen also knew that regulators relied on lab tests— indirect observations rather than direct, on-road assessments. The system had all the ingredients of complexity: it was a black box with complicated inner workings and only indirect measurements of what's going on.

Much like Enron several years earlier, Volkswagen used complexity to cheat. And it would have gotten away with it, too, if it weren't for those meddling outsiders.

VOLKSWAGEN WAS no stranger to scandal. In 1993, Ferdinand Piëch, Volkswagen's hard-charging CEO, poached a star executive, Jose Lopez, from General Motors. Lopez had slashed costs at GM, saving the automaker billions. Piëch believed that Lopez could do the same at Volkswagen. But when Lopez left GM with three other executives, GM accused him of stealing seventy cartons of confidential documents. The resulting legal battle dragged on for years, and Volkswagen officials stonewalled the press. Eventually, VW settled the civil case by paying $100 million and agreeing to buy nearly a billion dollars' worth of parts from GM. Chairman Piëch, for his part, weathered the controversy.

Scandal struck again in the mid-2000s. A headline in the *Guardian* read: "Bribery, Brothels, Free Viagra: VW Trial Scandalises Germany." The story was like a parody of corporate malfeasance: Volkswagen managers used "a company slush fund to pay for high-class prostitutes and to sponsor the mistresses of trade union officials, as well as regular visits to brothels, cash gifts for wives and even free supplies of Viagra." In addition, Volkswagen paid €2 million in illegal bonuses to the head of its powerful works council.

Richard Milne, a *Financial Times* reporter who covered Volkswagen in the mid-2000s, returned to Wolfsburg, Germany, to cover the emissions cheating scandal. "People inside the company always expected there to be another scandal because of the culture and the power structures at Volkswagen," Milne told us. "But I don't think anybody expected it to be about something technical. That blindsided a lot of people, because Volkswagen had this real reputation for engineering excellence. I think people basically expected a bribery scandal times two."

Instead, they got emissions cheating. GM's Bob Lutz has an idea of how it happened. He once sat next to Piëch at an event where

Volkswagen had just debuted a new model of the Volkswagen Golf. Lutz admired the Golf's tight tolerances on the car's components— the narrow gaps between the doors and the body for example. He expressed his admiration to Piëch:

> LUTZ: I wish we could get close to [those tolerances] at Chrysler.
>
> PIËCH: I'll give you the recipe. I called all the body engineers, stamping people, manufacturing, and executives into my conference room. And I said, "I am tired of all these lousy body fits. You have six weeks to achieve world-class body fits. I have all your names. If we do not have good body fits in six weeks, I will replace all of you. Thank you for your time today."
>
> LUTZ: That's how you did it?
>
> PIËCH: Yes. And it worked.

But Volkswagen didn't just suffer from an authoritarian culture. As a corporate governance expert noted, "Volkswagen is well known for having a particularly poorly run and structured board: insular, inward-looking, and plagued with infighting." On the firm's twenty-member supervisory board, ten seats were reserved for Volkswagen workers, and the rest were split between senior managers and the company's largest shareholders. Both Piëch and his wife, a former kindergarten teacher, sat on the board. *There were no outsiders.*

This kind of insularity went well beyond the boardroom. As Milne put it, "Volkswagen is notoriously anti-outsider in terms of culture. Its leadership is very much homegrown." And that leadership is grown in a strange place. Wolfsburg, where Volkswagen has its headquarters, is the ultimate company town. "It's this incredibly peculiar place," according to Milne. "It didn't exist eighty years ago. It's on a wind-swept plain between Hanover and Berlin. But it's the richest town in Germany—thanks to Volkswagen. VW permeates everything. They've got their own butchers, they've got their own theme park; you don't escape VW there. And everybody comes through this system."

EVEN MONTHS AFTER we had interviewed Dan Carder, something from our conversation kept coming back to us. When we asked him whether he'd wanted to keep digging into Volkswagen's emissions, he responded, "It doesn't matter what I want." That's because Carder's lab is chronically underfunded. The Volkswagen on-road testing proved to be extremely complicated and costly, and Carder ended up having to fund the project with tens of thousands of dollars from other sources. His group won't see a penny from the billions of dollars that will come from the Volkswagen settlement. In 2016, Carder was named one of *Time* magazine's one hundred most influential people, but he still struggled to pay for his research, equipment, and staff.

That's a travesty, because what people like Carder want and think *should matter*. They help us understand complex systems because they notice things that insiders either can't or don't want to see. And they are able to ask inconvenient questions that keep our systems safe and honest. As Charles Perrow put it, "Society should not seal organizations off." Instead, we should open up our systems, let outsiders in, and listen to what they tell us.

# IV.

The space shuttle *Challenger* exploded shortly after its launch on a chilly January morning in 1986. The story of the accident is now well known. O-rings, intended to seal joints in the solid rocket boosters that helped propel the shuttle into orbit, didn't work because of the cold. Engineers knew that low temperatures affected O-rings, but after a tense conference call the night before the launch, they decided to proceed anyway.

According to the traditional explanation, NASA managers pushed for the launch because of deadlines and production pressures. But as sociologist Diane Vaughan studied the *Challenger* accident, she found a more subtle explanation, something she called *normalization of deviance*. As NASA grappled with the complexity of shuttle missions over the years, its definition of which risks were acceptable had quietly and gradually changed. With each launch, problems that were once unexpected became more and more expected—and ultimately accepted. Managers and engineers would often identify a part of the system as risky—as they did with the joints of the solid rocket booster—but then issue a waiver that the shuttle could fly without having resolved the problem.

"Each time, evidence initially interpreted as a deviation from expected performance was reinterpreted as within the bounds of acceptable risk," Vaughan observed. This shift allowed engineers and managers "to carry on as if nothing was wrong when they continually faced evidence that something *was* wrong." What used to be a deviation became the norm.

Nine years prior to the *Challenger* launch, engineers at aerospace company Morton Thiokol, the company that had designed and built the solid rocket booster, recommended that the joints be redesigned. The joints were necessary because the booster, which stood fourteen stories high, was too long to be shipped to the launchpad as one piece. But the redesign process was slow and budgets were limited, so in the meantime, engineers used a variety of fixes and took comfort in the fact that each joint was protected by both a primary and a secondary O-ring.

Nine months before the disaster, O-ring erosion affected another *Challenger* launch. On that flight, both the primary and secondary O-rings for a similar booster joint were severely damaged. Roger Boisjoly, a Thiokol engineer, wrote a memo to his bosses to highlight the problem. "The mistakenly accepted position on the joint problem was to fly without fear of failure and to run a series of design evaluations," he wrote. "This position is now drastically changed. If the same scenario should occur . . . the result would be a catastrophe of the highest order."

Beyond the concerns of Thiokol's engineers, someone within NASA also raised concerns. An employee named Richard Cook flagged the O-ring problem in a memo he wrote the year before the disaster. "There is little question," Cook wrote, "that flight safety has been and is still being compromised by potential failure of the seals, and it is acknowledged that failure during launch would certainly be catastrophic." Though he worked at NASA, Cook had an outsider's perspective. He'd been at the organization for only a few months, and he wasn't even an engineer—he was a budget analyst. So when he spoke with NASA engineers, they freely shared their concerns and conclusions with him, rather than becoming defensive or challenging his ideas. He was more like a confidant than an engineering adversary. As Simmel noted in his famous essay, an outsider "often receives the most surprising openness—confidences which sometimes have the character of a confessional and which would be carefully withheld from a more closely related person."

Cook channeled those concerned confessions into his memo. But his warnings—like the concerns of Boisjoly and other Thiokol engineers—fell on deaf ears.

On January 28, 1986, the *Challenger* was launched. Almost immediately, the O-rings that sealed the lowest joint on the right booster broke down. Flames shot past them and blasted the shuttle's external fuel tank. Oxygen and hydrogen began to leak. Just seventy-three seconds after liftoff, the external fuel tank exploded and, about ten miles above Earth, the *Challenger* erupted into a ball of flame.

SEVENTEEN YEARS after the *Challenger* accident, history repeated itself. Moments after the launch of the space shuttle *Columbia*, foam insulation from the fuel tank broke off, struck the left wing, and punched a hole in the shuttle's heat-resistant tiles. The rest of the launch went fine—but when the *Columbia* reentered Earth's atmosphere, hot gases penetrated the wing, and the spacecraft broke into thousands of pieces.

Though the engineering details were different, the organizational factors behind the two accidents were eerily similar. Long before the *Columbia* accident, NASA knew that foam could break off. In fact, foam debris had repeatedly hit the shuttle in previous years, and the heat-resistant tiles had to be replaced before each launch. But NASA managers viewed this as a routine maintenance problem, and they were comfortable with the risk. Normalization of deviance had struck again.

After the *Columbia* accident, NASA knew that something had to change. And it was clear that treating only the symptom—the foam-shedding issue—wouldn't be enough. Many of the problems were organizational, and as the chairman of the Accident Investigation Board put it, "We are quite convinced that these organizational matters are just as important as the foam."

NASA directed its research centers to figure out how to combat the normalization of deviance. In response, managers at Jet Propulsion Laboratory (JPL), NASA's premier unmanned space exploration group, sought to harness the power of outsiders. Like the medieval Italian cities that brought in judges, JPL tried to reduce bias and entanglement. But JPL managers didn't do this by bringing in external consultants or auditors. Instead, they tried to learn from outsiders *within* the organization.

JPL does some of the most complex engineering work in the world. Its mission statement is "Dare Mighty Things" or, less formally, "If it's not impossible, we're not interested."

Over the years, JPL engineers have had their share of failures. In 1999, for example, they lost two spacecraft destined for Mars—one because of a software problem onboard the *Mars Polar Lander* and the other because of confusion about whether a calculation used the English or the metric system.

After these failures, JPL managers began to use outsiders to help them manage the risk of missions. They created risk review boards made up of scientists and engineers who worked at JPL, NASA, or contractors—but who weren't associated with the missions they reviewed and didn't buy into the same assumptions as mission insiders.

But JPL's leaders wanted to go even further. Every mission that JPL runs has a project manager responsible for pursuing groundbreaking science while staying within a tight budget and meeting an ambitious schedule. Project managers walk a delicate line. When under pressure, they might be tempted to take shortcuts when designing and testing critical components. So senior leaders created the Engineering Technical Authority (ETA), a cadre of outsiders within JPL. Every project is assigned an ETA engineer, who makes sure that the project manager doesn't make decisions that put the mission at risk.

If an ETA engineer and a project manager can't agree, they take their issue to Bharat Chudasama, the manager who runs the ETA program. When an issue lands on his desk, Chudasama tries to broker a technical solution. He can also try to get project managers more money, time, or people. And if he can't resolve the issue, he brings it to his boss, JPL's chief engineer. This setup ensures that ETA engineers have a clear way to escalate their concerns outside the traditional bureaucracy.

ETA engineers embody Simmel's outsider. They are skilled enough to understand the technology, close enough to understand the group, but detached enough to bring a different perspective. The fact that they're embedded in the organization, but with their own reporting lines, means that project managers can't dismiss their concerns or ignore them.

This approach isn't rocket science. In fact, the creation of outsiders within an organization has a long history. For centuries, when the Roman Catholic Church was considering whether to declare a person a saint, it was the job of the Promoter of the Faith, popularly known as the Devil's Advocate, to make a case against the candidate and prevent any rash decisions. The Promoter of the Faith wasn't involved in the decision-making process until he presented his objections, so he was an outsider free from the biases of those who had made the case for a candidate in the first place.

A modern-day example of this approach is the Devil's Advocate Office at Aman, Israel's military intelligence agency. This special unit is made up of respected officers whose job is to criticize other departments' assessments and consider totally different assumptions. They entertain the possibility of worst-case scenarios and question the views of the defense establishment. Their memos go directly to all major decision makers, sidestepping the agency's chain of command. "Creative" is usually not the first word that comes to mind when describing military intelligence analyses, but as a former division head at the agency put it, "The Devil's Advocate Office ensures that Aman's intelligence assessments are creative and do not fall prey to groupthink."

The sportswriter Bill Simmons proposed something similar for sports teams. "I'm becoming more and more convinced that every professional sports team needs to hire a Vice President of Common Sense," Simmons wrote. "One catch: the VP of CS doesn't attend meetings, scout prospects, watch any film or listen to any inside information or opinions; he lives the life of a common fan. They just bring him in when they're ready to make a big decision, lay everything out and wait for his unbiased reaction."

All these approaches share the same basic principle: we leave some people out of the decision-making process so they can then bring an outsider's perspective on it and find problems that insiders would miss. And you don't even need a big organization to use this approach.

Consider the case of Sasha Robson, a young accountant in Toronto who was looking to buy a small condo—her first home—a few years ago. On a sweltering summer day, after five weeks of intense house hunting, Sasha felt that she'd finally found a promising property in a condo tower overlooking Lake Ontario. Full of anticipation, she took a waterfront stroll on her way to the building, enjoying an iced coffee and the cool breeze coming from the lake. The condo was beautifully staged with seashells, beach photos, and a cool vintage surfboard. "It smelled like a beach house, like saltwater and coconut ice cream, and you got this totally laid-back vibe," Sasha told us. There was also a great balcony with a lush lemon tree and a planter box full of fresh herbs. After viewing the unit, Sasha and her real estate agent toured the rest of the building to check out the common areas and the large outdoor swimming pool. On a lounge chair by the pool, she noticed a young woman reading a book and soaking up the afternoon sun. "That's when I decided that this was the condo I wanted, the life I wanted." And the timing seemed good, too; Sasha was tired of the search process and had started to feel guilty for making her agent tour condos with her weekend after weekend.

But before making a final decision, she emailed the condo's brochure to her friend Kristina, who had just moved to Europe after living in Toronto for ten years. To avoid biasing Kristina's reactions, Sasha sent her the listing not only for the waterfront condo but also four other properties in the same price range and didn't disclose which one she favored.

Kristina replied within a few hours, and her response came as a shock: she ranked Sasha's dream condo *fourth* out of the five properties. "The outdoor pool seems really nice, but don't forget that this is Toronto," Kristina wrote. "What you can do in July isn't representative of most of the year." She also felt that the space was too small for the price and worried that new condo towers might soon be raised around the building and obscure the lake views.

Instead of the waterfront property, Kristina's first choice was a downtown condo with more space and a better layout. Sasha had seen that condo a week earlier, but at the time, two students were renting it, and the place was so messy that she couldn't picture herself living there. But Kristina's email made her realize that it was a better long-term option. She ended up buying it and still lives there.

"It was painful to read Kristina's email at the time, but it was good advice—it brought me back to reality from my beach fantasy," Sasha told us. "Kristina wasn't a part of my search, she didn't know how tired I was of the whole thing, she didn't see the beautiful staging of that waterfront condo. She was actually thousands of miles away, so she could look at it as an outsider in this cold and very rational way—in a way I couldn't."

## Chapter Ten

# SURPRISE!

### "You expect a hallway, and there's a wall."

## I.

Steve Jobs was furious. He paced. He fumed. He wanted to get going, to leave the dusty Carmel Valley Airport in the small Piper Arrow plane chartered for him, former Apple CEO Mike Markkula, and some boxes of computer equipment. And he was used to getting his way.

The trouble started when Brian Schiff, the Arrow's twenty-year-old pilot, sized up the two passengers and the equipment that they wanted to bring with them. They had a lot of gear, and the Arrow could carry only so much weight.

Not only that, it was a hot summer afternoon. You might remember from high school physics that as air heats up, it gets thinner. That's why hot air balloons float and why steam rises from a pot of simmering water. On a hot day, that phenomenon works against small planes, robbing them of lift. There's just less air to flow over their wings. And thinner air has less oxygen, so the plane's engine becomes less effective—it just can't burn as much fuel. To make matters worse, Carmel Valley Airport had a short runway and was flanked on three sides by rising terrain, so the plane would need to climb quickly after takeoff. Brian's gut told him that everything would be working against them.

Rather than load up and hope for the best, Brian decided to add up all the weight they would be carrying and calculate the airplane's performance. It's something that every pilot is trained to do, but it's not always done before a flight.

"I'm going to have to crunch the numbers on this," Brian told Jobs and Markkula. "I'm not sure we can do this safely."

That's when Jobs flew off the handle. Brian remembers it to this day:

> I can still picture myself with the owner's manual of the Arrow, doing a weight and balance calculation on the wing of the airplane. Of course it's hot and sunny, and I'm sweating, and that's adding to the pressure. And Steve Jobs is looking over my shoulder, as if to be able to tell what I'm looking at, as if to tell if it's OK or not. And he's kind of prodding me along and saying, "Well, what do you think? What do you think? Can we go? Can we go?"
>
> I was a young skinny little punk, and I looked like a kid and Jobs is . . . a menacing presence, you know? He is. And I was just—I was nervous and if I were to say my hands weren't shaking, I'd probably be wrong.

Brian's calculation confirmed his intuition. They might be able to go, but it was just too close to the edge for his comfort. He had been taught to fly with a big margin of safety, and that day they just didn't have it.

He told Jobs and Markkula that they couldn't go. Jobs erupted. He insisted that the flight could be done safely: "We just did this last week!"

But Brian wouldn't budge. "You know, it wasn't me last week," he told Jobs. "I don't know how much gear you had then, and I don't know the temperature or the wind, and I don't know all the details of last week. All I can tell you is that this isn't going to work."

It was a gutsy call. Markkula was Brian's boss—he owned the whole charter company. And Jobs was a titan of Silicon Valley. It would have been easier to say yes, to just load up and take off. By pushing back, Brian might have gotten fired. But he knew there was more at stake than just a job. "I would rather lose my job and be alive than, in the interest of keeping my job, injure or kill myself or anybody else."

Brian proposed a solution: he would fly to the nearby Monterey airport, with its long runway, cooler temperatures, headwind, and no obstacles. Everything would be in their favor there. For the passengers, it would only be a twenty-five-minute drive to meet him there.

Jobs was furious, but Markkula talked him into the compromise. The trio met up at the Monterey airport and had an uneventful, if tense, flight to San Jose. Not a word was spoken.

When they landed, Jobs stormed out of the plane. As Brian unloaded the gear, one of the service guys came up to him and said, "Brian—Markkula wants to see you in his office."

"Here it comes, I'm done," Brian thought. "But I don't care. I know I did the right thing." On his way to Markkula's office, he braced himself for the worst.

The meeting went something like this:

> MARKKULA: Brian, have a seat. . . . How much are we
> paying you to fly the Arrow?
> BRIAN: Fifty dollars a day.
> MARKKULA: Well, anybody that's willing to stand up to
> Steve Jobs in the interest of safety is exactly who we
> want around here. We're going to double your pay.

Not many have the courage and conviction to put
him in his place and keep him there. I'm proud of you.

When we talked with Brian about that day, he looked back on it
with a kind of fondness. "I was floored by the whole thing. I think
that if Markkula had actually fired me and yelled at me, maybe I
wouldn't be an airline pilot today. That was a fork in the road. Being
rewarded for doing the right thing just cemented things for me.

"With Jobs, it would have been so easy to just say okay, whatever
you say, let's go. And that happens. It happens so much—and we see
accidents as a result."

But Brian stopped and took his time to revise his plan. In a complex system, that's often the right thing to do. Pausing gives us a
chance to understand what's going on and decide how to change
course. But we often fail to pause even when we can. We press on
even when our original plan no longer makes sense.

Pilots call this *get-there-itis*. The formal name is *plan continuation
bias*, and it's a common factor in airline accidents. And the closer we
are to our goal, the stronger this bias becomes. Pilots might notice
signs that they should abandon their plan and divert to another
airport—the weather is getting worse and there isn't much fuel
left—but it's hard to stop when the destination airport is only fifteen
minutes away.

Get-there-itis affects all of us, not just pilots. We become so fixated on getting there—whether "there" is an airport or the end of a
big project—that we can't stop even when the circumstances change.
Daniel Tremblay, a young IT consultant in Canada, experienced
get-there-itis while working on a project to develop new business
software. "We should've known that it wasn't a good idea to push
ahead because the response we got halfway into the project was very
weak, not even lukewarm," he told us. "Even clients who like to su-
garcoat things told us it wasn't a good idea."

Despite the warning signs, the team kept going. "We thought we were so close," Tremblay recalled. "It was like, OK, just two more weeks or three, a couple more all-nighters, and we'll be done. We can't stop now!" But the project went on much longer, and in the end, no one was interested in buying the final product. Tremblay lost his job. "The project was a total flop, and I still don't know what we were thinking," he told us. "It's like we couldn't stop because we could see the light at the end of the tunnel. But why did we go so far in the tunnel in the first place?"

Is it possible to avoid plan continuation bias? Brian Schiff's father was a decorated pilot and prolific writer on aviation safety, and Brian learned the importance of resisting get-there-itis at an early age. But how can we instill this lesson in an organization?

Individual feedback certainly helps. Markkula's unexpectedly positive reaction became a critical moment in Brian's career. But it's even better if the praise is public—if it sends a message to everyone in the organization. Consider this story shared by organizational researchers Catherine Tinsley, Robin Dillon, and Peter Madsen:

> An enlisted seaman on an aircraft carrier discovered during a combat exercise that he'd lost a tool on the deck. He knew that an errant tool could cause a catastrophe if it were sucked into a jet engine, and he was also aware that admitting the mistake could bring a halt to the exercise—and potential punishment. . . . He reported the mistake, the exercise was stopped, and all aircraft aloft were redirected to bases on land, at a significant cost. Rather than being punished for his error, the seaman was commended by his commanding officer in a formal ceremony for his bravery in reporting it.

*A formal ceremony!* It's an incredible response. Celebrate the guy whose dumb mistake forced us to call off the exercise and scour every inch of a huge deck to find a lost tool! Would that happen in your organization? Would you celebrate someone who told you to stop everything and abandon your plan because he'd made a careless mistake?

Symbolic gestures like the deck ceremony can convey a powerful message: if you see a problem with pushing ahead, then stop—or tell your boss and colleagues to stop. In a complex, tightly coupled system, stopping can prevent disaster. It can give us a chance to notice unexpected threats and figure out what to do about them before things get completely out of hand.

But in some situations, stopping isn't an option. The system we are dealing with might be so tightly coupled that, if we don't keep going, things will fall apart right away. In the middle of a critical surgery, or when trying to regain control of a runaway nuclear reactor or a stalling airplane, we can't just pause. What can we do then?

# II.

A small boy with a history of asthma was brought to the emergency department at a children's hospital in the Midwest. He was having trouble breathing, and it was getting worse. A few minutes after he arrived, he stopped breathing altogether. In the trauma bay, a doctor sealed a bag-valve mask over the boy's face and began to squeeze the bag to force air into his lungs. Then, suddenly, the boy's pulse was gone. The ER team—three doctors and five nurses—started CPR. But a minute and a half later, still no pulse. And the bag-valve mask didn't seem to be helping. The boy's chest wasn't rising. The team was puzzled. *What's going on with this kid?*

They intubated the boy, placing a breathing tube down his throat. The doctor who inserted the tube could see it pass through the vocal cords perfectly. The tube was in the right place, and nothing was blocking the boy's airway. But minutes passed and still no chest rise. "Nothing happening," a nurse said.

The team pulled out the tube and started using the bag-valve mask again. But even as they squeezed the bag, the boy's chest was still not moving. No rise, no fall. And the clock was ticking. The team grew desperate. Eventually, they decided to use a defibrillator to restart the boy's heart. But still no pulse and no chest rise. "Just spinning our wheels," one of the doctors said. And the wheels continued to spin for another three minutes.

Finally, a nurse recalled a mnemonic that listed all the reasons for the failure to ventilate: DOPE. *D* stands for displacement or dislodgement of the tube, but the tube was in the right place. *O* is for obstruction—something is blocking the tube—but that didn't seem to be the case, either. *P* is for pneumothorax, a collapsed lung, and the team had already ruled that out. There was only one possibility left. "*E*, equipment!" the nurse cried out. "We got equipment failure!"

She was right. The bag-valve mask—or bag, as it's simply called—was broken. Even though it looked fine, it supplied no oxygen. But by the time the team figured this out and replaced the bag, the boy had been without oxygen for more than ten minutes. In real life, he would have died. Fortunately, this was just a simulation, which the hospital ran as part of a training program for emergency department teams. The patient wasn't a real boy. It was a medical manikin hooked up to a massive computer that simulated the physiological responses of a real patient.

All teams started with the same scenario: a boy with a history of asthma was brought into the hospital and eventually stopped breathing. And all teams faced the same surprise: the bag-valve mask was broken. But only some of the teams solved the problem quickly enough.

This simulation involved a great deal of tight coupling and complexity. Time was running out fast, and since the patient was unconscious, the teams had to rely on what they could see, hear, and feel to figure out what was wrong. And because all teams faced the same unexpected event, the simulation yielded a treasure trove of data about how different teams handled a complex crisis under pressure.

So how did some of the teams detect the equipment problem and save the boy's life? What did they do differently from the teams that failed? To find out, Marlys Christianson—a physician turned management scholar at the University of Toronto—painstakingly analyzed hours and hours of video recordings of the teams.

A few teams found the solution very quickly—for example, when a team member happened to notice right away that the bag didn't sound or feel right. "These teams had the good fortune of having the right team member at the right place at the right time," Christianson told us. "The fastest team was one where a nurse squeezed the bag a couple of times and said, 'This isn't working. It's broken!' So he just threw it over his head backwards—it spiraled like a football and landed on the ground—and he grabbed a new bag."

But most teams didn't arrive at the solution right away. They missed some cues and went down the wrong path—as we often do in a crisis. And, ultimately, only about half of those teams were able to overcome their false start. The rest of the teams never discovered that the bag was broken.

What made the difference? Here's Christianson:

What seems to matter is whether a team is able to balance the work of taking care of the patient with the work of making sense of the situation. Obviously, teams need to keep doing the tasks—like resuscitation and giving medications—so stopping all the time to think about the situation is a bad idea. But focusing only on the tasks and never stopping to make sense of what's happening is also bad. And some teams became really fixated on one or the other.

In contrast, the best teams found a balance. "They focused not only on coordinating the tasks, but would also say things like, 'You know, can we step back for a second? Do you think there's something else going on? Let's check in on where we were!'" Christianson told us. "The most striking thing about these teams was this pattern—this cycle—of moving from tasks to monitoring to diagnosis and then back to tasks again."

The cycle Christianson describes often starts with a task, such as intubating the patient. The next step is monitoring: you check if performing the task had the expected effect. If it didn't, then you move on to the next step and come up with a new possible diagnosis. And then you go back to tasks because you need to *do* something—for example, administer medications or replace the bag—to test your new theory.

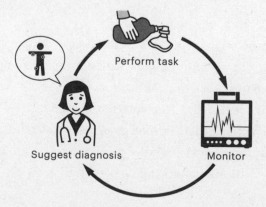

Perform task

Monitor

Suggest diagnosis

"If you look at the teams that were effective, they all have that cycle, and often they have it multiple times as they quickly move through various diagnoses," Christianson told us. "It's rapid cycling—you move through all of the steps quickly, so you can test multiple diagnoses in a short time."

Rapid cycling worked especially well when team members *narrated* what they were thinking and doing at each step. "On some of the best teams," Christianson noted, "people were saying, out loud, 'Hey, if this person has this kind of problem, then we'd expect to see these kinds of changes, say, in blood pressure or $O_2$ sats.'" This sort of live narrative made it clear to everyone what others were thinking and helped the team move to the next step quickly.

In teams that solved the puzzle, a typical conversation sequence looked something like this—with the dots representing conversations about tasks, monitoring, or a diagnosis.

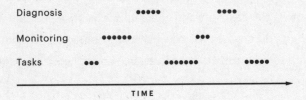

These teams talked about tasks, then discussed what they learned from monitoring the results, and then came up with a new diagnosis. And then went back to tasks again.

But many teams failed to complete the cycles. "The teams that didn't do well often had really long stretches of task talk," says Christianson. "Or they wouldn't always go all the way up to diagnosis—they'd just go task, monitoring, and back to task. So they never figured it out."

IN THE HOSPITAL SIMULATION, time was measured in seconds and minutes. But Christianson's findings hold some lessons even for situations when the time frame is in weeks and months. If you've ever been involved in a big, intense project, you know how easy it is to become overwhelmed by tasks. There's always something urgent to do and a deadline that's coming too soon. And once you get a task done, the next deadline is already close. There's never time to pause, and it's easy to lose sight of the big picture. We just keep our heads down, focus on the tasks, and push ahead.

Remember Target Canada? As business reporter Joe Castaldo put it, "Everyone knew the launch was a disaster and the company had to stop opening stores so it could fix its operational problems, but no one actually said so." They just focused on the tasks at hand and kept going—much like an ER team that never figured out that the bag was broken.

But there's a better way. Consider the entry of foreign firms into China. Experts estimate that nearly half of foreign companies withdraw from China within two years of entering. That's a grim statistic, but it masks an important fact. "Some of these firms didn't really fail in the long run," points out Chris Marquis, a management professor who specializes in China. "Many firms—including large multinationals—made mistakes early on and suffered big losses, and might have even pulled out, but then some of them were able to regroup and adjust their approach."

Take American toymaker Mattel, which opened a flagship Barbie store in Shanghai in 2009. The multimillion-dollar House of Barbie—a six-story, hot-pink building that housed the world's largest collection of Barbie dolls—struggled, and Mattel closed the store just two years later. Here's Marquis and his coauthor Zoe Yang:

The company came with all the best intentions of adapting to the local market, developing a doll with Asian features named Ling. However, the company's market researchers couldn't have predicted that Chinese girls would prefer blonde Barbie to the doll that looked like them.

It was an unpleasant surprise. Like the bag-valve mask in the emergency room, the strategy focused on the Ling doll was *supposed* to work.

But Mattel didn't stay on the wrong path for long. Its executives used an approach similar to the cycle Christianson noticed during the hospital simulation. When their monitoring of the situation made it clear that they had gotten things wrong, they came up with a new assessment of the market—a new diagnosis—and then reentered China to test it. This time, Mattel lowered the price of its dolls and introduced a "Violin Soloist" Barbie—a blonde doll that came with a violin, a bow, and sheet music.

The new price was palatable to many more parents—and so was the Barbie with the violin. "Mattel began to understand that

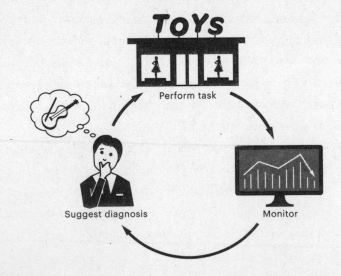

Perform task

Monitor

Suggest diagnosis

Chinese parents want their children well-educated and well-groomed," notes Helen Wang, an expert on consumer trends in China. "The 'Violin Soloist' Barbie certainly feeds into that kind of mentality. Tiger moms are more likely to buy the doll, in the hope that their daughters would want to be more like Barbie."

While some other large firms left the country after initial stumbles, Mattel didn't give up. It also didn't stick with its original diagnosis. Like the best hospital teams, it kept going through the steps of the cycle.

The same kind of process can also help with modern family life. "With four kids and eight pets, life was chaotic," wrote David and Eleanor Starrs in a delightfully wonky paper titled "Agile Practices for Families: Iterating with Children and Parents." For years, the Starrs were caught up in a whirlwind of kids, coats, pets, and lunchboxes. Getting the kids ready for school, for example, often turned into a nightmare. But rather than accept the status quo, they decided to take a step back. They started having family meetings every Sunday night. And that changed everything.

Each meeting starts with three questions:

1. What went well this week?
2. What things should be improved next week?
3. What will we commit to changing next week?

Before they had family meetings, they were just trying to keep up with the tasks that were right in front of them. But now they could do more; they had a way to complete the cycle. They looked at what worked, what didn't, and what they could improve. Each week they monitored the situation, diagnosed the problems, and came up with new strategies to try. And they didn't just assume that their solutions would work; they repeated the cycle every week. As a result, they tried lots of solutions—from a morning checklist to points that reward good behavior—and continued to refine their system. The solutions the Starrs came up with might seem obvious; many of us have tried them ourselves. But the devil is in the details. And by using the cycle, the Starrs figured out those details.

A few years after the Starrs had started their experiment, *New York Times* columnist Bruce Feiler visited the family. He observed a morning scene that many parents would envy: Eleanor sat in a reclining chair, sipping coffee and chatting with her kids as they went about their morning routines. The kids made their own breakfast, fed the pets, did their chores, gathered their things for school, and headed out to the bus. Feiler was blown away: "It was one of the most astonishing family dynamics I have ever seen."

Modern families, like ER teams and companies, don't have all the answers. But what we do have is the ability to *try* things, see what works, and reevaluate. It's the same iterative process, but instead of evaluating vital signs or sales numbers, we're checking on things in our own lives.

# III.

The SWAT team spent a lot of time preparing for the raid. First, the officers learned everything they could about the suspected drug house. They studied all the photos, videos, and floorplans they could get their hands on. They memorized every room and every turn. They then came up with a detailed plan of how to get in and where everyone would go once inside. They rehearsed and refined the plan until they knew it inside out. When the day of the raid arrived, they were ready. But when they rammed down the door, they could tell something was amiss. *The place didn't look like the floorplan.*

The suspects had modified the layout, so the rooms were not where they were supposed to be. It was a nasty surprise. As one officer recalled, "You expect a hallway, and there's a wall."

On the set of an indie horror film, the crew got ready to shoot a dramatic slaughter scene: on the top floor of a large mansion, a victim would be electrocuted while falling into a hot tub. But the crew forgot one crucial detail. They filled the tub all the way, so when the actor fell into it, the water overflowed, spread all over the floor, and then cascaded down through the glass chandelier in the mansion's entryway. A production assistant yelled into his walkie-talkie: "I'm on the first floor and there is water dripping on my head!" Then everything went dark. The water shorted out the power in the whole building.

SWAT teams and film crews deal with surprises all the time. And when the unexpected happens, they don't just stop. If a house isn't configured as expected, SWAT officers still press on. When the power goes out, film crews figure out how to resume shooting as soon as possible. In these fields, surprises are a normal part of the job, and people are pretty good at handling them. How do they do it?

To answer that question, management scholars Beth Bechky and Gerardo Okhuysen dug into the habits of a SWAT team and several film crews. While Okhuysen interviewed SWAT officers and played fly-on-the-wall during their briefings and training sessions, Bechky moonlighted as a production assistant on film sets and took notes on everything she observed.

When the two researchers compared notes, they discovered a common thread. In both cases, people readily *shifted roles* to handle surprises. Consider how the SWAT team dealt with a surprise similar to the one described above—entering a house to find something they didn't expect. Here's the researchers' description:

[SWAT officer] Glenn described how finding a couch in the team's path during an entry surprised the SWAT team. Ordinarily, the lead officer in an entry team rushed ahead to achieve maximum coverage. In this case, though, the couch was a dangerous obstacle because, as Glenn put it, "Someone could be on the other side, just waiting for us." He then described how the team responded to the surprise by using role shifting. Instead of running to the right as originally planned, Glenn ran left and stopped at a vantage point where he could "cover" the couch. Peter, who was second in the stack and whose role was to run left, immediately ran to the right around the couch while being covered by Glenn, executing the task originally assigned to Glenn.

In other words, the team instantly changed its plan. And this quick role shift didn't require any talking. Peter knew exactly what Glenn's original job was. As Glenn put it, "We know what *everyone* is supposed to do."

Role shifts are common on film sets, too. Surprises come up, so sometimes a crew just can't shoot the scenes it had planned for the day. And switching to a different set of scenes requires that people move flexibly between jobs. Other times, an essential crew member is missing because of illness or a personal crisis. But because every day of shooting is so expensive, and schedules are so tight, production can't stop.

Here's a telling story that Bechky heard from two crew members, who spent the previous weekend shooting a commercial at a water reservoir:

[One of the two crew members] was hired as a set production assistant but ended up also performing the craft service job, and the other was hired as the assistant production office co-ordinator but also worked as the chauffeur (a task normally assigned to a teamster). A third crew member performed the tasks of the entire art department, as well as filling in for the scenic department. As one of them described, "They just looked at him one afternoon and said, 'We need you to manu-facture pond scum right now.'"

*Your job title doesn't matter—you need to make pond scum right now!*
On another production, an aerial camera operator didn't show up for work. This was a setback, but not for long. "Are you capable of operating this camera?" the cinematographer asked people. When a crew member said yes, he became the aerial camera operator. Of course, this meant that now *his* original role wasn't filled. But then someone else stepped into that role, too, and the shooting resumed.

But role shifting is easier said than done. Clearly, it requires that several people in a group know how to accomplish a particular task. But it also means everyone needs to understand how the various tasks fit into the bigger picture.

In the film industry, this knowledge often comes from how peo-ple naturally progress through their careers. Many rookies start as production assistants and work on tasks that cut across different de-partments, from costumes to lighting and sound. Others work on many projects and in several different departments in the span of just a few months. As a production coordinator put it, "If I want to produce, I am on that track. If, instead, I want to be an AD [assistant director], I am also on that track. You get a lot of exposure as a pro-duction coordinator, so you can do a bunch of things."

SWAT teams make a specific point to achieve something simi-lar through cross-training. New officers, for example, need to learn how to use a sniper's rifle and scope even if they aren't planning to become snipers. They don't need to become expert marksmen, but they need to understand what snipers see and how they work. As a SWAT trainer put it, "You are supposed to know everybody else's job."

*Know everybody else's job?* That's not at all how we usually do things. In fact, it's the opposite. Here's a succinct diagnosis by Tim Brown, the CEO of IDEO, the famous design-consulting firm:

> Most companies have lots of people with different skills. The problem is, when you bring people together to work on the same problem, if all they have are those individual skills . . . it's very hard for them to collaborate. What tends to happen is that each individual discipline represents its own point of view. It basically becomes a negotiation at the table as to whose point of view wins, and that's when you get gray compromises where the best you can achieve is the lowest common denominator between all points of view. The results are never spectacular but, at best, average.

*At best, average*—it doesn't sound catastrophic. And on a normal day, it might not be. But when teams without much cross-training face a surprise in a complex system, a meltdown can result. It's a lesson that stock exchange Nasdaq learned after the initial public offering (IPO) of Facebook shares. Check out these headlines:

**FACEBOOK IPO: WHAT THE %$#! HAPPENED?**

**NASDAQ "EMBARRASSED" OVER FACEBOOK IPO**

**MINUTE BY MINUTE, NASDAQ CHAOS ENGULFED FACEBOOK IPO**

## NASDAQ: "ARROGANCE" CONTRIBUTED TO
## FACEBOOK IPO FLOP

In the weeks leading up to the start of trading, bankers traveled around the country hyping Facebook's stock; the company was ultimately valued at over $100 billion. Nasdaq, Facebook's primary exchange, spent weeks testing its own systems to ensure that it could handle what would be the busiest IPO in history.

On the morning of May 18, 2012, at precisely 11:05, Nasdaq planned to execute the first trade in the stock through a process it called the opening cross. The cross was an auction of sorts—buyers and sellers entered orders, and Nasdaq calculated a price that would cause as many shares as possible to change hands.

As the start of trading approached, hundreds of thousands of orders poured in, like a mob of gamblers trying to place bets on a horse race before the starting pistol fires. But when 11:05 arrived, nothing happened, and no one knew why.

With billions of dollars poised to change hands and the spotlight on, Nasdaq managers scrambled to diagnose the problem. They dialed into an emergency conference call to troubleshoot. But they didn't really understand how the technology worked, and Nasdaq clearly faced a technology failure. After a few minutes, a group of programmers—who were not on the call—narrowed the problem down to something called the validation check.

Years before, when the programmers wrote the computer program that runs trading, they included a validation check, a safety feature that independently calculated how many shares would trade in an opening auction. On May 18, the trading program and the validation check didn't match, so trading wouldn't start.

The engineers shared their findings with their boss, the senior vice president (SVP) who ran the exchange technology group. Before that moment, the SVP had never even heard of the validation check, but he relayed the description of the problem to his fellow managers. The most senior Nasdaq executive on the call told him to figure out whether the programmers could run the opening cross anyway.

Here's the Securities and Exchange Commission describing what happened next:

> First, NASDAQ attempted to change the commands in its IPO Cross system to override the validation check. This attempt was unsuccessful. Next, the engineers reported to [the SVP] their belief that NASDAQ could complete the cross if . . . [they] *removed several lines of code that configured the validation check function.*

It was a radical solution. Even though no manager understood *why* the validation check stopped the cross, they wanted the programmers to change the system—on the fly—to skip the check.

Five minutes later, programmers removed the check, and trading started. But Nasdaq's system was incredibly complicated, and the workaround caused a series of unexpected failures. It turned out that the validation check had been correct: there was a bug that caused the opening cross to ignore orders for more than *twenty minutes*, an eternity on Wall Street. At the start of trading, people bought $3 billion worth of Facebook stock. But for hours, Nasdaq couldn't even tell how much stock each trader bought. Traders blamed Nasdaq for hundreds of millions of dollars of losses. Nasdaq itself, though legally prohibited from trading stock, ended up accidentally selling $125 million worth of Facebook shares. The mistake exposed Nasdaq to litigation, fines, and ridicule.

SWAT officers trained with the sniper rifle to understand what snipers could see. And their trainer told them that they had to know something about *everybody else's* job. Nasdaq managers needed the same kind of training. They didn't need to be programmers, and they didn't need to be able to write the computer code for the validation check. But they *did* need to understand what it was—and why they shouldn't bypass it.

SWAT: *You expect a hallway, and there's a wall.*

Nasdaq: *You expect trading, and there's a validation check.*

The SWAT team figured out how to go around the wall. Nasdaq managers tried to run through it.

Epilogue

# THE GOLDEN AGE OF MELTDOWNS

"Going to hell in a handbasket."

W. B. Yeats wrote his famous apocalyptic poem, "The Second Coming," in the aftermath of World War I. In recent years, references to the poem have skyrocketed in newspapers and on social media. Lines from the first stanza have been especially popular:

> Turning and turning in the widening gyre
> The falcon cannot hear the falconer;
> Things fall apart; the centre cannot hold;
> Mere anarchy is loosed upon the world,
> The blood-dimmed tide is loosed, and everywhere
> The ceremony of innocence is drowned;
> The best lack all conviction, while the worst
> Are full of passionate intensity.

People have quoted these lines in reference to terror attacks, financial crises, political upheaval, climate change, and epidemics. As the *Wall Street Journal* put it, the poem gives us a "highbrow way of saying 'the world is going to hell in a handbasket.'"

It can certainly seem that way, particularly if you're reading this book! But the truth is more nuanced. As Steven Pinker and Andrew Mack point out, "News is about things that happen, not things that don't happen." An uneventful flight or a quiet day on a drilling rig doesn't make headlines. "Since the human mind estimates probability by the ease with which it can recall examples," Pinker and Mack explain, "newsreaders will always perceive that they live in dangerous times."

It's not that things are worse today; it's that they're *different*. In the past half century, humanity has pushed its technological boundaries. We've harnessed nuclear power, drilled miles into the earth to extract oil, and developed a global financial system. These systems give us tremendous capabilities. But they also move us into the danger zone, and when they fail, they can kill people, devastate the environment, and destabilize economies. It's not that we're less safe on a daily basis; it's that we're more vulnerable to unexpected system failures.

Take hospitals. Remember the overdose that nearly killed Pablo Garcia? It happened because of computerized prescriptions, a pharmacy robot, and bedside barcode scanners. That system eliminated small errors due to messy handwriting and distracted nurses. But it opened the door to nasty surprises.

Or think about driverless cars. They will almost certainly be safer than human drivers. They'll eliminate accidents due to fatigued, distracted, and drunk driving. And if they're well engineered, they won't make the silly mistakes that we make, like changing lanes while another car is in our blind spot. At the same time, they'll be susceptible to meltdowns—brought on by hackers or by interactions in the system that engineers didn't anticipate.

But as we have seen in this book, there are solutions. We can design safer systems, make better decisions, notice warning signs, and learn from diverse, dissenting voices. Some of these solutions might seem obvious: Use structured tools when you face a tough decision. Learn from small failures to avoid big ones. Build diverse teams and listen to skeptics. And create systems with transparency and plenty of slack. Hardly shocking, right?

Yet many of these ideas are rarely used in practice—even in the face of our greatest challenges. We celebrate intuition in wicked environments. We ignore voices of concern and fail to act on warning signs about climate change, famines, and imminent terrorist attacks. Homogeneous teams run some of our most important financial institutions, government agencies, and military organizations. Our food supply chains are more complex and less transparent than ever before. And complexity and tight coupling in how we manage and store nuclear weapons make it far too easy for things to go wrong even in our most dangerous systems.

Closer to home, has your team or your organization fully embraced the ideas we've seen in *Meltdown*? If it has, that's great. But we suspect the answer is either "no" or "not entirely." And that's a missed opportunity because many of these solutions don't require massive budgets or fancy technologies. We can all run a premortem, use predetermined criteria, and make predictions using the SPIES method. We can all use Perrow's matrix to figure out which part of our organization or project is most prone to a nasty surprise—and what we might do about it. And we can all do a better job of listening to skeptics and speaking up when something doesn't feel right. You don't need to be a CEO to make a difference. And many of these approaches work even in our personal lives, when we're making decisions about where to live, what job to take, and how to work together as a family.

While it might be obvious that we should learn from warning signs, encourage dissent, and foster diversity, it's much less obvious *how* to do those things effectively. Putting these solutions into practice can be tough; it often goes against our natural instincts. We tend to celebrate intuition and self-confidence, want to hear good news, and feel comfortable around people who look and think like us. But managing complex, coupled systems requires the opposite— careful and humble decision making, the open sharing of bad news, and an emphasis on doubt, dissent, and diversity.

One reason people resist these ideas is that they assume that avoiding failure means taking fewer risks; they assume that preventing meltdowns requires sacrificing innovation and efficiency. Indeed, there are trade-offs. Adding slack to a system or redesigning it to cut complexity can mean higher costs and fewer capabilities. And there's a lot of value in talking about these trade-offs explicitly—and using complexity and coupling as basic parameters when we consider costs, benefits, and risks.

But the things that help us manage complex systems don't always involve painful trade-offs. In fact, there's now plenty of research showing that many of the solutions we've seen in this book— structured decision tools, diverse teams, and norms that encourage healthy skepticism and dissent—tend to fuel, rather than squelch, innovation and productivity. Adopting these solutions is a win-win.

That's why we decided to write this book. We wanted people to realize that preventing meltdowns was within their grasp.

IN THE MIDDLE AGES, humanity faced a grave threat. In October 1347, a fleet of trading ships arrived in Sicily. Most of the sailors were dead; the rest were coughing and vomiting blood. Other ships ran aground before reaching port because everyone aboard had died. It was the start of the Black Death, an epidemic that would go on to kill tens of millions. The disease, which originated in Asia, moved west along the Silk Road with traders and Mongol soldiers. The Mongol army used it as a weapon, catapulting infected bodies over the walls of a trading city it had besieged. The epidemic soon spread to Africa and the Middle East.

The world was ripe for the spread of the disease. New trade routes connected cities and encouraged movement. People lived in closer quarters than ever before. But humanity wouldn't develop antibiotics, epidemiology, sanitation, or the germ theory of disease for centuries. It was what one historian called "the golden age of bacteria." We were vulnerable to epidemics, but our ability to understand—let alone prevent—them lagged far behind.

Today, we are in the golden age of meltdowns. More and more of our systems are in the danger zone, but our ability to manage them hasn't quite caught up. The result: things fall apart.

But times are changing. We now know how to bring the golden age of meltdowns to a close. We just need the conviction to try.

# ACKNOWLEDGMENTS

A book is a complex system. Sentences and paragraphs form an elaborate web, and the narrative thread easily unravels if you tinker with it in the wrong places. Though book writing involves more slack than many other systems, there's still some tight coupling. An accidentally deleted interview transcript is hard to recover, and you can't meet a deadline once you missed it. To avoid meltdowns, writers can't go it alone: they need to rely on feedback from strangers, learn from diverse views, and listen to dissenting voices.

We are fortunate to have had a wonderful team at Penguin Press, led by Ann Godoff and Scott Moyers, to help us navigate the complexities of writing. Our extraordinary editor, Emily Cunningham, provided discerning feedback, gentle guidance, and unwavering support. She taught us how to write for a broad audience and had a profound influence on the direction of this book. Jennifer Eck, Megan Gerrity, Karen Mayer, and Claire Vaccaro helped shepherd the book to publication with great care, expertise, and professionalism. Matt Boyd, Sarah Hutson, and Grace Fisher were wonderful advocates of *Meltdown* and worked tirelessly to spread the word about the book. A few miles to the north, Diane Turbide at Penguin Canada was a source of inspiration, encouragement, and insights, and her colleagues Frances Bedford and Kara Carnduff worked as a seamless team to promote the book in Canada.

At the Wylie Agency, Kristina Moore and James Pullen gave us invaluable feedback on our initial ideas and worked tirelessly to find a great home for the book. Special thanks go to James for taking a very early interest in our work and suggesting the title *Meltdown*.

We are grateful to the *Financial Times* and McKinsey and Company, whose Bracken Bower Prize competition gave us an initial spur to start writing, and we thank the competition judges—Vindi Banga, Lynda Gratton, Jorma Ollila, and Stephen Rubin—who saw value in our proposal. The prize introduced us to a community of thinkers whose work we used to admire only from afar. Andrew Hill, Dominic Barton, Lionel Barber, and Anne-Marie Slaughter were a great source of support and encouragement. Martin Ford and Sean Silcoff read early drafts and took the time to write detailed comments that dramatically improved the book. Dick Thaler gave us sage advice on how to navigate the publishing world.

We owe a huge debt to the Rotman School of Management at the University of Toronto. Not one but two Rotman deans became early champions of our work. Roger Martin was an incredibly generous mentor and gave us the kind of advice that only someone who'd written ten books can provide. Tiff Macklem was a constant source of encouragement and perceptive questions, and the lessons he'd learned during the global financial crisis helped inspire Chapter Ten. András's colleagues at Rotman created a wonderful community in which to work and think, and we learned a great deal from the students who took Catastrophic Failure in Organizations and shared their insights in the classroom.

Few people were more persistently enthusiastic about the book than Ken McGuffin, Steve Arenburg, and Rod Lohin. In 2015, it was Ken who encouraged us to apply for the Bracken Bower Prize. A year later, Steve organized a public lecture that gave us a chance to get important early feedback from a diverse audience. Rod saw potential in our idea the first time he heard about it, and under his guidance, the Michael Lee-Chin Family Institute for Corporate Citizenship provided generous funding for our research.

Many people gave us extremely valuable feedback on our book proposal and manuscript. Adam Grant encouraged us to focus on solutions and include everyday disasters among our examples. Andrea Ovans had fantastic input on the managerial implications of our ideas. Our friends Matthew Clark and Jonathan Worth have always been a source of gentle encouragement and helpful questions, and Matthew's comments on our proposal were transformational. With a keen and critical eye, he guided us in the right direction and helped sharpen our focus on systems. Joe Badaracco, Vjeko Begic, Alex Berlin, Illya Bomash, Tom Callaghan, Karen Christensen, Kara Fitzsimmons, Andrea Flores, Richard Florida, Patricia Foo, Jack Gallagher, Joshua Gans, Andy Greenberg, Alex Guth, Clay Kaminsky, Sarah Kaplan, Carl Kay, Ed Koubek, Tor Krever, Inna Livitz, Jamie Malton, Simona Malton, Nicole Martin, Paul Mariz, Chris Marquis, David Mayer, Jessica Moffett Rose, Pat O'Brien, Eoghan O'Donnell, Kim Pernell, Thom Rose, Heather Rothman, Maureen Sarna, Julia Twarog, Jim Weatherall, Matt Weinstock, and Michele Wucker all provided support and helpful feedback. We'd also like to thank the Joint Engineering Board at NASA's Jet Propulsion Laboratories for their input and Brian Muirhead, Bharat Chudasama, Chris Jones, and Howard Eisen for their generosity with their time and feedback. We are thankful to Anton Ioukhnovets, who created the book's interior graphics, and to Christopher King, who designed the cover.

We are deeply indebted to the researchers, accident investigators, and many other heroes who shared their wisdom with us. We are fortunate to have had a chance to learn from them. They are quoted in the book or mentioned in the notes, but we wanted to give special thanks to three of them here. Charles Perrow's research is brilliant, and learning from him was a humbling and powerful experience.

The weekend we spent with Chick in New Haven in July 2016 was a key moment in the genesis of this book and one of the most rewarding parts of the project. Our friend Ben Berman—a thinker with a rare combination of brilliance, kindness, and humility—was incredibly generous with his ideas throughout this journey. And huge thanks to Marlys Christianson, who patiently taught us about her research, helped us find examples, and introduced us to other scholars in her field.

Our deepest gratitude goes to our families. Our parents taught us to love books at a young age. Torvald was a source of incredible joy and inspiration for Chris, and Soren's impending arrival helped set a firm deadline for the book. Pelu was András's loyal writing companion. Most of all, we are thankful to Linnéa and Marvin, who patiently listened to many iterations of our ideas and asked penetrating questions. They helped us avoid our own meltdowns and stood by us in good times and bad. We couldn't have written this book without them.

# NOTES

## Prologue: A Day Like Any Other

1 **It was a warm Monday:** Details of the accident were drawn from the National Transportation Safety Board's Railroad Accident Report NTSB/RAR-10/02, "Collision of Two Washington Metropolitan Area Transit Authority Metrorail Trains Near Fort Totten Station," Washington, DC, June 22, 2009, https://www.ntsb.gov /investigations/AccidentReports/Reports/RAR1002.pdf. Details about the Wherleys and others came from Christian Davenport, "General and Wife, Victims of Metro Crash, Are Laid to Rest," *Washington Post*, July 1, 2009, http://www.wash ingtonpost.com/wp-dyn/content/article/2009/06/30/AR2009063002664.html? sid=ST2009063003813; Eli Saslow, "In a Terrifying Instant in Car 1079, Lives Became Forever Intertwined," *Washington Post*, June 28, 2009, http://www.wash ingtonpost.com/wp-dyn/content/article/2009/06/27/AR2009062702417 .html; and Gale Curcio, "Surviving Against All Odds: Metro Crash Victim Tells Her Story," *Alexandria Gazette Packet*, April 29, 2010, http://connectionarchives .com/PDF/2010/042810/Alexandria.pdf.

1 **he was the general who:** Davenport, "General and Wife." See also the National Commission on Terrorist Attacks upon the United States, *The 9/11 Commission Report: Final Report of the National Commission on Terrorist Attacks upon the United States* (Washington, DC: Government Printing Office, 2011), 44.

4 **several airlines have grounded:** This happened to numerous airlines during the course of writing this book. See, for example, Alice Ross, "BA Computer Crash: Passengers Face Third Day of Disruption at Heathrow," *Guardian*, May 29, 2017, https:// www.theguardian.com/business/2017/may/29/ba-computer-crash-passen gers-face-third-day-of-disruption-at-heathrow; "United Airlines Systems Outage Causes Delays Globally," *Chicago Tribune*, October 14, 2016, http://www.chicagotri bune.com/business/ct-united-airlines-systems-outage-20161014-story.html; and Chris Isidore, Jethro Mullen, and Joe Sutton, "Travel Nightmare for Fliers After Power Outage Grounds Delta," CNN Money, August 8, 2016, http://money.cnn.com /2016/08/08/news/companies/delta-system-outage-flights/index.html?iid=EL.

6 **In many ways, Berman explained:** Personal interview with Ben Berman on January 10, 2016.

6 **likelihood of a failure:** Air Transport Action Group, "Aviation Benefits Beyond Borders," April 2014, https://aviationbenefits.org/media/26786/ATAG__Aviation Benefits2014_FULL_LowRes.pdf.

7 **learned the grim details:** Our description of the ValuJet 592 accident and the investigation is based on our interview with Ben Berman on January 10, 2016; the

National Transportation Safety Board's Aircraft Accident Report NTSB/AAR-97 /06, "In-Flight Fire and Impact with Terrain, ValuJet Airlines Flight 592 DC-9-32, N904VJ, Everglades, Near Miami, Florida, May 11, 1996," August 19, 1997, https:// www.ntsb.gov/investigations/AccidentReports/Reports/AAR9706.pdf; and William Langewiesche, "The Lessons of ValuJet 592," *Atlantic*, March 1998, https://www.the atlantic.com/magazine/archive/1998/03/the-lessons-of-valujet-592/306534/. Langewiesche's article provides a thorough overview of the accident and an insightful discussion of its underlying causes.

8 **a shipping ticket from SabreTech:** A copy of the original shipping ticket appears in NTSB/AAR-97/06, 176. For clarity, we present a simplified version here.

9 **"If this seems confusing":** Langewiesche, "The Lessons of ValueJet 592."

10 **Jasmine Garsd, a producer:** Michel Martin, "When Things Collide," National Public Radio, June 23, 2009, http://www.npr.org/sections/tellmemore/2009/06 /when_things_collide.html.

## Chapter One: The Danger Zone

16 **plot of *The China Syndrome*:** *The China Syndrome*, directed by James Bridges, written by Mike Gray, T. S. Cook, and James Bridges, Columbia Pictures, 1979.

16 **one executive called it:** David Burnham, "Nuclear Experts Debate 'The China Syndrome,'" *New York Times*, March 18, 1979, http://www.nytimes.com/1979/03/18/ archives/nuclear-experts-debate-the-china-syndrome-but-does-it-satisfy-the.html.

16 **"I have a premonition":** Dick Pothier, "Parallels Between 'China Syndrome' and Harrisburg Incident Disturbing," *Evening Independent*, 7A, April 2, 1979.

16 **a handsome twenty-six-year-old:** Ira D. Rosen, "Grace Under Pressure in Harrisburg," *Nation*, April 21, 1979.

16 **"Oh, they're having some problem":** Tom Kauffman, "Memories Come Back as NEI Staffer Returns to Three Mile Island," Nuclear Energy Institute, March 2009, http://www.nei.org/News-Media/News/News-Archives/memories-come-back -as-nei-staffer-returns-to-three.

16 **Inside, the control room was crowded:** For insights into the details of the Three Mile Island accident, we are indebted to Victor Gilinsky, former commissioner of the U.S. Nuclear Regulatory Commission (NRC), and Thomas Wellock, the historian for the NRC. Our description of the accident draws on Charles Perrow, *Normal Accidents: Living with High-Risk Technologies* (Princeton, NJ: Princeton University Press, 1999); J. Samuel Walker, *Three Mile Island: A Nuclear Crisis in Historical Perspective* (Berkeley and Los Angeles: The University of California Press, 2004); John G. Kemeny et al., "The Need for Change: The Legacy of TMI," Report of the President's Commission on the Accident at Three Mile Island (Washington, DC: Government Printing Office, 1979); U.S. Nuclear Regulatory Commission, "Backgrounder on the Three Mile Island Accident," February 2013, https://www.nrc.gov/reading-rm/doc-collections/fact-sheets/3mile-isle.html; "Looking Back at the Three Mile Island Accident," National Public Radio, March 15, 2011, http://www.npr.org/2011/03/15/134571483/Three-Mile-Island-Accident -Different-From-Fukushima-Daiichi; Victor Gilinsky, "Behind the Scenes of Three Mile Island," *Bulletin of the Atomic Scientists*, March 23, 2009, http://the bulletin.org/behind-scenes-three-mile-island-0; and Mark Stencel, "A Nuclear Nightmare in Pennsylvania," *Washington Post*, March 27, 1999, http://www.washing tonpost.com/wp-srv/national/longterm/tmi/tmi.htm.

16 **half of the nuclear fuel:** Victor Gilinsky, in a note in response to fact-checking questions (May 17, 2017), clarified that the fact that half of the nuclear fuel had melted was only discovered several years later, after the pressure vessel was opened. He wrote: "The estimates at the time of the accident were that any melting would have been minimal. The accident reports a year or so later hardly mention fuel melting."

16 **It was the worst nuclear accident:** Many sources describe the Three Mile Island meltdown as the worst or most significant nuclear accident in U.S. history. The event is rated at Level 5 on the International Nuclear and Radiological Event Scale, indicating an "accident with wider consequences." At the same time, as Thomas Wellock pointed out in response to a fact-checking email (May 16, 2017), "there were other accidents on developmental reactors owned by the Atomic Energy Commission that led to injuries and, in one case, three deaths." In any case, the Three Mile Island meltdown was the most significant accident in *commercial* nuclear power history in the United States.

17 **send in terminal cancer patients:** Gilinsky, "Behind the Scenes of Three Mile Island." In response to a fact-checking email (May 16, 2017), Thomas Wellock provided the following clarification: "There was never a serious discussion of having someone risk their lives to run in and open a valve somewhere, not just because it would risk someone's life, but because there was no need to do so. Valves to vent containment did not require a building entry, and it would have been unwise to vent the reactor vessel given its high temperatures and pressures . . . I think [the president's science aide] simply misunderstood Gilinsky's briefing and suggested something that was unnecessary and dangerous. So while the story is useful in understanding [the science aide's] state of mind, it is not a helpful guide to what was really happening at the plant."

18 **water that was supposed to cover:** This was a tremendously complicated accident, and we have skipped over many details. For example, immediately after the main feedwater pumps had quit, the turbine also stopped, by design. At that point, also by design, auxiliary feedwater pumps turned on, but the flow of water from these pumps was blocked by two valves that, after maintenance work a couple of days earlier, had accidentally been left in a closed position. Later in the accident, as the temperature rose and the coolant turned into steam, the pumps that forced coolant through the core began to shake violently, so operators shut them off, which compounded the problems due to the loss of coolant. As the water heated up, it escaped through the stuck-open valve as steam. For a more detailed description of the accident, see Walker, *Three Mile Island.*

18 **For a while, the computer monitoring:** B. Drummond Ayres Jr., "Three Mile Island: Notes from a Nightmare," *New York Times,* April 16, 1979, http://www .nytimes.com/1979/04/16/archives/three-mile-island-notes-from-a-nightmare -three-mile-island-a.html.

19 **"It was difficult to process":** Gilinsky, "Behind the Scenes of Three Mile Island."

19 **The man was Charles Perrow:** Our description of Perrow's theories and the development of his ideas is based on our personal interviews with him on July 23 and 24, 2016, as well as Perrow, *Normal Accidents.*

19 **A** *New Yorker* **cartoonist:** This cartoon appeared on the cover of *The Sociologist's Book of Cartoons* (New York: Cartoon Bank, 2004).

20 **"achieved iconic status.":** Kathleen Tierney, "Why We Are Vulnerable," *American Prospect,* June 17, 2007, http://prospect.org/article/why-we-are-vulnerable.

20 **"the undisputed 'master of disaster.'":** Professor Dalton Conley's endorsement for Charles Perrow, *The Next Catastrophe: Reducing Our Vulnerabilities to Natural, Industrial, and Terrorist Disasters* (Princeton, NJ: Princeton University Press, 2007);

it appears on the Princeton University Press page for the book (http://press
.princeton.edu/quotes/q9442.html).

20 **"The testimony of the operators":** Charles Perrow, "An Almost Random Career," in Arthur G. Bedeian, ed., *Management Laureates: A Collection of Autobiograph-
ical Essays*, vol. 2 (Greenwich, CT: JAI Press, 1993), 429–30.

20 **"a toxic and corrosive group":** Perrow, *Normal Accidents*, viii.

21 **One scholar described him as:** Laurence Zuckerman, "Is Complexity Interlinked
with Disaster? Ask on Jan. 1; A Theory of Risk and Technology Is Facing a Millen-
nial Test," *New York Times*, December 11, 1999, http://www.nytimes.com/1999/12
/11/books/complexity-interlinked-with-disaster-ask-jan-1-theory-risk-tech
nology-facing.html.

21 **intense but constructive criticism:** Perrow was relentless in his own research,
too, but some of the organizations he tried to study were suspicious of his motives.
"The managers would sometimes take me to a fancy lunch with many rounds of
Martinis and start making racist comments," he told us. "They wanted to test how
I'd react, to see if I was a typical left-wing sociologist or someone they could trust.
But I figured out what they were doing. So I went along with it to get the data."
With a grin, he added, "And they wanted to see if I could handle Martinis. It turns
out I liked them." Personal interview with Charles Perrow on July 23, 2016.

21 **"Chick's critical appraisals of my work":** Lee Clarke, *Mission Improbable: Using
Fantasy Documents to Tame Disaster* (Chicago and London: The University of Chicago Press, 1999), xi–xii.

22 **"retrospective errors," he called them:** Charles Perrow, "Normal Accident at
Three Mile Island," *Society* 18, no. 5 (1981): 23.

22 **The failure was driven:** For an important perspective on how systems shape the
world, see Donella Meadows, *Thinking in Systems: A Primer* (White River Junction,
VT: Chelsea Green Publishing, 2008).

24 **the butterfly effect from chaos theory:** Edward N. Lorenz, "Deterministic Non-
periodic Flow," *Journal of the Atmospheric Sciences*, 20, no. 2 (1963): 130–41; and
Edward N. Lorenz, *The Essence of Chaos* (Seattle: University of Washington Press,
1993), 181–84.

26 **Perrow's initial sketch:** Our depiction of Perrow's matrix of complexity and coupling is adapted and simplified from Figure 3.1 in Perrow, *Normal Accidents*, 97.

26 **"In the post office, mail":** Perrow, *Normal Accidents*, 98.

27 **"A normal accident,":** Charles Perrow, "Getting to Catastrophe: Concentrations,
Complexity and Coupling," *Montréal Review*, December 2012, http://www.themon
trealreview.com/2009/Normal-Accidents-Living-with-High-Risk-Technologies
.php.

27 **"It is normal for us to die,":** Perrow, *Normal Accidents*, 5.

28 **In the winter of 2012:** Our story of the Starbucks Twitter fiasco draws on "Starbucks
Twitter Campaign Hijacked by Tax Protests," *Telegraph*, December 17, 2012, http://
www.telegraph.co.uk/technology/twitter/9750215/Starbucks-Twitter-cam
paign-hijacked-by-tax-protests.html; Felicity Morese, "Starbucks PR Fail at Natural
History Museum After #SpreadTheCheer Tweets Hijacked," *Huffington Post
UK*, December 17, 2012, http://www.huffingtonpost.co.uk/2012/12/17/starbucks
-pr-rage-natural-history-museum_n_2314892.html; and "Starbucks' #SpreadThe
Cheer Hashtag Backfires as Twitter Users Attack Coffee Giant," *Huffington Post*, December 17, 2012, http://www.huffingtonpost.com/2012/12/17/starbucks-spread-the
-cheer_n_2317544.html.

32 **gourmet food magazine *Bon Appétit*:** Emily Fleischaker, "Your 10 Funniest
Thanksgiving Bloopers + the Most Common Disasters," *Bon Appétit*, November 23,

2010, http://www.bonappetit.com/entertaining-style/holidays/article/your-10-fun
niest-thanksgiving-bloopers-the-most-common-disasters.

32 **"Hundreds of you sent":** Ibid.

32 **"If you break down the turkey":** Ben Esch, "We Asked a Star Chef to Rescue You
from a Horrible Thanksgiving," *Uproxx*, November 21, 2016, http://uproxx.com/life
/5-ways-screwing-up-thanksgiving-dinner. Jason Quinn isn't the only expert who
favors simplifying the system in this way. Sam Sifton, the food editor of the *New York
Times* and author of *Thanksgiving: How to Cook It Well* (New York: Random House,
2012), for example, recommends a similar approach when time and oven space are
limited (see Sam Sifton, "Fastest Roast Turkey," *NYT Cooking*, https://cooking.ny
times.com/recipes/1016948-fastest-roast-turkey). Similarly, J. Kenji López-Alt, author of *The Food Lab: Better Home Cooking Through Science* (New York: W. W. Norton,
2015), explains how to roast a turkey in parts to reduce complexity and ensure that the
different parts are all cooked to the correct temperature (see J. Kenji López-Alt,
"Roast Turkey in Parts Recipe," *Serious Eats*, November 2010, http://www.serious
eats.com/recipes/2010/11/turkey-in-parts-white-dark-recipe.html).

## Chapter Two: Deep Waters, New Horizons

35 **When Erika Christakis hit send:** Our coverage of the controversy at Yale
builds on Conor Friedersdorf, "The Perils of Writing a Provocative Email at Yale,"
*Atlantic*, May 26, 2016, https://www.theatlantic.com/politics/archive/2016/05/the
-peril-of-writing-a-provocative-email-at-yale/484418. Throughout this section,
we refer to Erika and Nicholas Christakis as "co-masters," which is an informal
term. Technically, Nicholas, a sociologist and physician, was the master of the college; Erika was a lecturer in early childhood education. Since these events occurred,
the name of the position has been changed from "master" to "head of college."

35 **a broader conversation about race:** That conversation came to include Yale directly.
See Justin Wm. Moyer, "Confederate Controversy Heads North to Yale and John C.
Calhoun," *Washington Post*, July 6, 2015, https://www.washingtonpost.com/news
/morning-mix/wp/2015/07/06/confederate-controversy-heads-north-to-yale-and
-john-c-calhoun. In 2017, Calhoun College was renamed Grace Hopper College.

36 **a group of students confronted him:** Our description of the confrontation draws
on Conor Friedersdorf's above-mentioned article in the *Atlantic* and a smartphone
video available on YouTube that captured the confrontation. Nicholas's quotes were
transcribed from the audio. "Yale Halloween Costume Controversy," YouTube play-
list, posted by TheFIREorg, https://www.youtube.com/playlist?list=PLvIqJIL2k
OMefn77xg6-6yrvek5kbNf3Z.

37 **resigned from their positions as co-masters:** See "Yale University Statement
on Nicholas Christakis," May 25, 2016, https://news.yale.edu/2016/05/25/yale
-university-statement-nicholas-christakis-may-2016.

37 **a wealthy town in Connecticut:** See, for example, Blake Neff, "Meet the Privileged
Yale Student Who Shrieked at Her Professor," *Daily Caller*, November 11, 2015,
http://dailycaller.com/2015/11/09/meet-the-privileged-yale-student-who-shrieked
-at-her-professor.

38 **inspector named Patrick Regan:** Patrick J. Regan, "Dams as Systems: A Holistic
Approach to Dam Safety," conference paper, 30th U.S. Society on Dams conference, Sacramento, 2010.

38 **"If the sensor is giving erroneous":** Ibid., 5. Of course, some dam operations do
use video, but it's not used in all cases, nor is it foolproof.

**38  At a California dam:** See the description of the Nimbus Dam incident in Regan, "Dams as Systems."

**39  finance became a perfect example:** Of course, the global financial system was no stranger to failure even before the developments in recent decades. See, for example, Liaquat Ahamed, *Lords of Finance: The Bankers Who Broke the World* (New York: Random House, 2009); and Ben S. Bernanke, "Nonmonetary Effects of the Financial Crisis in the Propagation of the Great Depression," *American Economic Review* 73, no. 3 (1983): 257–76.

**39  That same kind of price spiral:** For a deep account of the crash of 1987, Long-Term Capital Management, and modern finance more broadly (including the role of complexity and tight coupling), see Richard Bookstaber's excellent book, *A Demon of Our Own Design* (Hoboken, NJ: Wiley, 2007).

**40  As Andrew Ross Sorkin detailed:** Another great writer who analyzed the financial crisis is, of course, Michael Lewis. See, for example, "Wall Street on the Tundra," *Vanity Fair*, April 2009, http://www.vanityfair.com/culture/2009/04/iceland200904; and *The Big Short: Inside the Doomsday Machine* (New York: W. W. Norton, 2011).

**40  "exceeds the complexity":** This Perrow quote is from a 2010 interview, which was conducted by Tim Harford and reported in Harford's insightful book, *Adapt: Why Success Always Starts with Failure* (New York: Farrar, Straus, and Giroux, 2011).

**40  a slow summer day on Wall Street:** Our account of Knight's failure is based on our interviews with Knight CEO Tom Joyce on January 21, 2016; "John Mueller" (pseudonym) on January 14, 2016; and other traders. We've also drawn on the SEC's report regarding Knight's trading mistake. See "In the Matter of Knight Capital LLC," Administrative Proceeding File No. 3-15570, October 16, 2013. It's important to note that, unlike National Transportation Safety Board reports, whose purpose is to ascertain the causes of an accident, the SEC's report lays out the basis for an enforcement action against Knight Capital. We also drew from contemporary reporting, including an interview with Tom Joyce on "Market Makers," Bloomberg Television, August 2, 2012; Nathaniel Popper, "Knight Capital Says Trading Glitch Cost It $440 Million," *New York Times*, August 2, 2012, https://dealbook.nytimes.com/2012/08/02/knight-capital-says-trading-mishap-cost-it-440-million/; and David Faber and Kate Kelly with Reuters, "Knight Capital Reaches $400 Million Deal to Save Firm," CNBC, August 6, 2012, http://www.cnbc.com/id/48516238.

**42  more than $15 million *per minute*:** At 10:00 a.m. Knight was probably down closer to $200 million (Tom Joyce, personal correspondence, May 16, 2017). But because traders across Wall Street knew that Knight needed to trade out of the erroneous positions, Knight's losses worsened. Throughout the day, Knight's traders worked to shrink the portfolio before eventually trading out of the balance with Goldman Sachs in a late-afternoon block trade.

**43  The use of computers drove down:** While there are many examples of the downsides of "high-frequency" or algorithmic trading, there are also benefits. Since the processing of trades by banks and brokers has a high fixed cost, more trading and increased use of technology lowers the marginal cost of a trade. In addition, the presence of automated trading narrows the spread between the bid and offer of a stock, which reduces prices for consumers. See, for example, Terrence Hendershott, Charles M. Jones, and Albert J. Menkveld, "Does Algorithmic Trading Improve Liquidity?" *Journal of Finance* 66, no. 1 (2011): 1–33. Algorithmic trading also supports low-cost instruments like index funds, which many investors hold as exchange-traded funds (ETFs) or mutual funds in retirement accounts. While debates rage over whether high-frequency trading is better for "mom and pop" traders, it has certainly reduced the cost of access.

43 **On May 6, 2010:** Chris Clearfield and James Owen Weatherall, "Why the Flash Crash Really Matters," *Nautilus*, April 23, 2015, http://nautil.us/issue/23 /dominoes/why-the-flash-crash-really-matters.

48 **Less than twelve hours later:** Our description of the Deepwater Horizon accident draws on several sources: National Commission on the BP Deepwater Horizon Oil Spill and Offshore Drilling, *Deep Water: The Gulf Oil Disaster and the Future of Offshore Drilling*, Report to the President (Washington, DC: Government Publishing Office, 2011); David Barstow, David Rohde, and Stephanie Saul, "Deepwater Horizon's Final Hours," *New York Times*, December 25, 2010, http://www.nytimes.com /2010/12/26/us/26spill.html; Earl Boebert and James M. Blossom, *Deepwater Horizon: A Systems Analysis of the Macondo Disaster* (Cambridge, MA: Harvard University Press, 2016); Peter Elkind, David Whitford, and Doris Burke, "BP: 'An Accident Waiting to Happen,'" *Fortune*, January 24, 2011, http://fortune.com/2011/01/24/bp-an-accident -waiting-to-happen; and BP's "Deepwater Horizon Accident Investigation Report," September 8, 2010, http://www.bp.com/content/dam/bp/pdf/sustainability/issue -reports/Deepwater_Horizon_Accident_Investigation_Report.pdf.

48 **from thirty miles away:** "Understanding the Initial Deepwater Horizon Fire," *Hazmat Management*, May 10, 2010, http://www.hazmatmag.com/environment /understanding-the-initial-deepwater-horizon-fire/1000370689.

49 **ignoring worrisome pressure readings:** National Commission on the BP Deepwater Horizon Oil Spill and Offshore Drilling, *Deep Water*, 105–9.

49 **skipping cement integrity tests:** Ibid., 3–4.

49 **"Safety meeting after safety meeting":** David Barstow, Rob Harris, and Haeyoun Park, "Escape from the Deepwater Horizon," *New York Times* video, 6:34, December 26, 2010, https://www.nytimes.com/video/us/1248069488217/escape-from-the -deepwater-horizon.html.

49 **The crew even helped make:** Ibid.

50 **"Senior BP management":** Andrew B. Wilson, "BP's Disaster: No Surprise to Folks in the Know," CBS News, June 22, 2010, http://www.cbsnews.com/news/bps -disaster-no-surprise-to-folks-in-the-know.

50 *worrying about coffee spills***:** Elkind, Whitford, and Burke, "BP."

50 **"Notwithstanding the tragic loss of life":** Proxy Statement Pursuant to Section 14(a), filed by Transocean with the U.S. Securities and Exchange Commission on April 1, 2011, https://www.sec.gov/Archives/edgar/data/1451505/00010474691100 3066/a2202839zdef14a.htm.

52 **fancy new IT system called Horizon:** Much of the section on the UK Post Office and its Horizon system draws on statements that Members of Parliament made during an adjournment debate in the House of Commons on December 17, 2014 (*Parliamentary Debates*. Commons, 6th ser., vol. 589 [2014], http://hansard.parlia ment.uk/Commons/2014-12-17/debates/14121741000002/PostOfficeMediation Scheme), particularly the statements made by MPs James Arbuthnot, Andrew Bridgen, Katy Clark, Jonathan Djanogly, Sir Oliver Heald, Huw Irranca-Davies, Kevan Jones, Ian Murray, Albert Owen, Gisela Stuart, and Mike Wood. We also draw on Second Sight, "Interim Report into Alleged Problems with the Horizon System," July 8, 2013; and Second Sight, "Initial Complaint Review and Mediation Scheme: Briefing Report—Part Two," April 9, 2015, http://www.jfsa.org.uk/uploads/5/4/3/1 /54312921/report_9th_april_2015.pdf.

In 2017, a Group Litigation Order against the Post Office was approved by the President of the Queen's Bench Division of the High Court; the Post Office is defending the case. See Freeths, "Group Litigation Order against Post Office Limited Is Approved," March 28, 2017, http://www.freeths.co.uk/news/group-liti gation-order-against-post-office-limited-is-approved; and HM Courts & Tribunals

Service, "The Post Office Group Litigation," March 21, 2017, https://www.gov.uk/guidance/group-litigation-orders#the-post-office-group-litigation.

52 **"one of the biggest IT projects":** The Post Office, "Post Office Automation Project Complete," PR Newswire, June 21, 2001, http://www.prnewswire.co.uk/news-releases/post-office-automation-project-complete-153845715.html.

52 **Decent Lives Destroyed by the Post Office:** Neil Tweedie, "Decent Lives Destroyed by the Post Office: The Monstrous Injustice of Scores of Sub-Postmasters Driven to Ruin or Suicide When Computers Were Really to Blame," *Daily Mail*, April 24, 2015, http://www.dailymail.co.uk/news/article-3054706/Decent-lives-destroyed-Post-Office-monstrous-injustice-scores-sub-postmasters-driven-ruin-suicide-computers-really-blame.html.

52 **Post Office Under Fire Over IT System:** Tim Ross, "Post Office Under Fire Over IT System," *Telegraph*, August 2, 2015, http://www.telegraph.co.uk/news/uknews/royal-mail/11778288/Post-Office-under-fire-over-IT-system.html.

52 **Subpostmasters Fight to Clear Names:** Rebecca Ratcliffe, "Subpostmasters Fight to Clear Names in Theft and False Accounting Case," *Guardian*, April 9, 2017, https://www.theguardian.com/business/2017/apr/09/subpostmasters-unite-to-clear-names-theft-case-post-office.

53 **shortfalls in cash and stamps:** *Parliamentary Debates*, Commons, 6th ser., vol. 589 (2014), http://hansard.parliament.uk/Commons/2014-12-17/debates/14121741000002/PostOfficeMediationScheme. As MP James Arbuthnot noted during the debate, "In 2000, the Post Office introduced the Horizon accounting system. A spate of concerns began to arise shortly afterwards. Sub-postmasters across the country experienced discrepancies in their accounts, which they had to balance at the end of each day. Some of those accounts were over what they ought to have been, and some were under what they ought to have been. Some sub-postmasters found themselves closing their post offices on a Saturday with one balance and opening on a Monday to discover that the balance was entirely different." Arbuthnot also described the following case during the debate: "[My constituent Jo Hamilton] first found that there was a discrepancy of, I think, £2,000. She rang up the help desk, which told her to press certain buttons, and immediately the discrepancy doubled to £4,000. Eventually the discrepancy rose and rose to more than £30,000. There was no proper investigation by the Post Office." During the same debate, MP Albert Owen made the following statement: "The Horizon system has been looked at as there have been problems with it. Many sub-postmasters and sub-postmistresses, some of whom are now retired—their post offices have closed for whatever reason—indicated to me in the early stages in 2001–02 that there were issues of concern at that time in rural areas, when the system was going offline and being rebooted. I therefore find it hard to accept that the Post Office has concluded that there was nothing wrong with the system." Likewise, MP Ian Murray observed that "we continue to hear about the significant problems experienced by sub-postmasters up and down the country." And MP Huw Irranca-Davies stated: "My constituent was asked in 2008 to repay more than £5,000 to Post Office Ltd as a result of discrepancies of the like we have heard about today. He claims that it was the fault of the Horizon computer system, but also the fault of a lack of training, support and follow-up when difficulties arose." See also Second Sight, "Initial Complaint Review and Mediation Scheme," Freeths, "Group Litigation Order against Post Office Limited is Approved"; HM Courts & Tribunals Service, "The Post Office Group Litigation"; Gill Plimmer, "MPs Accuse Post Office over 'Fraud' Ordeal of Sub-Postmasters," *Financial Times*, December 9, 2014, https://www.ft.com/content/89e1bdf6-7fb1-11e4-adff-00144feabdc0; Michael Pooler, "Sub-Postmasters Fight Back over Post Office Accusations of Fraud," *Financial Times*, January 31, 2017, https://www.ft.com/con

tent/6b6e4afc-e7af-11e6-893c-082c54a7f539; and Gill Plimmer and Andrew Bounds, "Dream Turns to Nightmare for Post Office Couple in Fraud Ordeal," *Financial Times*, December 12, 2014, https://www.ft.com/content/91080df0-814c-11e4-b956 -00144feabdc0.

**53   caused ATMs to behave strangely:** Second Sight, "Initial Complaint Review and Mediation Scheme: Briefing Report—Part Two", April 9, 2015, http://www.jfsa.org .uk/uploads/5/4/3/1/54312921/report_9th_april_2015.pdf; Testimony of Ian Henderson, "Post Office Mediation," HC 935, Business, Innovation and Skills Committee, February 3, 2015, http://data.parliament.uk/writtenevidence/committee evidence.svc/evidencedocument/business-innovation-and-skills-committee/post -office-mediation/oral/17926.html; and Tweedie, "Decent Lives Destroyed by the Post Office."

**53   according to the *Financial Times*:** Plimmer and Bounds, "Dream Turns to Nightmare" and Second Sight, "Initial Complaint Review and Mediation Scheme." These conclusions are consistent with several statements that MPs made in the House of Commons during the December 17, 2014 adjournment debate (*Parliamentary Debates*, Commons, 6th ser., vol. 589 [2014]). Consider, for example, the statements by MP Huw Irranca-Davies, who emphasized "problems with the interface between Horizon and existing schemes" and "the lack of support and training," and the statements by MP Mike Wood, who noted that "the responsibility for any shortfall or shortcoming rests contractually with the postmaster or postmistress."

**53   Tom Brown had seen a lot:** Tom Brown's story was discussed by MP Kevan Jones during an adjournment debate in the House of Commons (*Parliamentary Debates*, Commons, 6th ser., vol. 589 [2014]). See also related statements made during the same debate by MPs James Arbuthnot, Katy Clark, and Huw Irranca-Davies about the support systems associated with Horizon. As Katy Clark stated, for example, "The general point that comes through is that the support systems provided by the Post Office are inadequate. Wrong advice and assistance is regularly given by the help desks that are there to try to deal with such situations as they arise." At the same debate, MP Huw Irranca-Davies stated: "I have three cases in a very small constituency. All three are different in their nature, but they all consistently say the same things. They have all had problems with the interface between Horizon and existing schemes. They have all had problems with downtime on Horizon during the period in which it was introduced, which messed up their calculations. The lack of support and training given when that happened was appalling. They all say that the subsequent lack of training and support when incidents arose was appalling. They have all had to dip into their own pockets, as sub-postmasters have to, to make good on this." See also Second Sight, "Initial Complaint Review and Mediation Scheme," 25.

**53   "fully confident that the Horizon":** Post Office statement quoted in Karl Flinders, "Post Office Faces Legal Action Over Alleged Accounting System Failures," *Computer Weekly*, February 8, 2011, http://www.computerweekly.com/news/1280095088 /Post-Office_faces-legal-action-over-alleged-accounting-system-failures. In a fact-checking email on August 11, 2017, a representative from the Post Office wrote that "Like any other IT system, Horizon is not perfect but it is robust and reliable."

**53   "across 11,600 branches":** This statement comes from a member of the Post Office's communication team in an email on August 11, 2017. In our view, it's clear that Horizon successfully serves thousands of sub-postmasters processing millions of transactions, and our inclusion of Horizon is not meant to imply that the entire system has failed. A complex and tightly coupled system can lead to surprising and costly failures even if the system works properly in the vast majority of cases; an airline crash, like the ValuJet 592 accident, can be a system failure without implying that the modern aviation system as a whole is a failure.

53 **the Post Office accused:** *Parliamentary Debates*, Commons, 6th ser., vol. 589 [2014]; see the statements made by MPs James Arbuthnot and Albert Owen. See also Freeths, "Group Litigation Order against Post Office Limited is Approved"; HM Courts & Tribunals Service, "The Post Office Group Litigation"; and Pooler, "Sub-Postmasters Fight Back."

54 **it even brought criminal charges:** *Parliamentary Debates*, Commons, 6th ser., vol. 589 (2014); see the statements made by MPs James Arbuthnot, Huw Irranca-Davies, Kevan Jones, and Albert Owen. See also Freeths, "Group Litigation Order against Post Office Limited is Approved"; HM Courts & Tribunals Service, "The Post Office Group Litigation"; Pooler, "Sub-Postmasters Fight Back"; and Ratcliffe, "Subpostmasters Fight to Clear Names."

54 **I had to remortgage the house:** Jo Hamilton's case was discussed in depth during a debate in the House of Commons by MP James Arbuthnot (*Parliamentary Debates*, Commons, 6th ser., vol. 589 [2014]); Jo Hamilton's quote comes from Matt Prodger, "MPs Attack Post Office Sub-Postmaster Mediation Scheme," BBC News, December 9, 2014, http://www.bbc.com/news/business-30387973 and the accompanying audio file.

54 **After some Members of Parliament:** *Parliamentary Debates*, Commons, 6th ser., vol. 589 (2014); see, in particular, the statements by MP James Arbuthnot.

54 **Second Sight found that the problems:** Henderson, "Post Office Mediation." See also Second Sight, "Initial Complaint Review and Mediation Scheme" and Charlotte Jee, "Post Office Obstructing Horizon Probe, Investigator Claims," *Computerworld UK*, February 3, 2015, http://www.computerworlduk.com/infrastructure /post-office-obstructing-horizon-probe-investigator-claims-3596589.

54 **shortfalls might be explained by:** Second Sight, "Initial Complaint Review and Mediation Scheme," 14–19.

54 **ATMs run by the Bank of Ireland:** Ibid.

54 **complexity of the Horizon system:** *Parliamentary Debates*, Commons, 6th ser., vol. 589 (2014). For example, as MP James Arbuthnot noted, "The thing that I am worried about most is that it is often impossible to find those flaws in the software that could have caused some of these problems." During the same debate, Jo Swinson, the Parliamentary Under-Secretary of State for Business, Innovation and Skills, observed that "many of the cases are incredibly complex, understandably so, because they are dealing with systems and many transactions." In addition, as the *Financial Times* noted, "IT experts say it is extremely difficult to track this type of computer failure, especially when the systems are complex and the problems are being investigated in hindsight" (Plimmer, "MPs Accuse Post Office"). See also Second Sight, "Initial Complaint Review and Mediation Scheme" and Plimmer and Bounds, "Dream Turns to Nightmare."

54 **ended up bankrupt or jailed:** *Parliamentary Debates*, Commons, 6th ser., vol. 589 (2014), particularly the statements made by MPs James Arbuthnot, Andrew Bridgen, Sir Oliver Heald, Kevan Jones, and Ian Murray about the experiences of sub-postmasters in their constituencies. See also Pooler, "Sub-Postmasters Fight Back"; and Plimmer and Bounds, "Dream Turns to Nightmare."

54 **Horizon's bewildering complexity:** *Parliamentary Debates*, Commons, 6th ser., vol. 589 (2014); Second Sight, "Initial Complaint Review and Mediation Scheme"; and Plimmer, "MPs Accuse Post Office."

55 **disputing the conclusions of:** Alexander J. Martin, "Subpostmasters Prepare to Fight Post Office Over Wrongful Theft and False Accounting Accusations," *The Register*, April 10, 2017, https://www.theregister.co.uk/2017/04/10/subpostmasters _prepare_to_fight_post_office_over_wrongful_theft_and_false_accounting _accusations; and "The UK's Post Office Responds to Horizon Report," *Post &*

*Parcel*, April 20, 2015, http://postandparcel.info/64576/news/the-uks-post-office-responds-to-horizon-report.

55 **"After two years of investigation":** "Post Office IT System Criticised in Report," BBC News, September 9, 2014, http://www.bbc.com/news/uk-29130897. See also Karl Flinders, "Post Office IT Support Email Reveals Known Horizon Flaw," *Computer Weekly*, November 18, 2015, http://www.computerweekly.com/news/4500257572/Post-Office-IT-support-email-reveals-known-Horizon-flaw.

55 **the Post Office is defending:** HM Courts & Tribunals Service, "The Post Office Group Litigation" and Michael Pooler, "Post Office Faces Class Action Over 'Faulty' IT System," *Financial Times*, August 2, 2017, https://www.ft.com/content/f420f2f8-75fa-11e7-a3e8-60495fe6ca71.

55 **Criminal Cases Review Commission is investigating:** Pooler, "Post Office Faces Class Action Over 'Faulty' IT System."

55 **"complete and utter nonsense.":** Statement by MP Kevan Jones. *Parliamentary Debates*, Commons, 6th ser., vol. 589 (2014). See also statements made by MPs James Arbuthnot, Andrew Bridgen, Katy Clark, Jonathan Djanogly, Sir Oliver Heald, Huw Irranca-Davies, Ian Murray, Albert Owen, Gisela Stuart, and Mike Wood during the same debate, as well as Plimmer and Bounds, "Dream Turns to Nightmare."

55 **"Some people have been jailed":** This quote is from Alan Bates, who set up the group Justice for Sub-Postmasters Alliance, cited in Steve White, "Post Office Wrongly Accused Sub-Postmaster of Stealing £85,000 in Five Years of 'Torture,'" *Mirror*, August 16, 2013, http://www.mirror.co.uk/news/uk-news/post-office-wrongly-accused-sub-postmaster-2176052.

## Chapter Three: Hacking, Fraud, and All the News That's Unfit to Print

57 **Barnaby Jack took the stage:** Jack's presentation "Jackpotting: Automated Teller Machines" was widely publicized, and there is a video of his talk and slides at https://www.youtube.com/watch?v=4StcW9OPpPc, posted by DEFCONconference, November 8, 2013.

58 **hackers stole forty million:** The story was covered extensively in major news outlets, but Brian Krebs broke news of the breach with his story ("Sources: Target Investigating Data Breach," *Krebs on Security*, December 18, 2013, https://krebsonsecurity.com/2013/12/sources-target-investigating-data-breach/) and then followed that up with a number of in-depth articles on the breach itself.

59 **Whatever happens, don't panic:** This section draws on our interview with Andy Greenberg on August 12, 2016, and his articles, including "Hackers Remotely Kill a Jeep on the Highway—With Me in It," *Wired*, July 21, 2015, https://www.wired.com/2015/07/hackers-remotely-kill-jeep-highway; "After Jeep Hack, Chrysler Recalls 1.4M Vehicles for Bug Fix," *Wired*, July 24, 2015, https://www.wired.com/2015/07/jeep-hack-chrysler-recalls-1-4m-vehicles-bug-fix; and "Hackers Reveal Nasty New Car Attacks—With Me Behind the Wheel (Video)," *Forbes*, August 12, 2013, https://www.forbes.com/sites/andygreenberg/2013/07/24/hackers-reveal-nasty-new-car-attacks-with-me-behind-the-wheel-video/#60fde1d9228c.

60 **Chrysler acknowledged the security flaw:** Greenberg, "After Jeep Hack, Chrysler Recalls 1.4M Vehicles for Bug Fix." Fiat Chrysler also worked with Sprint, the cellular network provider, to prevent hackers from reaching the Jeep in the first place.

60 **malicious actors that connect things together:** Personal interview with Andy Greenberg on August 12, 2016.

61 **Jack turned his attention to:** Stilgherrian, "Lethal Medical Device Hack Taken to Next Level," *CSO Online*, October 21, 2011, https://www.cso.com.au/article /404909/lethal_medical_device_hack_taken_next_level; David C. Klonoff, " Cybersecurity for Connected Diabetes Devices," *Journal of Diabetes Science and Technology* 9, no. 5 (2015): 1143–47; and Jim Finkle, "U.S. Government Probes Medical Devices for Possible Cyber Flaws," Reuters, October 22, 2014, http://www .reuters.com/article/us-cybersecurity-medicaldevices-insight-idUSKCN0IB0DQ 20141022.

61 **Jack also hacked implantable defibrillators:** Darren Pauli, "Hacked Terminals Capable of Causing Pacemaker Deaths," *IT News*, October 17, 2012, https://www .itnews.com.au/news/hacked-terminals-capable-of-causing-pacemaker-deaths -319508. Interestingly, Jack's research and legacy have been carried on by another New Zealander, Justine Bone, who is the CEO of the medical device security firm MedSec. Bone's firm claimed to have uncovered security vulnerabilities in implantable defibrillators manufactured by device maker St. Jude Medical. St. Jude denies that there is a problem and has sued MedSec for false statements. See Michelle Cortez, Erik Schatzker, and Jordan Robertson, "Carson Block Takes on St. Jude Medical Claiming Hack Risk," *Bloomberg*, August 25, 2016, https://www.bloomberg .com/news/articles/2016-08-25/carson-block-takes-on-st-jude-medical-with -claim-of-hack-risk; and *St Jude Medical Inc v. Muddy Waters Consulting LLC et al.*, Federal Civil Lawsuit, Minnesota District Court, Case No. 0:16-cv-03002.

61 **made the attack seem *too difficult*:** Barnaby Jack, "'Broken Hearts': How Plausible Was the Homeland Pacemaker Hack?" IOActive Labs Research, February 25, 2013, http://blog.ioactive.com/2013/02/broken-hearts-how-plausible-was.html.

62 **hacker could wreak havoc:** For an exploration of the relationship between increasingly complex modern systems and the potential for crippling, unanticipated terrorist attacks, see Thomas Homer-Dixon, "The Rise of Complex Terrorism," *Foreign Policy* 128, no. 1 (2002): 52–62.

62 **complexity creates opportunities for wrongdoing:** For a rigorous introduction to theories of wrongdoing in organizations inspired, in part, by Charles Perrow's work, see Donald Palmer, *Normal Organizational Wrongdoing* (New York: Oxford University Press, 2013).

64 **The company was Enron:** Our section on Enron draws from the deep reporting of Bethany McLean and Peter Elkind in *The Smartest Guys in the Room: The Amazing Rise and Scandalous Fall of Enron* (New York: Portfolio, 2003); the fantastic 2005 documentary film based on the book, *Enron: The Smartest Guys in the Room* (directed by Alex Gibney); Bethany McLean's article "Is Enron Overpriced?" *Fortune*, March 5, 2001, http://money.cnn.com/2006/01/13/news/companies/enron original_fortune; and Kurt Eichenwald's *Conspiracy of Fools: A True Story* (New York: Broadway Books, 2005). We also drew on documents from the bankruptcy proceedings that followed the collapse, including court-appointed examiner Neal Batson's extensive report prepared for *In re: Enron Corp. et al.*, U.S. Bankruptcy Court, Southern District of New York and appendices, November 4, 2003.

65 **"One way to hide a log":** Bethany McLean, "Why Enron Went Bust," *Fortune*, December 24, 2001, http://archive.fortune.com/magazines/fortune/fortune_arch ive/2001/12/24/315319/index.htm.

65 **One strategy exploited price caps:** Enron's strategies were described in two legal memos: Christian Yoder and Stephen Hall, "re: Traders' Strategies in the California Wholesale Power Markets/ISO Sanctions," Stoel Rives (firm), December 8, 2000; and Gary Fergus and Jean Frizell, "Status Report on Further Investigation and Analysis of EPMI Trading Strategies," Brobeck (firm) (undated).

65 **come up with a reason to go down:** See *Enron: The Smartest Guys in the Room* (Gibney), which includes tapes of phone calls from Enron traders.

66 **$40 billion in added energy costs:** Christopher Weare, *The California Electricity Crisis: Causes and Policy Options* (San Francisco: Public Policy Institute of California, 2003).

66 **the business of doing deals:** Rebecca Mark quoted in V. Kasturi Rangan, Krishna G. Palepu, Ahu Bhasin, Mihir A. Desai, and Sarayu Srinivasan, "Enron Development Corporation: The Dabhol Power Project in Maharashtra, India (A)," Harvard Business School Case 596–099, May 1996 (Revised July 1998).

68 **There was no slowing down:** For an important take on how mark-to-market accounting also has a negative effect on the ability of investment organizations to take a long-term view, see Donald Guloien and Roger Martin, "Mark-to-Market Accounting: A Volatility Villain," *Globe and Mail*, February 13, 2013, https://www.theglobeandmail.com/globe-investor/mark-to-market-accounting-a-volatility-villain/article8637443.

69 **convoluted transactions to hide the debt:** For details of these transactions, see Appendix D of the Batson report.

69 **laws and regulation are vague:** Peter Elkind, "The Confessions of Andy Fastow," *Fortune*, July 1, 2013, http://fortune.com/2013/07/01/the-confessions-of-andy-fastow.

69 **"Running a pipeline business":** This quote is from an email from Carmen Marino, a managing director at Credit Suisse First Boston, detailed in Appendix F of the Batson report.

70 **paid over $2 billion:** Julie Creswell, "J.P. Morgan Chase to Pay Enron Investors $2.2 Billion," *New York Times*, June 15, 2005, http://www.nytimes.com/2005/06/15/business/jp-morgan-chase-to-pay-enron-investors-22-billion.html.

70 **an address at Harvard Business School:** Owen D. Young, "Dedication Address," *Harvard Business Review* 5, no. 4 (July 1927), https://iiif.lib.harvard.edu/manifests/view/drs:8982551$1i. Thanks to Malcolm Salter, "Lawful but Corrupt: Gaming and the Problem of Institutional Corruption in the Private Sector" (unpublished research paper, Harvard Business School, 2010) for the reference to Young's address.

71 **"You have a complex set of rules":** Elkind, "The Confessions of Andy Fastow."

71 **Similar accounting scandals:** Sean Farrell, "The World's Biggest Accounting Scandals," *Guardian*, July 21, 2015, https://www.theguardian.com/business/2015/jul/21/the-worlds-biggest-accounting-scandals-toshiba-enron-olympus; "India's Enron," *Economist*, January 8, 2009, http://www.economist.com/node/12898777; "Europe's Enron," *Economist*, February 27, 2003, http://www.economist.com/node/1610552; "The Enron Down Under," *Economist*, May 23, 2002, http://www.economist.com/node/1147274.

75 **They were all written by Jayson Blair:** The original articles, now with corrections appended, are still available on the *New York Times* website. See Jayson Blair, "Retracing a Trail: The Investigation; U.S. Sniper Case Seen as a Barrier to a Confession," *New York Times*, October 30, 2002, http://www.nytimes.com/2002/10/30/us/retracing-trail-investigation-us-sniper-case-seen-barrier-confession.html; Jayson Blair, "A Nation at War: Military Families; Relatives of Missing Soldiers Dread Hearing Worse News," *New York Times*, March 27, 2003, http://www.nytimes.com/2003/03/27/us/nation-war-military-families-relatives-missing-soldiers-dread-hearing-worse.html; and Jayson Blair, "A Nation at War: Veterans; In Military Wards, Questions and Fears from the Wounded," *New York Times*, April 19, 2003, http://www.nytimes.com/2003/04/19/us/a-nation-at-war-veterans-in-military-wards-questions-and-fears-from-the-wounded.html.

75 **And they were all fabricated:** The research from this section draws on the paper's own coverage, written by Dan Barry, David Barstow, Jonathan D. Glater, Adam Liptak, and Jacques Steinberg, "Correcting the Record; Times Reporter Who Resigned Leaves Long Trail of Deception," *New York Times*, May 11, 2003, http://www .nytimes.com/2003/05/11/us/correcting-the-record-times-reporter-who-resigned -leaves-long-trail-of-deception.html; Seth Mnookin, "Scandal of Record," *Vanity Fair*, December 2004, http://www.vanityfair.com/style/2004/12/nytimes200412; and the Siegal Committee, "Report of the Committee on Safeguarding the Integrity of Our Journalism," July 28, 2003, http://www.nytco.com/wp-content/uploads /Siegal-Committe-Report.pdf.

75 **a drinking and drug problem:** Jayson Blair, interview by Katie Couric, "A Question of Trust," *Dateline NBC*, NBC, March 17, 2004, http://www.nbcnews.com/id /4457860/ns/dateline_nbc/t/question-trust/#.WZHenRIrKu6.

75 **"We have to stop Jayson":** Barry et al., "Correcting the Record."

76 **mixed up his notes:** Mnookin, "Scandal of Record."

76 **"People would kill to get":** Ibid.

77 **echoes of Chick Perrow's ideas:** William Woo, "Journalism's 'Normal Accidents,'" *Nieman Reports*, September 15, 2003, http://niemanreports.org/articles /journalisms-normal-accidents.

77 **unobservability is a key ingredient:** Dominic Lasorsa and Jia Da, "Newsroom's Normal Accident? An Exploratory Study of 10 Cases of Journalistic Deception," *Journalism Practice* 1, no. 2 (2007): 159–74.

77 **sheer volume of information:** In response to the Jayson Blair scandal, the *Times* established the position of public editor to give readers a way to raise complaints independent of the normal bureaucracy. See Margaret Sullivan, "Repairing the Credibility Cracks," *New York Times*, May 4, 2013, http://www.nytimes.com/2013/05/05 /public-editor/repairing-the-credibility-cracks-after-jayson-blair.html. In 2017, the *Times* eliminated the position.

## Chapter Four: Out of the Danger Zone

81 **Glitz. Glamour. Complexity. Confusion:** For the Oscars story, we drew on Jim Donnelly, "Moonlight Wins Best Picture After 2017 Oscars Envelope Mishap," March 3, 2017, http://oscar.go.com/news/winners/after-oscars-2017-mishap-moon light-wins-best-picture; Yohana Desta, "Both Oscar Accountants 'Froze' During Best Picture Mess," *Vanity Fair*, March 2, 2017, http://www.vanityfair.com/holly wood/2017/03/pwc-accountants-froze-backstage; Jackson McHenry, "Everything We Know About That Oscars Best Picture Mix-up," *Vulture*, February 27, 2017, http://www.vulture.com/2017/02/oscars-best-picture-mixup-everything-we-know .html; and the broadcast of the 89th Academy Awards itself.

82 **described the setup in a blog:** Brian Cullinan and Martha Ruiz, "These Accountants Are the Only People Who Know the Oscar Results," *Huffington Post*, January 31, 2017, http://www.huffingtonpost.com/entry/oscar-results-balloting-pwc_us _5890f00ee4b02772c4e9cf63.

82 **It's not rocket science:** Valli Herman, "Was Oscar's Best Picture Disaster Simply the Result of Poor Envelope Design?" *Los Angeles Times*, February 27, 2017, http:// www.latimes.com/entertainment/envelope/la-et-envelope-design-20170227-story .html.

84  **what had gone through her mind:** Michael Schulman, "Scenes from the Oscar-Night Implosion," *New Yorker*, February 27, 2017, http://www.newyorker.com/culture/culture-desk/scenes-from-the-oscar-night-implosion.

84  **category names on the envelopes:** Marc Friedland, the designer in several previous years, took great pains to avoid any envelope confusion. "I can't say our envelope would have prevented it, but we put measures in to make it as foolproof as possible, such as really legible, very big type," he told the *Los Angeles Times*. See Herman, "Oscar's Best Picture Disaster." In past years, category names on the envelopes were often printed in black on a cream-colored background, providing sharp contrast and legibility even backstage.

85  **"safety systems are the biggest single source":** Charles Perrow, "Organizing to Reduce the Vulnerabilities of Complexity," *Journal of Contingencies and Crisis Management* 7, no. 3 (1999): 152.

85  **One study of bedside alarms:** Barbara J. Drew, Patricia Harris, Jessica K. Zègre-Hemsey, Tina Mammone, Daniel Schindler, Rebeca Salas-Boni, Yong Bai, Adelita Tinoco, Quan Ding, and Xiao Hu, "Insights into the Problem of Alarm Fatigue with Physiologic Monitor Devices: A Comprehensive Observational Study of Consecutive Intensive Care Unit Patients," *PLOS ONE* 9, no. 10 (2014): e110274, https://doi.org/10.1371/journal.pone.0110274.

86  **It's counterintuitive: safety features reduce safety:** For a compelling in-depth treatment of how safety systems—and the sense of safety they foster—can lead to failure, see Greg Ip, *Foolproof: Why Safety Can Be Dangerous and How Danger Makes Us Safe* (New York: Little, Brown and Company, 2015).

86  **In his book *The Digital Doctor*:** Robert Wachter, *The Digital Doctor: Hope, Hype and Harm at the Dawn of Medicine's Computer Age* (New York: McGraw-Hill Education, 2015).

86  **"Computerized ordering would make":** Ibid., 130.

87  **During a discussion about the overdose:** Bob Wachter, "How to Make Hospital Tech Much, Much Safer," *Wired*, April 3, 2015, https://www.wired.com/2015/04/how-to-make-hospital-tech-much-much-safer.

87  **"The matrix tells you where":** Personal interview with "Gary Miller" (pseudonym) on February 9, 2017.

88  **"You don't need to predict it":** Of course, ideally, we could predict the details of future meltdowns with some accuracy. For more on the fascinating topic of prediction, see Philip E. Tetlock and Dan Gardner, *Superforecasting: The Art and Science of Prediction* (New York: Random House, 2016).

88  **"The Airbus A330 is unbelievably beautiful":** Thijs Jongsma, "That's Why I Love Flying the Airbus 330," *Meanwhile at KLM*, July 1, 2015, https://blog.klm.com/thats-why-i-love-flying-the-airbus-330.

90  **"When we fly the Boeing 737":** Personal interview with Ben Berman on March 9, 2017.

91  **In 2009, Air France Flight 447:** For detailed analyses of this accident, see Chapter 3 in Charles Duhigg, *Smarter, Faster, Better* (New York: Random House, 2016); and William Langewiesche, "The Human Factor," October 2014, http://www.vanityfair.com/news/business/2014/10/air-france-flight-447-crash.

91  **not enough "lift" to hold up the plane:** Federal Aviation Administration, *The Pilot's Handbook of Aeronautical Knowledge* (Washington, DC: Federal Aviation Administration, 2016). Technically, a stall can happen at any attitude, but both these planes crashed because the pilots pitched the nose up too high.

91  **"The two sidesticks don't move":** Personal interview with Ben Berman on March 9, 2017.

92 **cause of the accident was traced:** Peter Valdes-Dapena and Chloe Melas, "Fix Ready for Jeep Gear Shift Problem That Killed Anton Yelchin," CNN Money, June 22, 2016, http://money.cnn.com/2016/06/22/autos/jeep-chrysler-shifter-recall-fix /index.html.

92 **The lack of feedback confused:** Ibid. At the time of Yelchin's death, the Jeep was subject to a voluntary recall.

93 **They treat the boring logistical issues:** For an insightful account of how logistical problems and related issues can lead to complex, interconnected breakdowns on Mount Everest, see Michael A. Roberto, "Lessons from Everest: The Interaction of Cognitive Bias, Psychological Safety, and System Complexity," *California Management Review* 45, no. 1 (2002): 136–58.

93 **very few gastrointestinal issues:** Alpine Ascents International, "Why Climb with Us," Logistics and Planning: Base Camp, accessed August 29, 2017, https://www .alpineascents.com/climbs/mount-everest/why-climb-with-us.

94 **In other systems, people have found:** Our discussion of the hierarchy of alerts in aviation draws on Robert Wachter's excellent book *The Digital Doctor*, and we are indebted to Captain Ben Berman for helping us craft the technical details of this section. Any errors that remain are, of course, our own.

95 **"We formed a committee":** Wachter, "How to Make Hospital Tech Much, Much Safer."

96 **Gary Miller, the management consultant:** Personal interview with "Gary Miller" (pseudonym) on February 9, 2017.

## Chapter Five: Complex Systems, Simple Tools

99 *Dwellings built on high ground:* Danny Lewis, "These Century-Old Stone 'Tsunami Stones' Dot Japan's Coastline," *Smithsonian Magazine*, August 31, 2015, http:// www.smithsonianmag.com/smart-news/century-old-warnings-against-tsunamis -dot-japans-coastline-180956448. We are indebted to Julia Twarog for her nuanced translation.

99 **But after World War:** Martin Fackler, "Tsunami Warnings, Written in Stone," *New York Times*, April 20, 2011, http://www.nytimes.com/2011/04/21/world/asia /21stones.html.

100 **Two hundred miles south of Aneyoshi:** For a detailed account of the Fukushima Daiichi nuclear disaster, see International Atomic Energy Agency, "The Fukushima Daiichi Accident—Report by the Director General," 2015, http://www-pub.iaea .org/MTCD/Publications/PDF/Pub1710-ReportByTheDG-Web.pdf.

100 **The Onagawa Nuclear Power Plant:** Risa Maeda, "Japanese Nuclear Plant Survived Tsunami, Offers Clues," October 19, 2011, http://www.reuters.com/article /us-japan-nuclear-tsunami-idUSTRE79J0B420111020.

100 **Three Stanford researchers:** Phillip Y. Lipscy, Kenji E. Kushida, and Trevor Incerti, "The Fukushima Disaster and Japan's Nuclear Plant Vulnerability in Comparative Perspective," *Environmental Science & Technology* 47, no. 12 (2013): 6082–88.

101 **"The Onagawa power plant's 14 meter":** Ibid., 6083.

101 **came to a chilling conclusion:** For a broader exploration of why we tend to underprepare for natural disasters and other catastrophic risks, see Robert Meyer and Howard Kunreuther, *The Ostrich Paradox: Why We Underprepare for Disasters* (Philadelphia: Wharton Digital Press, 2017).

102 **"Research on these types of forecasts":** Don Moore and Uriel Haran, "A Simple Tool for Making Better Forecasts," May 19, 2014, https://hbr.org/2014/05/a -simple-tool-for-making-better-forecasts. For more on overconfidence, see Don A.

Moore and Paul J. Healy, "The Trouble with Overconfidence," *Psychological Review* 115, no. 2 (2008): 502–17.

103 **It's called SPIES:** Don A. Moore, Uriel Haran, and Carey K. Morewedge, "A Simple Remedy for Overprecision in Judgment," *Judgment and Decision Making* 5, no. 7 (2010): 467–76.

104 **Our studies consistently show:** Moore and Haran, "A Simple Tool for Making Better Forecasts."

104 **"TEPCO did not think":** Akira Kawano, "Lessons Learned from the Fukushima Accident and Challenge for Nuclear Reform," November 26, 2012, http://nas-sites .org/fukushima/files/2012/10/TEPCO.pdf. See also Dennis Normile, "Lack of Humility and Fear of Public Misunderstandings Led to Fukushima Accident," *Science*, November 26, 2012, http://www.sciencemag.org/news/2012/11/lack-humility -and-fear-public-misunderstandings-led-fukushima-accident.

105 **psychologists call a wicked environment:** For this section, we are indebted to Daniel Kahneman and Gary Klein's excellent article "Conditions for Intuitive Expertise: A Failure to Disagree," *American Psychologist* 64, no. 6 (2009): 515–26; their discussion "Strategic Decisions: When Can You Trust Your Gut?" *McKinsey Quarterly* 13 (2010): 1–10; Gary Klein, "Developing Expertise in Decision Making," *Thinking & Reasoning* 3, no. 4 (1997): 337–52; Paul E. Meehl, *Clinical Versus Statistical Prediction: A Theoretical Analysis and a Review of the Evidence* (Minneapolis: University of Minnesota Press, 1954); James Shanteau, "Competence in Experts: The Role of Task Characteristics," *Organizational Behavior and Human Decision Processes* 53 (1992): 252–66; and Robin Hogarth's work, including Robin M. Hogarth, Tomás Lejarraga, and Emre Soyer, "The Two Settings of Kind and Wicked Learning Environments," *Current Directions in Psychological Science* 24, no. 5 (2015): 379–85; and Robin M. Hogarth, *Educating Intuition* (Chicago: University of Chicago Press, 2001).

105 **fire captain who relies on his sixth sense:** Though this story is covered in *Blink*, it is originally from Gary Klein's excellent book *Sources of Power* (Cambridge, MA: MIT Press, 1998), 32.

105 **people who work in wicked environments:** Chip Heath and Dan Heath explain this distinction beautifully in their book *Decisive: How to Make Better Choices in Life and Work* (New York: Crown Business, 2013). For an in-depth discussion of research on the conditions under which intuitive expertise exists, see Kahneman and Klein, "Conditions for Intuitive Expertise." For an important perspective on why common sense can be helpful in everyday situations but fails easily when it comes to thinking about complex systems—from markets to global institutions—see Duncan J. Watts, *Everything Is Obvious (Once You Know the Answer): How Common Sense Fails Us* (New York: Crown Business, 2011).

106 **judgments don't get much better:** Shai Danziger, Jonathan Levav, and Liora Avnaim-Pesso, "Extraneous Factors in Judicial Decisions," *Proceedings of the National Academy of Sciences* 108, no. 17 (2011): 6889–92; David White, Richard I. Kemp, Rob Jenkins, Michael Matheson, and A. Mike Burton, "Passport Officers' Errors in Face Matching," *PLOS ONE* 9, no. 8 (2014): e103510, https://doi.org /10.1371/journal.pone.0103510; and Aldert Vrij and Samantha Mann, "Who Killed My Relative? Police Officers' Ability to Detect Real-Life High-Stake Lies," *Psychology, Crime and Law* 7, no. 1–4 (2001): 119–32.

106 **Meteorologists, for example, are good:** For this observation, we are indebted to Mark Simon and Susan M. Houghton, "The Relationship Between Overconfidence and the Introduction of Risky Products: Evidence from a Field Study," *Academy of Management Journal* 46, no. 2 (2003): 139–49. The underlying meteorological research is reported in two studies: Allan H. Murphy and Robert L. Winkler, "Reliability of Subjective Probability Forecasts of Precipitation and Temperature,"

*Journal of the Royal Statistical Society, Series C (Applied Statistics)* 26, no. 1 (1977): 41–47; and Allan H. Murphy and Robert L. Winkler, "Subjective Probabilistic Tornado Forecasts: Some Experimental Results," *Monthly Weather Review* 110, no. 9 (1982): 1288–97.

106 **even their rain forecasts:** Jerome P. Charba and William H. Klein, "Skill in Precipitation Forecasting in the National Weather Service," *Bulletin of the American Meteorological Society* 61, no. 12 (1980): 1546–55.

107 **there are tools we can use:** For a deeper introduction to the various tools we can use to improve our decisions in complex environments, see Atul Gawande, *The Checklist Manifesto: How to Get Things Right* (New York: Metropolitan Books, 2009); Dan Ariely, *Predictably Irrational: The Hidden Forces That Shape Our Decisions* (New York: HarperCollins, 2009); Richard H. Thaler and Cass R. Sunstein, *Nudge: Improving Decisions About Health, Wealth, and Happiness* (New Haven, CT: Yale University Press, 2008); and Dilip Soman, *The Last Mile: Creating Social and Economic Value from Behavioral Insights* (Toronto: University of Toronto Press, 2015).

107 **Consider how doctors diagnose:** P. Sujitkumar, J. M. Hadfield, and D. W. Yates, "Sprain or Fracture? An Analysis of 2000 Ankle Injuries," *Emergency Medicine Journal* 3, no. 2 (1986): 101–6.

107 **a team of Canadian physicians:** Ian G. Stiell, Gary H. Greenberg, R. Douglas McKnight, Rama C. Nair, I. McDowell, and James R. Worthington, "A Study to Develop Clinical Decision Rules for the Use of Radiography in Acute Ankle Injuries," *Annals of Emergency Medicine* 21, no. 4 (1992): 384–90. We have simplified their diagram, which appears as Figure 2 in their article.

108 **turned every doctor into an expert:** For another interesting discussion of how doctors become experts, see Atul Gawande's *Complications* (New York: Picador, 2002), in which he discusses the success rate of hernia repairs at Shouldice Hospital outside of Toronto. At Shouldice, surgeons focus exclusively on hernia repairs and perform more of them in a year than many general surgeons do during their entire careers.

108 **Lisa, a young mom in Seattle:** Personal interview with "Lisa" (pseudonym) on May 21, 2017.

109 **called a pairwise wiki survey:** This method has been developed by Princeton sociologist Matthew Salganik and his research group; their free, open-source website (www.allourideas.org) allows anyone to create a pairwise wiki survey. For the research behind the tool, see Matthew J. Salganik and Karen E. C. Levy, "Wiki Surveys: Open and Quantifiable Social Data Collection," *PLOS ONE* 10, no. 5 (2015): e0123483, https://doi.org/10.1371/journal.pone.0123483.

111 **Target was well known in Canada:** Our description of the birth and fall of Target Canada draws heavily from Joe Castaldo's in-depth article ("The Last Days of Target," *Canadian Business*, January 2016, http://www.canadianbusiness.com/the-last-days-of-target-canada) and our personal interview with Castaldo on October 12, 2016.

112 **"Simply put, we were losing money":** Ian Austen and Hiroko Tabuchi, "Target's Red Ink Runs Out in Canada," *New York Times*, January 15, 2015, https://www.nytimes.com/2015/01/16/business/target-to-close-stores-in-canada.html.

112 **a Canadian playwright has written:** The play, *A Community Target*, written by Robert Motum, is based on interviews with about fifty former Target Canada employees. "90% of the text is completely verbatim—with just small edits for clarity," Motum wrote in response to a fact-checking email (June 17, 2017). "The first half of the play delves into the specific problems of Target. . . . The second half of the play branches out and invites us to reflect on Canada's current retail ecology. Overall, it's a story about the people who worked for Target—and the community they shared."

112 **"When you want to open":** Joe Castaldo in an interview on Minnesota Public Radio with *MPR News* host Tom Weber, "The Downfall of Target Canada," Minnesota Public Radio, January 29, 2016, https://www.mprnews.org/story/2016/01 /29/target-canada-failure.

113 **Castaldo called it an "unforgiving beast.":** Castaldo, "The Last Days of Target."

113 **"Why did Target's distribution centers":** Personal interview with Joe Castaldo on October 12, 2016.

114 **"We almost didn't see what":** Castaldo, "The Last Days of Target."

114 **Target's annual report described:** "Target 2010 Annual Report," http://media .corporate-ir.net/media_files/irol/65/65828/Target_AnnualReport_2010.pdf.

116 **method called the *premortem*:** Gary Klein, "Performing a Project Premortem," *Harvard Business Review* 85, no. 9 (2007): 18–19.

116 **If a project goes poorly:** Kahneman and Klein, "Strategic Decisions."

117 **A landmark 1989 study:** Deborah J. Mitchell, J. Edward Russo, and Nancy Pennington, "Back to the Future: Temporal Perspective in the Explanation of Events," *Journal of Behavioral Decision Making* 2, no. 1 (1989): 25–38.

117 **Consider predicting the winner:** Ibid., 34–35.

117 **"The logic is that":** Kahneman and Klein, "Strategic Decisions."

118 **Jill Bloom, a smart and hardworking:** Personal interview with "Jill Bloom" (pseudonym) on May 29, 2017. Before running a premortem, Bloom and her husband had both heard Chris (one of the authors of this book) talk about the technique at a variety of social occasions.

119 **"Most decision makers will trust":** Kahneman and Klein, "Strategic Decisions."

## Chapter Six: Reading the Writing on the Wall

121 *What in the world was wrong:* For our reporting of the Flint water crisis, we drew on many sources, including Julia Laurie, "Meet the Mom Who Helped Expose Flint's Toxic Water Nightmare," *Mother Jones*, January 21, 2016, http://www.mother jones.com/politics/2016/01/mother-exposed-flint-lead-contamination-water -crisis; LeeAnne Walters's testimony to the Michigan Joint Committee on the Flint Water Public Health Emergency, March 29, 2016 (via ABC News, http://abcnews .go.com/US/flint-mother-emotional-testimony-water-crisis-affected-childrens /story?id=38008707); Lindsey Smith, "This Mom Helped Uncover What Was Really Going On with Flint's Water," Michigan Radio, December 14, 2015, http://michiganradio.org/post/mom-helped-uncover-what-was-really-going -flint-s-water; the excellent radio documentary by Lindsey Smith, "Not Safe to Drink," Michigan Radio, http://michiganradio.org/topic/not-safe-drink; Gary Ridley, "Flint Mother at Center of Lead Water Crisis Files Lawsuit," *Mlive*, March 3, 2016, http://www.mlive.com/news/flint/index.ssf/2016/03/flint_mother_at_center _of_lead.html; Ryan Felton, "Flint Residents Raise Concerns over Discolored Water," *Detroit Metro Times*, August 13, 2014, http://www.metrotimes.com/detroit /flint-residents-raise-concerns-over-discolored-water/Content?oid=2231724; Ron Fonger, "Flint Starting to Flush Out 'Discolored' Drinking Water with Hydrant Releases," *Mlive*, July 30, 2014, http://www.mlive.com/news/flint/index.ssf /2014/07/flint_starting_to_flush_out_di.html; Ron Fonger, "State Says Flint River Water Meets All Standards but More Than Twice the Hardness of Lake Water," *Mlive*, May 23, 2014, http://www.mlive.com/news/flint/index.ssf/2014/05/state _says_flint_river_water_m.html; Ron Fonger, "Flint Water Problems: Switch Aimed to Save $5 Million—But at What Cost?" *Mlive*, January 23, 2015, http://www.mlive .com/news/flint/index.ssf/2015/01/flints_dilemma_how_much_to_spe.html;

Matthew M. Davis, Chris Kolb, Lawrence Reynolds, Eric Rothstein, and Ken Sikkema, "Flint Water Advisory Task Force Final Report," Flint Water Advisory Task Force, 2016, https://www.michigan.gov/documents/snyder/FWATF_FINAL_RE PORT_21March2016_517805_7.pdf; Miguel A. Del Toral, "High Lead Levels in Flint, Michigan—Interim Report," Environmental Protection Agency, June 24, 2015, http://flintwaterstudy.org/wp-content/uploads/2015/11/Miguels-Memo.pdf; and an internal email from Miguel A. Del Toral, "Re: Interim Report on High Lead Levels in Flint," Environmental Protection Agency (see Jim Lynch, "Whistle-Blower Del Toral Grew Tired of EPA 'Cesspool,'" *Detroit News*, March 28, 2016, http://www.detroitnews.com/story/news/michigan/flint-water-crisis/2016/03/28 /whistle-blower-del-toral-grew-tired-epa-cesspool/82365470/).

122 **"Water is an absolute vital service":** Dominic Adams, "Closing the Valve on History: Flint Cuts Water Flow from Detroit After Nearly 50 Years," *Mlive*, April 25, 2014, http://www.mlive.com/news/flint/index.ssf/2014/04/closing_the_valve_on_his tory_f.html.

122 **difference in water quality:** Ibid.

123 **prompting the state to buy:** Merrit Kennedy, "Lead-Laced Water in Flint: A Step-by-Step Look at the Makings of a Crisis," National Public Radio, April 20, 2016, http://www.npr.org/sections/thetwo-way/2016/04/20/465545378/lead-laced -water-in-flint-a-step-by-step-look-at-the-makings-of-a-crisis.

123 **outbreak of Legionnaires' disease:** Elisha Anderson, "Legionnaires'-Associated Deaths Grow to 12 in Flint Area," *Detroit Free Press*, April 11, 2016, http://www .freep.com/story/news/local/michigan/flint-water-crisis/2016/04/11/legionnaires -deaths-flint-water/82897722.

123 **rusting the engine blocks:** Mike Colias, "How GM Saved Itself from Flint Water Crisis," *Automotive News*, January 31, 2016, http://www.autonews.com/article/2016 0131/OEM01/302019964/how-gm-saved-itself-from-flint-water-crisis.

124 **Beyond just ignoring warning signs:** State officials designed the sampling procedure, which many local utilities adopted. See Rebecca Williams, "State's Instructions for Sampling Drinking Water for Lead 'Not Best Practice,'" Michigan Radio, November 17, 2015, http://michiganradio.org/post/states-instructions-sampling-drink ing-water-lead-not-best-practice.

125 **thoroughly vacuuming a room:** Julianne Mattera, "Missed Lead: Is Central Pa.'s Water Testing Misleading?" *Penn Live*, February 1, 2016, http://www.pennlive .com/news/2016/02/lead_in_water_flint_water_samp.html.

126 **keep the overall lead level:** Mark Brush, "Expert Says Michigan Officials Changed a Flint Lead Report to Avoid Federal Action," Michigan Radio, November 5, 2015, http://michiganradio.org/post/expert-says-michigan-officials-changed-flint -lead-report-avoid-federal-action.

126 **not just about my family:** LeeAnne Walters's testimony to the Michigan Joint Committee on the Flint Water Public Health Emergency.

126 *sixty dollars per day:* This according to the report, prepared by engineering consulting firms Rowe and LAN, "Analysis of the Flint River as a Permanent Water Supply for the City of Flint," July 2011, http://www.scribd.com/doc/64381765 /Analysis-of-the-Flint-River-as-a-Permanent-Water-Supply-for-the-City-of -Flint-July-2011; see, in particular, "Opinion of Probable Cost" in Appendix 8, https://www.scribd.com/document/64382181/Analysis-of-the-Flint-River-as-a -Permanent-Water-Supply-for-the-City-of-Flint-July-2011-Appendices-1-to-8. Though some estimates in the press put the cost at just over $100 per day, we couldn't find calculations to support that figure.

127 **Michigan's budget allocated hundreds:** "Michigan Governor Signs Budget Tripling State Spending on Flint Water Emergency," *Chicago Tribune*, June 29, 2016,

http://www.chicagotribune.com/news/nationworld/midwest/ct-flint-water-crisis
-20160629-story.html.
127 **"When the treated river water":** Darnell Earley as quoted in Adams, "Closing
the Valve on History." Earley was the emergency manager, appointed by the
Michigan governor, who oversaw the switch to the Flint River. He maintained that
the decision to change water sources was made by the previous emergency
manager and local politicians before he had been appointed. See Ron Fonger,
"Ex-Emergency Manager Says He's Not to Blame for Flint River Water Switch,"
*Mlive*, October 13, 2015, http://www.mlive.com/news/flint/index.ssf/2015/10/ex_
emergency_manager_earley_sa.html.
127 **denial is far too common:** Perrow, *Normal Accidents*, 214.
128 **It was a clever system:** Technical details of the Washington, DC, Metro system
and the accident in particular come from NTSB/RAR-10/02. At the time of the
Metro Train 112 accident, operations were controlled from what is now the Washington Metropolitan Area Transit Authority's downtown DC headquarters. The
control facility has since been moved to a nearby suburb.
129 **underlying technology was out of date:** NTSB/RAR-10/02, 20–23. While the
Metro's signaling system is also used by other transit operators, it relies on analog
signals that can be affected by noise, transmission power, and a host of other
variables.
129 **the sensors had failed to detect:** NTSB/RAR-10/02, 44.
130 **The workers stayed to see:** NTSB/RAR-10/02, 40–41. The workers told the
NTSB that the first train had been detected, but a review of the recorded data revealed that the track circuits hadn't seen see any trains that morning.
131 **As had happened for the:** NTSB/RAR-10/02, 81. When the track circuit lost detection, the train received a 0 mph speed command. All of the trains prior to Train
214 managed to coast out of the troubled block of track and go on as normal.
133 **two crashes for every *ten million*:** "How Aviation Safety Has Improved," Allianz
Expert Risk Articles, http://www.agcs.allianz.com/insights/expert-risk-articles/how
-aviation-safety-has-improved.
133 **driving is a hundred times riskier:** See, for example, Ian Savage, "Comparing the
Fatality Risks in United States Transportation Across Modes and Over Time," *Research in Transportation Economics* 43, no. 1 (2013): 9–22. Allianz's "How Aviation
Safety Has Improved" report puts the per-mile spread even higher.
133 **they navigate by following a set:** Federal Aviation Administration, *The Pilot's
Handbook of Aeronautical Knowledge*. Aircraft can also navigate using airways defined
by GPS coordinates or fly direct to their destination.
134 **Trans World Airlines Flight 514:** This section draws from the National Transportation Safety Board's Aircraft Accident Report NTSB-AAR-75-16, "Trans World Airlines, Inc, Boeing 727-231 N54328, Berryville, Virginia, December, 1 1974," http://
libraryonline.erau.edu/online-full-text/ntsb/aircraft-accident-reports/AAR75-16
.pdf. We've adapted the figures from that report and simplified them.
134 **read aloud from the approach plate:** The actual plate is displayed in NTSB-
AAR-75-16, 59. Our profile view does not include the missed approach point, and
we're also ignoring the concept of approach minimums in our discussion.
135 **the crew discussed the next steps:** Quotes are from the cockpit voice recorder.
See NTSB-AAR-75-16, 4.
137 **the brain works quickly to:** See, for example, Karl E. Weick, "The Vulnerable
System: An Analysis of the Tenerife Air Disaster," *Journal of Management* 16, no. 3
(1990): 571–93; and Karl E. Weick, Kathleen M. Sutcliffe, and David Obstfeld,
"Organizing and the Process of Sensemaking," *Organization Science* 16, no. 4 (2005):
409–21.

**139** **"pilots have become so accustomed":** NTSB-AAR-75-16, 12.

**139** **sent a notice to its pilots:** NTSB-AAR-75-16, 23.

**141** **aggressive descent to a lower altitude:** NASA, "Automation Dependency," *Callback*, September 2016, https://asrs.arc.nasa.gov/publications/callback/cb_440.html.

**141** **described the dangers of complacency:** NASA, "The Dangers of Complacency," *Callback*, March 2017, https://asrs.arc.nasa.gov/publications/callback/cb_446.html.

**141** **generates counterintuitive findings:** Perrow, "Organizing to Reduce the Vulnerabilities of Complexity," 153.

**142** **In an experiment, we asked:** We based this experiment on the excellent work of Robin L. Dillon and Catherine H. Tinsley, "How Near-Misses Influence Decision Making Under Risk: A Missed Opportunity for Learning," *Management Science* 54, no. 8 (2008): 1425–40. Dillon and Tinsley's experiment used a fictitious NASA mission as the basis for the decisions involved. We are indebted to engineer Vjeko Begic for his help in crafting the scenario we used in our version of the experiment.

**144** **Researchers call this learning process:** More broadly, "anomalizing" refers to the process of noticing and making sense of anomalies—discrepancies between what we had planned and how the situation is actually unfolding—to anticipate threats and crises. For a rigorous introduction to the concept, see Michelle A. Barton, Kathleen M. Sutcliffe, Timothy J. Vogus, and Theodore DeWitt, "Performing Under Uncertainty: Contextualized Engagement in Wildland Firefighting," *Journal of Contingencies and Crisis Management* 23, no. 2 (2015): 74–83.

**144** **The first step is to gather data:** For our understanding of how organizations learn from near misses and other warning signs, we are indebted to Catherine H. Tinsley, Robin L. Dillon, and Peter M. Madsen, "How to Avoid Catastrophe," *Harvard Business Review* 89, no. 4 (2011): 90–97. For a rigorous introduction to learning from close calls and near misses, see Scott D. Sagan, *The Limits of Safety* (Princeton, NJ: Princeton University Press, 1995). For more on the importance of seeking to know what we don't know, see Karlene H. Roberts and Robert Bea, "Must Accidents Happen? Lessons from High-Reliability Organizations," *The Academy of Management Executive* 15, no. 3 (2001): 70–78.

**144** **At an Illinois hospital:** Edward Doyle, "Building a Better Safety Net to Detect—and Prevent—Medication Errors," *Today's Hospitalist*, September 2006, https://www.todayshospitalist.com/Building-a-better-safety-net-to-detect-and-prevent-medication-errors.

**145** **In response, managers:** Ibid.

**145** **mistakes are a normal part:** For more on how reducing the stigma of failure can facilitate learning, see Amy C. Edmondson, "Strategies for Learning from Failure," *Harvard Business Review* 89, no. 4 (2011): 48–55.

**145** **"If you're going to shoot the messenger":** Personal interview with Ben Berman on March 9, 2017.

**145** **"The measure of a safe organization":** Wachter, "How to Make Hospital Tech Much, Much Safer."

**146** **But what do I do:** For an important take on how organizations can learn from ambiguous warning signs, see Michael A. Roberto, Richard M.J. Bohmer, and Amy C. Edmondson, "Facing Ambiguous Threats," *Harvard Business Review* 84, no. 11 (2006): 106–13.

**146** **Danish organizational researcher:** Personal interview with Claus Rerup on April 13, 2017.

**146** **Rerup conducted an in-depth:** Claus Rerup, "Attentional Triangulation: Learning from Unexpected Rare Crises," *Organization Science* 20, no. 5 (2009): 876–93.

147 **work with every unit at least once:** Some units have facilitations every three years, others every year. But, at minimum, each unit is facilitated once every six years. See Novo Nordisk, "The Novo Nordisk Way: The Essentials," http://www .novonordisk.com/about-novo-nordisk/novo-nordisk-way/the-essentials.html.

148 **in a recent year, 95 percent:** Novo Nordisk, 2014 Annual Report, http://www .novonordisk.com/content/dam/Denmark/HQ/Commons/documents/Novo-Nor disk-Annual-Report-2014.pdf, 12.

148 **just one person: a trusted advisor:** Vanessa M. Strike and Claus Rerup, "Mediated Sensemaking," *Academy of Management Journal* 59, no. 3 (2016): 885. See also Vanessa M. Strike, "The Most Trusted Advisor and the Subtle Advice Process in Family Firms," *Family Business Review* 26, no. 3 (2013): 293–313.

## Chapter Seven: The Anatomy of Dissent

149 **In the fall of 1846:** To tell the story of Ignác Semmelweis throughout this chapter, we have drawn heavily from Sherwin B. Nuland, *The Doctors' Plague: Germs, Childbed Fever, and the Strange Story of Ignác Semmelweis* (New York and London: W. W. Norton, 2003).

150 **"When I heard the bell":** Ibid., 84.

153 **Semmelweis called a "cadaverous smell.":** Ignaz (Ignác) Semmelweis, *The Etiology, Concept, and Prophylaxis of Childbed Fever*, trans. and ed. K. Codell Carter (Madison: University of Wisconsin Press, 1983), 88.

153 **"I have handled cadavers":** Nuland, *The Doctors' Plague*, 104.

153 **"The remedy does not lie":** Ibid.

154 **functional magnetic resonance imaging:** Vasily Klucharev, Kaisa Hytönen, Mark Rijpkema, Ale Smidts, and Guillén Fernández, "Reinforcement Learning Signal Predicts Social Conformity," *Neuron* 61, no. 1 (2009): 140–51.

154 **"We show that a deviation":** Elizabeth Landau, "Why So Many Minds Think Alike," January 15, 2009, http://www.cnn.com/2009/HEALTH/01/15/social.con formity.brain.

154 **"This is likely an automatic process":** "Social Conformism Measured in the Brain for the First Time," Donders Institute for Brain, Cognition and Behaviour, January 15, 2009, http://www.ru.nl/donders/news/vm-news/more-news/.

154 **played out in a fascinating study:** Gregory S. Berns, Jonathan Chappelow, Caroline F. Zink, Giuseppe Pagnoni, Megan E. Martin-Skurski, and Jim Richards, "Neurobiological Correlates of Social Conformity and Independence During Mental Rotation," *Biological Psychiatry* 58, no. 3 (2005): 245–53.

155 **"the pain of independence.":** Ibid., 252.

155 **"Our brains are exquisitely tuned":** Landau, "Why So Many Minds Think Alike."

156 **"From the beginning, he had viewed":** Nuland, *The Doctors' Plague*, 120.

157 **"And being human, he was having":** Ibid., 121.

158 **Research shows that there is:** Jeremy P. Jamieson, Piercarlo Valdesolo, and Brett J. Peters, "Sympathy for the Devil? The Physiological and Psychological Effects of Being an Agent (and Target) of Dissent During Intragroup Conflict," *Journal of Experimental Social Psychology* 55 (2014): 221–27.

158 **conducted at the University of Wisconsin–Madison:** The study (Dan Ward and Dacher Keltner, "Power and the Consumption of Resources," unpublished manuscript, University of Wisconsin–Madison, 1998) is summarized in Dacher Keltner, Deborah H. Gruenfeld, and Cameron Anderson, "Power, Approach, and Inhibition," *Psychological Review* 110, no. 2 (2003): 265–84.

**159** **"Everybody takes one cookie,":** "How Do Humans Gain Power? By Sharing It," *PBS NewsHour*, June 9, 2016, http://www.pbs.org/newshour/bb/how-do-hu mans-gain-power-by-sharing-i.

**159** **signs of "disinhibited eating,":** Keltner, Gruenfeld, and Anderson, "Power, Approach, and Inhibition," 277.

**159** **"people with power tend":** Dacher Keltner, "The Power Paradox," *Greater Good Magazine*, December 1, 2007, https://greatergood.berkeley.edu/article/item/power _paradox.

**160** **they don't speak up:** For a rigorous introduction to the science of speaking up, see Amy Edmondson's groundbreaking research on psychological safety, employee voice, and learning, which has influenced much of the research covered in this chapter: Amy C. Edmondson, "Psychological Safety and Learning Behavior in Work Teams," *Administrative Science Quarterly* 44, no. 2 (1999): 350–83; Amy C. Edmondson, *Teaming: How Organizations Learn, Innovate, and Compete in the Knowledge Economy* (San Francisco: Jossey-Bass, 2012); Amy C. Edmondson and Zhike Lei, "Psychological Safety: The History, Renaissance, and Future of an Interpersonal Construct," *Annual Review of Organizational Psychology and Organizational Behavior* 1 (2014): 23–43; Amy C. Edmondson, "Speaking Up in the Operating Room: How Team Leaders Promote Learning in Interdisciplinary Action Teams," *Journal of Management Studies* 40, no. 6 (2003): 1419–52; and James R. Detert and Amy C. Edmondson, "Implicit Voice Theories: Taken-for-Granted Rules of Self-Censorship at Work," *Academy of Management Journal* 54, no. 3 (2011): 461–88.

**160** **research by Jim Detert:** For our understanding of research on speaking up, we are indebted to Jim Detert (personal interview on October 17, 2016).

**160** **"Whether you realize it or not":** James R. Detert and Ethan R. Burris, "Can Your Employees Really Speak Freely?" *Harvard Business Review* 94, no. 1 (2016): 84.

**160** **open-door policies had little effect:** Ibid.; see also James R. Detert and Ethan R. Burris, "Leadership Behavior and Employee Voice: Is the Door Really Open?" *Academy of Management Journal* 50, no. 4 (2007): 869–84.

**161** **"The subtext is 'It's not safe'":** Detert and Burris, "Can Your Employees Really Speak Freely?" 82.

**161** **tendency to berate his critics:** For research on the importance of managing one's emotions when speaking up—a skill that Semmelweis was evidently lacking at this time—see Adam M. Grant, "Rocking the Boat but Keeping It Steady: The Role of Emotion Regulation in Employee Voice," *Academy of Management Journal* 56, no. 6 (2013): 1703–23.

**161** **"Your teaching," he wrote:** John Waller, *Leaps in the Dark: The Making of Scientific Reputations* (New York: Oxford University Press, 2004), 155.

**162** **Robert, a large, muscular man:** "Robert" is a pseudonym. Robert's story is based on personal interviews with Richard Speers and his receptionist, Donna, who asked to be identified only by her first name, on May 5, 2016.

**164** **"I am puzzled by what":** Weick, "The Vulnerable System," 588.

**164** **study of accidents due to flight:** These results held up even when researchers took into account the possibility that captains might take control over the plane under dangerous weather conditions or in other crisis situations. See R. Key Dismukes, Benjamin A. Berman, and Loukia D. Loukopoulos, *The Limits of Expertise: Rethinking Pilot Error and the Causes of Airline Accidents* (Burlington, VT: Ashgate, 2007); and National Transportation Safety Board, *A Review of Flightcrew-Involved Major Accidents of US Air Carriers, 1978 Through 1990* (Washington, DC: National Transportation Safety Board, 1994).

165 **All this changed with a training:** For more on the history and effectiveness of Crew Resource Management, see Robert L. Helmreich and John A. Wilhelm, "Outcomes of Crew Resource Management Training," *International Journal of Aviation Psychology* 1, no. 4 (1991): 287–300; Robert L. Helmreich, Ashleigh C. Merritt, and John A. Wilhelm, "The Evolution of Crew Resource Management Training in Commercial Aviation," *International Journal of Aviation Psychology* 9, no. 1 (1999): 19–32; and Eduardo Salas, C. Shawn Burke, Clint A. Bowers, and Katherine A. Wilson, "Team Training in the Skies: Does Crew Resource Management (CRM) Training Work?" *Human Factors* 43, no. 4 (2001): 641–74. For our understanding of the changes in aviation and the evolution of Crew Resource Management in the past several decades, we are indebted to Captain Ben Berman.

166 **In the 1990s, just half:** Dismukes, Berman, and Loukopoulos, *The Limits of Expertise*, 283.

166 **In a 2014 article:** Richard D. Speers and Christopher A. McCulloch, "Optimizing Patient Safety: Can We Learn from the Airline Industry?" *Journal of the Canadian Dental Association* 80 (2014): e37.

167 **"create a kind of artifact":** Michelle A. Barton and Kathleen M. Sutcliffe, "Overcoming Dysfunctional Momentum: Organizational Safety as a Social Achievement," *Human Relations* 62, no. 9 (2009): 1340.

167 **called Project Aristotle:** For an in-depth description of this research study, see Chapter 2 in Duhigg, *Smarter, Faster, Better.*

167 **Other research shows that a bank's:** James R. Detert, Ethan R. Burris, David A. Harrison, and Sean R. Martin, "Voice Flows to and Around Leaders: Understanding When Units Are Helped or Hurt by Employee Voice," *Administrative Science Quarterly* 58, no. 4 (2013): 624–68.

167 **They called it "charm school":** Helmreich, Merritt, and Wilhelm, "Evolution of Crew Resource Management," 21.

167 **more and more accident investigations:** In response to fact-checking emails (May 16, 2017), Captain Berman emphasized that Crew Resource Management itself has evolved over time; since the early days of the program, airlines have reduced the use of psychological jargon and made their training exercises more directly applicable to crews.

168 **In a large hospital in Texas:** Detert and Burris, "Can Your Employees Really Speak Freely?," 84.

168 **"I've never done a perfect flight,":** Personal interview with Ben Berman on March 9, 2017.

168 **In the summer of 2011:** Melissa Korn, "Where I Work: Dean of BU's School of Management," *Wall Street Journal*, June 11, 2012, https://blogs.wsj.com/atwork/2012/06/11/where-i-work-dean-of-bus-school-of-management.

169 **Lawrence McDonald described:** "A Look Back at the Collapse of Lehman Brothers," *PBS NewsHour*, September 14, 2009, http://www.pbs.org/newshour/bb/business-july-dec09-solmanlehman_09-14.

170 **psychologist Matie Flowers:** Matie L. Flowers, "A Laboratory Test of Some Implications of Janis's Groupthink Hypothesis," *Journal of Personality and Social Psychology* 35, no. 12 (1977): 888–96. For ease of presentation, we collapsed Flowers's results across levels of group cohesiveness.

172 **Parenting expert Jane Nelsen:** Jane Nelsen, *Positive Discipline* (New York: Ballantine, 2006), 220.

173 **"It all goes back to the need":** Personal interview with Jim Detert on October 17, 2016.

## Chapter Eight: The Speed Bump Effect

175 **When Sallie Krawcheck:** "How 'Lehman Siblings' Might Have Stemmed the Financial Crisis," *PBS NewsHour*, August 6, 2014, http://www.pbs.org/newshour /making-sense/how-lehman-siblings-might-have-stemmed-the-financial-crisis.

176 **Half a dozen people sat:** Sheen S. Levine, Evan P. Apfelbaum, Mark Bernard, Valerie L. Bartelt, Edward J. Zajac, and David Stark, "Ethnic Diversity Deflates Price Bubbles," *Proceedings of the National Academy of Sciences* 111, no. 52 (2014): 18524–29. The stocks the participants traded had a calculable true (that is, fundamental or intrinsic) value. This allowed the researchers to measure the extent to which market prices deviated from the true value of assets.

177 **"The diverse markets were":** Personal interview with Evan Apfelbaum on November 4, 2016.

178 **"their mere presence changed the tenor":** Levine et al., "Ethnic Diversity Deflates Price Bubbles," 18528.

178 **"We tend to think":** Personal interview with Evan Apfelbaum on November 4, 2016.

179 **Apfelbaum and his colleagues:** Sarah E. Gaither, Evan P. Apfelbaum, Hannah J. Birnbaum, Laura G. Babbitt, and Samuel R. Sommers, "Mere Membership in Racially Diverse Groups Reduces Conformity," *Social Psychological and Personality Science* (2017): in press, https://doi.org/10.1177/1948550617708013.

180 **"It appears to be a 'benefit'":** Personal interview with Evan Apfelbaum on November 4, 2016.

181 **experiment in 2006, researchers:** Katherine W. Phillips, Gregory B. Northcraft, and Margaret A. Neale, "Surface-Level Diversity and Decision-Making in Groups: When Does Deep-Level Similarity Help?" *Group Processes & Intergroup Relations* 9, no. 4 (2006): 467–82.

181 **"The groups with racial diversity":** Katherine W. Phillips, "How Diversity Makes Us Smarter," *Scientific American*, October 1, 2014, https://www.scientificamerican .com/article/how-diversity-makes-us-smarter.

181 **racially mixed juries shared:** Samuel R. Sommers, "On Racial Diversity and Group Decision Making: Identifying Multiple Effects of Racial Composition on Jury Deliberations," *Journal of Personality and Social Psychology* 90, no. 4 (2006): 597–612.

182 **"A more diverse, less cohesive board":** Lawrence J. Abbott, Susan Parker, and Theresa J. Presley, "Female Board Presence and the Likelihood of Financial Restatement," *Accounting Horizons* 26, no. 4 (2012): 613. See also Anne-Marie Slaughter, "Why Family Is a Foreign-Policy Issue," *Foreign Policy*, November 26, 2012, http:// foreignpolicy.com/2012/11/26/why-family-is-a-foreign-policy-issue. As Slaughter put it, "Does it matter if the president has an all-testosterone team shaping America's place in the world? I'm sure it does, and in ways that hinder the country's ability to address the complex new challenges of our 21st-century planet."

182 **Diversity, in contrast, feels strange:** Phillips, "How Diversity Makes Us Smarter"; see also David Rock, Heidi Grant, and Jacqui Grey, "Diverse Teams Feel Less Comfortable—and That's Why They Perform Better," September 22, 2016, *Harvard Business Review*, https://hbr.org/2016/09/diverse-teams-feel-less-comfort able-and-thats-why-they-perform-better.

182 **The following conversation took place:** Lauren A. Rivera, *Pedigree: How Elite Students Get Elite Jobs* (Princeton, NJ: Princeton University Press, 2016), 227. "Henry" and "Will" are pseudonyms.

183 **"He's super polished, confident":** We are indebted to Lauren Rivera for sharing with us excerpts from her field notes about this discussion.

183 **When orchestras started using:** Claudia Goldin and Cecilia Rouse, "Orchestrating Impartiality: The Impact of 'Blind' Auditions on Female Musicians," *American Economic Review* 90, no. 4 (2000): 715–41. In recent years, there has been an increase in the use of various blind-audition technologies in other labor markets as well. Thus far, however, there has been little systematic research on the effectiveness of such interventions.

184 **the proportion of black men:** Our summary of research about the effectiveness of diversity programs draws heavily on Frank Dobbin and Alexandra Kalev, "Why Diversity Programs Fail," *Harvard Business Review* 94, no. 7 (2016): 52–60. For the underlying research, see Frank Dobbin, Daniel Schrage, and Alexandra Kalev, "Rage Against the Iron Cage: The Varied Effects of Bureaucratic Personnel Reforms on Diversity," *American Sociological Review* 80, no. 5 (2015): 1014–44; and Alexandra Kalev, Frank Dobbin, and Erin Kelly, "Best Practices or Best Guesses? Assessing the Efficacy of Corporate Affirmative Action and Diversity Policies," *American Sociological Review* 71, no. 4 (2006): 589–617.

185 **"You won't get managers on board":** Dobbin and Kalev, "Why Diversity Programs Fail," 54.

185 **"Our interviews suggest that managers":** Ibid., 57.

186 **While white men tend to find:** Ibid.

187 **hard problem with a soft solution:** For more on the difficulties and nuances of building and managing diverse organizations, see Emilio J. Castilla, "Gender, Race, and Meritocracy in Organizational Careers," *American Journal of Sociology* 113, no. 6 (2008): 1479–1526; Emilio J. Castilla and Stephen Benard, "The Paradox of Meritocracy in Organizations," *Administrative Science Quarterly* 55, no. 4 (2010): 543–676; Roberto M. Fernandez and Isabel Fernandez-Mateo, "Networks, Race, and Hiring," *American Sociological Review* 71, no. 1 (2006): 42–71; Roberto M. Fernandez and M. Lourdes Sosa, "Gendering the Job: Networks and Recruitment at a Call Center," *American Journal of Sociology* 111, no. 3 (2005): 859–904; Robin J. Ely and David A. Thomas, "Cultural Diversity at Work: The Effects of Diversity Perspectives on Work Group Processes and Outcomes," *Administrative Science Quarterly* 46, no. 2 (2001): 229–73; and Roxana Barbulescu and Matthew Bidwell, "Do Women Choose Different Jobs from Men? Mechanisms of Application Segregation in the Market for Managerial Workers," *Organization Science* 24, no. 3 (2013): 737–56.

188 **"five visionary tech entrepreneurs":** Laura Arrillaga-Andreessen, "Five Visionary Tech Entrepreneurs Who Are Changing the World," *New York Times*, October 12, 2015, http://www.nytimes.com/interactive/2015/10/12/t-magazine/elizabeth-holmes-tech-visionaries-brian-chesky.html?_r=0.

188 **"The Next Steve Jobs.":** *Inc.*, October 2015, https://www.inc.com/magazine/oct-2015.

188 **Theranos was valued:** Matthew Herper, "From $4.5 Billion to Nothing: Forbes Revises Estimated Net Worth of Theranos Founder Elizabeth Holmes," *Forbes*, June 1, 2016, https://www.forbes.com/sites/matthewherper/2016/06/01/from-4-5-billion-to-nothing-forbes-revises-estimated-net-worth-of-theranos-founder-elizabeth-holmes/#689b50603633.

188 **one hundred most influential people:** Henry Kissinger, "Elizabeth Holmes," *Time*, April 15, 2015, http://time.com/3822734/elizabeth-holmes-2015-time-100.

188 **"Turning a blood test into":** Arrillaga-Andreessen, "Five Visionary Tech Entrepreneurs."

188 **But John Carreyrou:** Charles Ornstein's interview with John Carreyrou for a ProPublica podcast: "How a Reporter Pierced the Hype Behind Theranos," Pro-

Publica, February 16, 2016, https://www.propublica.org/podcast/item/how-a-re
porter-pierced-the-hype-behind-theranos.

188 **It was a devastating report:** John Carreyrou, "Hot Startup Theranos Has Struggled with Its Blood-Test Technology," *Wall Street Journal*, October 15, 2015, https://
www.wsj.com/articles/theranos-has-struggled-with-blood-tests-1444881901.

189 **the drugstore chain Walgreens:** Kia Kokalitcheva, "Walgreens Sues Theranos
for $140 Million for Breach of Contract," *Fortune*, November 8, 2016, http://
fortune.com/2016/11/08/walgreens-theranos-lawsuit. In August 2017, the *Financial Times* reported that Theranos and Walgreens had reached a confidential agreement to settle the lawsuit; Walgreens said that "the matter has been resolved on
mutually acceptable terms" (Jessica Dye and David Crow, "Theranos Settles with
Walgreens over Soured Partnership," *Financial Times*, August 1, 2017, https://www
.ft.com/content/0d32febf-10f6-39cd-b520-c420c3d5391f).

189 **financial backers also sued:** Maya Kosoff, "More Fresh Hell for Theranos," *Vanity Fair*, November 29, 2016, http://www.vanityfair.com/news/2016/11/theranos
-lawsuit-investors-fraud-allegations.

189 **patients who'd received false results:** Jef Feeley and Caroline Chen, "Theranos
Faces Growing Number of Lawsuits Over Blood Tests," *Bloomberg*, October 14,
2016, https://www.bloomberg.com/news/articles/2016-10-14/theranos-faces-grow
ing-number-of-lawsuits-over-blood-tests.

189 **"world's most disappointing leaders":** "The World's 19 Most Disappointing
Leaders," *Fortune*, March 30, 2016, http://fortune.com/2016/03/30/most-disappoint
ing-leaders.

189 *Forbes* **revised her estimated net worth:** Herper, "From $4.5 Billion to Nothing."

189 **"It's impossible to comment":** Kevin Loria, "Scientists Are Skeptical About the
Secret Blood Test That Has Made Elizabeth Holmes a Billionaire," *Business Insider*,
April 25, 2015, http://www.businessinsider.com/science-of-elizabeth-holmes-the
ranos-2015-4.

189 **No peer-reviewed studies examined:** Nick Bilton, "Exclusive: How Elizabeth Holmes's House of Cards Came Tumbling Down," *Vanity Fair*, October 2016,
http://www.vanityfair.com/news/2016/09/elizabeth-holmes-theranos-exclusive.

189 **Ken Auletta asked Holmes to explain:** Ken Auletta, "Blood, Simpler," *New
Yorker*, December 15, 2014, http://www.newyorker.com/magazine/2014/12/15/blood
-simpler.

190 **"The more we tried to drill":** John Carreyrou, "At Theranos, Many Strategies
and Snags," *Wall Street Journal*, December 27, 2015, http://www.wsj.com/articles
/at-theranos-many-strategies-and-snags-1451259629.

190 **Google Ventures also considered:** Jillian D'Onfro, "Bill Maris: Here's Why
Google Ventures Didn't Invest in Theranos," *Business Insider*, October 20, 2015,
http://www.businessinsider.com/bill-maris-explains-why-gv-didnt-invest-in
-theranos-2015-10.

190 **"It's a board like no other,":** Jennifer Reingold, "Theranos' Board: Plenty of
Political Connections, Little Relevant Expertise," *Fortune*, October 15, 2015,
http://fortune.com/2015/10/15/theranos-board-leadership; and Roger Parloff, "A
Singular Board at Theranos," *Fortune*, June 12, 2014, http://fortune.com/2014/06
/12/theranos-board-directors.

191 **Jennifer Reingold called out:** Reingold, "Theranos' Board."

192 **thirteen hundred community banks:** Juan Almandoz and András Tilcsik, "When
Experts Become Liabilities: Domain Experts on Boards and Organizational Failure," *Academy of Management Journal* 59, no. 4 (2016): 1124–49.

193 **John Almandoz, a professor:** Personal interview with John Almandoz on December 3, 2016.

193 **He found three things:** For other risks associated with expert control, see Kim Pernell, Jiwook Jung, and Frank Dobbin, "The Hazards of Expert Control: Chief Risk Officers and Risky Derivatives," *American Sociological Review* 82, no. 3 (2017): 511–41.

193 **"The benefits of not having":** Almandoz and Tilcsik, "When Experts Become Liabilities," 1127.

193 **"If I got a board":** Ibid., 1128.

193 **"Everybody respects each other's ego":** Ibid.

194 **"Amateurs," Almandoz told us:** Personal interview with John Almandoz on December 3, 2016.

## Chapter Nine: Strangers in a Strange Land

195 **Dan Pacholke took a deep breath:** This section draws from the following sources: Detective Paul Lebsock, "Statement of Investigating Officer, Report Number: 15-173057," Spokane County, July 1, 2015; Senate Law and Justice Committee, "Majority Report: Investigation of Department of Corrections Early-Release Scandal," Washington State Senate, May 24, 2016, and witness statements; Carl Blackstone and Robert Westinghouse, "Investigative Report, Re: Department of Corrections, Early Release of Offenders," Yarmuth Wilsdon PLLC (firm), February 19, 2016; Joseph O'Sullivan and Lewis Kamb, "Fix to Stop Early Prison Releases Was Delayed 16 Times," *Seattle Times*, December 29, 2015, http://www.seattletimes .com/seattle-news/crime/fix-to-stop-early-prison-releases-delayed-16-times;   Joseph O'Sullivan, "In 2012, AG's Office Said Fixing Early-Prisoner Release 'Not So Urgent,'" *Seattle Times*, December 20, 2015, http://www.seattletimes.com/seattle -news/politics/in-2012-ags-office-called-early-prisoner-release-not-so-urgent; Kip Hill, "Teen Killed When Men Broke into Tattoo Shop, Witness Tells Police," *Spokesman-Review*, May 28, 2015, http://www.spokesman.com/stories/2015/may /28/teen-killed-when-men-broke-into-tattoo-shop; Kip Hill, "Mother of Slain Spokane Teenager Files $5 Million Claim Against State," *Spokesman-Review*, February 26, 2016, http://www.spokesman.com/stories/2016/feb/26/mother-of-slain -spokane-teenager-files-5-million-c; Nina Culver, "Second Suspect Arrested in Burglary, Murder of 17-Year-Old," *Spokesman-Review*, July 23, 2015, http://www .spokesman.com/stories/2015/jul/23/second-suspect-arrested-burgglary-murder -17-year-o; Mark Berman, "What Happened After Washington State Accidentally Let Thousands of Inmates Out Early," *Washington Post*, February 9, 2016, https:// www.washingtonpost.com/news/post-nation/wp/2016/02/09/heres-what -happened-after-the-state-of-washington-accidentally-let-thousands-of-inmates -out-early/; and Bert Useem, Dan Pacholke, and Sandy Felkey Mullins, "Case Study—The Making of an Institutional Crisis: The Mass Release of Inmates by a Correctional Agency," *Journal of Contingencies and Crisis Management* (in press). We are grateful to Senator Mike Padden (personal interview with Senator Padden on July 21, 2016) and to Erik Smith for their insights and generosity with their time. Thanks also to Dan Pacholke and Sandy Mullins, both of whom were involved in managing the crisis itself, for their discussion of the broader policy context of this story.

196 **caused by a coding error:** In response to a fact-checking email (June 30, 2017), a senate staffer argued that this wasn't a bug but rather a human error rooted in the DOC's misinterpretation of a 2002 court ruling. As a result, the staffer noted, the DOC had directed software developers to implement the system in a way that reflected its misinterpretation. The programmers did their job properly, and the

hardware and software performed as designed. But calling something a bug doesn't minimize its impact, restrict its causes, or imply that it was a trivial mistake.

197 **called "complex interdependencies":** Senate investigators' interview with Dr. Jay Ahn, February 21, 2016, from witness statements, "Majority Report: Investigation of Department of Corrections Early-Release Scandal."

197 **"'oh shit' moment":** Senate investigators' interview with Ira Feuer, February 19, 2016, from witness statements, "Majority Report: Investigation of Department of Corrections Early-Release Scandal."

198 **"They pull out all the stops":** Personal interview with Senator Mike Padden on July 21, 2016.

198 **Medina's mother filed a $5 million claim:** The claim was filed with the State of Washington on behalf of Medina's mother and Ceasar Medina's estate. The claim settled for $3.25 million in 2017. Personal interview with Chris Davis, of Davis Law Group P.S., on August 23, 2017.

198 **Simmel dazzled audiences:** For more on Simmel's life, ideas, and impact, see Lewis A. Coser, "Georg Simmel's Style of Work: A Contribution to the Sociology of the Sociologist," *American Journal of Sociology* 63, no. 6 (1958): 635–41; Lewis A. Coser, *Masters of Sociological Thought* (New York: Harcourt Brace Jovanovich, 1971); Donald N. Levine, Ellwood B. Carter, and Eleanor Miller Gorman, "Simmel's Influence on American Sociology," *American Journal of Sociology* 81, no. 4 (1976): 813–45; and Rosabeth Moss Kanter and Rakesh Khurana, "Types and Positions: The Significance of Georg Simmel's Structural Theories for Organizational Behavior," in Paul S. Adler, ed., *The Oxford Handbook of Sociology and Organization Studies: Classical Foundations* (New York: Oxford University Press, 2009), 291–306.

198 **"a purely honorary title":** Coser, *Masters of Sociological Thought*, 195.

199 **wrote a prominent historian:** This letter, written by Dietrich Schäfer, appears in English translation in Coser, "Georg Simmel's Style of Work," 640–41.

199 **It was called "The Stranger":** Georg Simmel, "The Stranger," in D. Levine, ed., *On Individuality and Social Forms* (Chicago: University of Chicago Press, 1971), 143–49.

199 **the power of strangers lay:** Ibid., 145–46.

200 **"Italian cities of recruiting":** Ibid., 145.

200 **"The citizens, seeing that there often":** Leandro Alberti is quoted in Lester K. Born, "What Is the Podestà?" *American Political Science Review* 21, no. 4 (1927): 863–71.

201 **Take Denny Gioia:** Dennis A. Gioia, "Pinto Fires and Personal Ethics: A Script Analysis of Missed Opportunities," *Journal of Business Ethics* 11, no. 5 (1992): 379–89. See also Jerry Useem's excellent article "What Was Volkswagen Thinking?" *Atlantic*, January/February 2016, https://www.theatlantic.com/magazine/archive/2016/01/what-was-volkswagen-thinking/419127.

201 **"It is difficult to convey":** Gioia, "Pinto Fires and Personal Ethics," 382.

201 **"Before I went to Ford":** Ibid., 388. For more on Denny Gioia and the Pinto case, see Malcolm Gladwell's fascinating essay "The Engineer's Lament," *New Yorker*, May 4, 2015, http://www.newyorker.com/magazine/2015/05/04/the-engineers-lament.

202 **The whole thing stumped:** For this section, we've drawn on Sonari Glinton, "How a Little Lab in West Virginia Caught Volkswagen's Big Cheat," National Public Radio, September 24, 2015, http://www.npr.org/2015/09/24/443053672/how-a-little-lab-in-west-virginia-caught-volkswagens-big-cheat; and Jason Vines's interview with Bob Lutz, *The Frank Beckmann Show*, WJR-AM, Detroit, Michigan, February 16, 2016.

202 **a diesel vehicle for the U.S.?:** Jason Vines's interview with Bob Lutz, *The Frank Beckmann Show*.

203  *Are they magicians*: Bob Lutz quoted by Alisa Priddle, "VW Scandal Puts Diesel Engines on Trial," *Detroit Free Press*, September 26, 2015, http://www.freep.com/story/money/cars/2015/09/26/vw-cheat-emissions-diesel-engine-fallout/72612616. Emphasis ours.

203  **"We have no idea"**: Jason Vines's interview with Bob Lutz, *The Frank Beckmann Show*.

203  **"Is it worth it?"**: Ibid.

203  **Dan Carder found the first part**: In this section, we draw on our personal interview with Dan Carder on November 9, 2016, and the report from the West Virginia University Center for Alternative Fuels, Engines, and Emissions by Gregory J. Thompson et al., "In-Use Emissions Testing of Light-Duty Diesel Vehicles in the United States" (2014), prepared for the International Council on Clean Transportation (ICCT). For the lab tests, the researchers collaborated with the California Air Resources Board, described later in the story.

205  **"It was experimental"**: Personal interview with Dan Carder on November 9, 2016.

205  *thirty-five times* **the allowed level**: Thompson et al., "In-Use Emissions Testing of Light-Duty Diesel Vehicles in the United States," 106.

205  **"We're funded only through our research"**: Personal interview with Dan Carder on November 9, 2016.

206  **It is noted that only three**: Thompson et al., "In-Use Emissions Testing of Light-Duty Diesel Vehicles in the United States."

206  **Alberto Ayala was one of**: Personal interview with Alberto Ayala on March 2, 2017. In response to a fact-checking email (May 17, 2017), a public information officer at the California Air Resources Board wrote:

> CARB was actually part (the other half really) of the emissions study along with WVU. ICCT wanted our engineers and facilities to be part of the research push from the start of the project. Alberto had heard from European regulators sometime before ICCT got involved, that there were unusually high emissions from the VW vehicles in the EU, and was part of that discussion all the way through. So CARB wasn't just handed the results of the study, we were an active part of obtaining those results. I believe we did the lab testing and WVU did the PEMs testing, running their data through our facility in El Monte.
>
> The point I'm trying to make is that CARB was not ever passive in this story, we were involved directly, beginning to end (if there ever really is an end to this case). We've simply had to hold our tongues on much of this because we were also the ones who had to carry on the actual regulatory investigation and court cases.

> After a request for clarification, he wrote (May 22, 2017): "We were already doing that investigation. Since we had already determined that the work was of interest to CARB, and needed to get done, then the decision point (the fork in the road) was, do we perform the work alone or do we do it in collaboration? We collaborate with many universities—in this case it was WVU."

207  **beyond just the on-road testing**: Personal interview with Alberto Ayala on March 2, 2017.

207  **the company cut costs**: Staff Report, "Bosch Warned VW About Illegal Software Use in Diesel Cars, Report Says," *Automotive News*, September 27, 2015, http://www.autonews.com/article/20150927/COPY01/309279989/bosch-warned-vw-about-illegal-software-use-in-diesel-cars-report-says.

208 **Volkswagen was no stranger to scandal:** Diana T. Kurylko and James R. Crate, "The Lopez Affair," *Automotive News Europe*, February 20, 2006, http://europe .autonews.com/article/20060220/ANE/60310010/the-lopez-affair.

208 **Scandal struck again:** Kate Connolly, "Bribery, Brothels, Free Viagra: VW Trial Scandalises Germany," *Guardian*, January 13, 2008, https://www.theguardian.com /world/2008/jan/13/germany.automotive.

208 **illegal bonuses to the head:** "Labor Leader Receives First Jail Sentence in VW Corruption Trial," *Deutsche Welle*, February 22, 2008, http://www.dw.com/en /labor-leader-receives-first-jail-sentence-in-vw-corruption-trial/a-3143471.

208 **returned to Wolfsburg:** On Volkswagen's culture, we draw from our personal interview with Richard Milne on March 2, 2017; and Bob Lutz, "One Man Established the Culture That Led to VW's Emissions Scandal," *Road & Track*, November 4, 2015, http://www.roadandtrack.com/car-culture/a27197/bob-lutz-vw-diesel-fiasco.

209 **He expressed his admiration:** Lutz, "One Man Established the Culture That Led to VW's Emissions Scandal."

209 **poorly run and structured board:** Lucy P. Marcus, "Volkswagen's Lost Opportunity Will Change the Car Industry," *Guardian*, October 25, 2015, https://www .theguardian.com/business/2015/oct/18/volkswagen-scandal-lost-oppor tunity-car-industry.

209 *There were no outsiders:* Richard Milne, "Volkswagen: System Failure," *Financial Times*, November 4, 2015, https://www.ft.com/content/47f233f0-816b-11e5-a01c -8650859a4767.

209 **notoriously anti-outsider in terms:** Personal interview with Richard Milne on March 2, 2017.

210 **extremely complicated and costly:** Jack Ewing, "Researchers Who Exposed VW Gain Little Reward from Success," *New York Times*, July 24, 2016, https://www .nytimes.com/2016/07/25/business/vw-wvu-diesel-volkswagen-west-virginia.html.

210 **"Society should not seal organizations off":** Perrow, "Organizing to Reduce the Vulnerabilities of Complexity," 155.

210 *Challenger* **exploded shortly after its launch:** For this section, we draw on the Presidential Commission on Space Shuttle *Challenger* Accident, *Report to the President by the Presidential Commission on the Space Shuttle Challenger Accident* (Washington, DC: Government Printing Office, 1986); and Diane Vaughan's excellent book, *The Challenger Launch Decision: Risky Technology, Culture, and Deviance at NASA*, enl. ed. (Chicago: University of Chicago Press, 2016). We're also indebted to Professor Vaughan for her review of a draft of this section. Any errors that remain are, of course, our own. For an insightful essay about the *Challenger* accident (including a discussion of Vaughan's research and Charles Perrow's ideas), see Malcolm Gladwell, "Blowup," *New Yorker*, January 22, 1996, http://www .newyorker.com/magazine/1996/01/22/blowup-2.

211 **she called** *normalization of deviance:* Vaughan, *The Challenger Launch Decision*, 62–64.

211 **within the bounds of acceptable risk:** Ibid., 120.

211 **as if nothing was wrong:** Ibid., 62.

212 **"The mistakenly accepted position":** Roger Boisjoly, "SRM O-Ring Erosion/ Potential Failure Criticality," Morton Thiokol interoffice memo, July 31, 1985, included in the report of the Presidential Commission on the *Challenger* Accident, Vol. 1, 249.

212 **flight safety has been and is:** Richard Cook, "Memorandum: Problem with SRB Seals," NASA, July 23, 1985. Included in the report of the Presidential Commission on the *Challenger* Accident, Vol. 4, 1–2.

212 **the most surprising openness:** Georg Simmel, "The Stranger," in *The Sociology of Georg Simmel*, translated and edited by Kurt H. Wolff (New York: The Free Press, 1950), 404.

213 **when the *Columbia* reentered:** For a more detailed look at the *Columbia* disaster and its aftermath, see William Starbuck and Moshe Farjoun, eds., *Organization at the Limit: Lessons from the Columbia Disaster* (Malden, MA: Blackwell, 2005); Julianne G. Mahler, *Organizational Learning at NASA: The Challenger and Columbia Accidents* (Washington, DC: Georgetown University Press, 2009); Diane Vaughan, "NASA Revisited: Theory, Analogy, and Public Sociology," *American Journal of Sociology* 112, no. 2 (2006): 353–93; Roberto, Bohmer, and Edmondson, "Facing Ambiguous Threats"; and "Strategies for Learning from Failure."

213 **Normalization of deviance had struck again:** Vaughan, *The Challenger Launch Decision*, xiv–xv.

213 **"We are quite convinced":** Admiral Harold Gehman, "*Columbia* Accident Investigation Board Press Briefing," August 26, 2003, https://govinfo.library.unt.edu /caib/events/press_briefings/20030826/transcript.html.

213 **managers at Jet Propulsion Laboratory:** We are indebted to a number of people at JPL, including the members of the Joint Engineering Board, and particularly Brian Muirhead, Bharat Chudasama, Chris Jones, and Howard Eisen. This section was developed after an extensive discussion on the JPL campus on September 13, 2016.

214 **have had their share of failures:** Arthur G. Stephenson et al., "Mars Climate Orbiter Mishap Investigation Board Phase I Report," November 10, 1999, ftp://ftp .hq.nasa.gov/pub/pao/reports/1999/MCO_report.pdf; and Arden Albee et al., "Report on the Loss of the Mars Polar Lander and Deep Space 2 Missions," March 22, 2000, https://spaceflight.nasa.gov/spacenews/releases/2000/mpl/mpl_report_1.pdf.

215 **when the Roman Catholic Church:** Theodore T. Herbert and Ralph W. Estes, "Improving Executive Decisions by Formalizing Dissent: The Corporate Devil's Advocate," *Academy of Management Review* 2, no. 4 (1977): 662–67; and Michael A. Roberto, *Why Great Leaders Don't Take Yes for an Answer: Managing for Conflict and Consensus* (Upper Saddle River, NJ: FT Press, 2013).

215 **"The Devil's Advocate Office ensures":** Yosef Kuperwasser, "Lessons from Israel's Intelligence Reforms," The Saban Center for Middle East Policy at the Brookings Institution, Analysis Paper no. 14 (2007): 4.

216 **Vice President of Common Sense:** Bill Simmons, "Welcome Back, Mailbag," May 19, 2016, http://www.espn.com/espn/print?id=2450419; see also Bill Simmons, "The VP of Common Sense Offers His Draft Advice," June 20, 2007, http://www .espn.com/espn/print?id=2910007.

216 **share the same basic principle:** As Wharton professor Adam Grant explains in his book *Originals* (New York: Viking, 2016), when you speak up only because it's your job to disagree, people take your concerns less seriously than if you voice a concern sincerely. (For the underlying research, see Charlan Nemeth, Keith Brown, and John Rogers, "Devil's Advocate Versus Authentic Dissent: Stimulating Quantity and Quality," *European Journal of Social Psychology* 31, no. 6 [2001]: 707–20; and Charlan Nemeth, Joanie B. Connell, John D. Rogers, and Keith S. Brown, "Improving Decision Making by Means of Dissent," *Journal of Applied Social Psychology* 31, no. 1 [2001]: 48–58.) This is an important point. To be clear, we do not advocate imposing a contrived role-playing exercise on a randomly chosen team member. Rather, we are suggesting that an outsider—someone who wasn't part of the decision-making process from the beginning—might bring a more objective view to bear on the issues and can identify problems that insiders have missed.

Indeed, research suggests that decision-making groups can benefit from receiving an outsider's critical input if it is in the form of a thoughtful, written critique that everyone on the team gets to consider before the deliberations (see, for example, Charles R. Schwenk, "Effects of Devil's Advocacy and Dialectical Inquiry on Decision Making: A Meta-Analysis," *Organizational Behavior and Human Decision Processes* 47, no. 1 [1990]: 161–76). Of course, as Grant points out, authentic dissent still tends to be more effective than artificial dissent. We agree: helping authentic dissenters speak up is a crucial task in the danger zone (see our Chapter Seven).

216 **Sasha Robson, a young accountant:** Personal interview with "Sasha Robson" (pseudonym) on June 5, 2017.

## Chapter Ten: Surprise!

219 **The trouble started when Brian Schiff:** We originally read about this story in Barry Schiff's excellent article "Saving Jobs," *AOPA Pilot*, April 5, 2016, https://www.aopa.org/news-and-media/all-news/2016/april/pilot/proficient. We reached out to Barry, and he kindly introduced us to his son, Captain Brian Schiff, who helped fill in the details for us (personal interview on November 2, 2016). Captain Brian Schiff's quotes come from that interview. For simplicity, we refer to the flight as a charter. Technically the plane was owned by Markkula's company and was flying under Part 91 of the FAA's rules; it wasn't strictly speaking a "charter" flight.

222 **common factor in airline accidents:** Dismukes, Berman, and Loukopoulos, *The Limits of Expertise.*

222 **Daniel Tremblay, a young IT consultant:** Personal interview with "Daniel Tremblay" (pseudonym) on April 6, 2017.

223 **Consider this story:** Tinsley, Dillon, and Madsen, "How to Avoid Catastrophe," 97. The story originally appeared in Martin Landau and Donald Chisholm, "The Arrogance of Optimism: Notes on Failure-Avoidance Management," *Journal of Contingencies and Crisis Management* 3, no. 2 (1995): 67–80.

224 **A small boy with a history:** For this story and our understanding of updating and trajectory management, we are indebted to Marlys Christianson (personal interview on January 16, 2017). For the research behind these ideas, see Marlys Christianson, "More and Less Effective Updating: The Role of Trajectory Management in Making Sense Again," *Administrative Science Quarterly* (forthcoming).

227 **the best teams found a balance:** A similar lesson about balance applies to leaders managing complex crises: they need to balance directing action and encouraging reflection, innovation, and dissent; see Faaiza Rashid, Amy C. Edmondson, and Herman B. Leonard, "Leadership Lessons from the Chilean Mine Rescue," *Harvard Business Review* 91, no. 7–8 (2012): 113–19.

229 **"Everyone knew the launch":** Castaldo, "The Last Days of Target."

229 **"Some of these firms didn't really":** Personal interview with Chris Marquis on February 24, 2017.

229 **Here's Marquis and his coauthor:** Christopher Marquis and Zoe Yang, "Learning the Hard Way: Why Foreign Companies That Fail in China Haven't Really Failed," *China Policy Review* 9, no. 10 (2014): 80–81.

230 **"Mattel began to understand":** Helen H. Wang, "Can Mattel Make a Comeback in China?" *Forbes*, November 17, 2013, https://www.forbes.com/sites/helenwang/2013/11/17/can-mattel-make-a-comeback-in-china/#434cc2961527.

231 **delightfully wonky paper:** David Starr and Eleanor Starr, "Agile Practices for Families: Iterating with Children and Parents," AGILE Conference, Chicago, Illinois (2009), http://doi.ieeecomputersociety.org/10.1109/AGILE.2009.53.

232 **Feiler was blown away:** Bruce Feiler, "Agile Programming—For Your Family," TED Talk, February 2013, https://www.ted.com/talks/bruce_feiler_agile_pro gramming_for_your_family?language=en.

232 **It's the same iterative process:** For a rigorous look at how to manage unexpected events, see Karl Weick and Kathleen Sutcliffe's magisterial book, *Managing the Unexpected: Resilient Performance in an Age of Uncertainty*, 2nd ed. (San Francisco: Jossey-Bass, 2007). For an in-depth case study of bouncing back from an unexpected large-scale disaster affecting a whole nation, see Michael Useem, Howard Kunreuther, and Erwann Michel-Kerjan, *Leadership Dispatches: Chile's Extraordinary Comeback from Disaster* (Palo Alto, CA: Stanford University Press, 2015).

232 **The SWAT team spent:** Our description of how SWAT teams and film crews handle surprises is based on Beth A. Bechky and Gerardo A. Okhuysen, "Expecting the Unexpected? How SWAT Officers and Film Crews Handle Surprises," *Academy of Management Journal* 54, no. 2 (2011): 239–61.

234 **Glenn described how finding a couch:** Ibid., 246.

234 **a telling story that Bechky:** Ibid., 247.

235 **an aerial camera operator didn't show:** Ibid., 246.

235 **"If I want to produce":** Ibid., 253.

236 **"You are supposed to know":** Ibid., 255.

236 **Tim Brown, the CEO of IDEO:** Morten T. Hansen, "IDEO CEO Tim Brown: T-Shaped Stars: The Backbone of IDEO's Collaborative Culture," January 21, 2010, http://chiefexecutive.net/ideo-ceo-tim-brown-t-shaped-stars-the-backbone -of-ideoaes-collaborative-culture__trashed.

236 **initial public offering (IPO) of Facebook:** Our description of this story draws on the SEC's report regarding the Facebook IPO error: "In the Matter of the NASDAQ Stock Market, LLC and NASDAQ Execution Services, LLC," Administrative Proceeding File No. 3-15339, May 29, 2013. It's important to note that, unlike National Transportation Safety Board reports, whose purpose is to ascertain the causes of an accident, the SEC's report lays out the basis for an enforcement action against Nasdaq. We've also drawn on background conversations we had with a senior Nasdaq official who was on the call and a senior technologist who left Nasdaq shortly before the IPO.

238 **Here's the Securities and Exchange Commission:** U.S. Securities and Exchange Commission, "NASDAQ Stock Market, LLC and NASDAQ Execution Services, LLC," Administrative Proceeding File No. 3-15339, May 29, 2013, https://www.sec .gov/litigation/admin/2013/34-69655.pdf, 6. Emphasis ours.

## Epilogue: The Golden Age of Meltdowns

241 **W. B. Yeats wrote his famous:** Jim Haughey, *The First World War in Irish Poetry* (Lewisburg, PA: Bucknell University Press, 2002), 182.

241 **"highbrow way of saying":** Ed Ballard, "Terror, Brexit and U.S. Election Have Made 2016 the Year of Yeats," *Wall Street Journal*, August 23, 2016, https://www.wsj .com/articles/terror-brexit-and-u-s-election-have-made-2016-the-year-of-yeats -1471970174.

242 **"News is about things that happen":** Steven Pinker and Andrew Mack, "The World Is Not Falling Apart," *Slate*, December 22, 2014, http://www.slate.com/arti cles/news_and_politics/foreigners/2014/12/the_world_is_not_falling_apart_the _trend_lines_reveal_an_increasingly_peaceful.html. For more on this fascinating topic, see Steven Pinker, *The Better Angels of Our Nature: Why Violence Has Declined* (New York: Viking, 2011).

242 **devastate the environment:** Jared Diamond, *Collapse: How Societies Choose to Fail or Succeed* (New York: Viking, 2005); Al Gore, *The Future: Six Drivers of Global Change* (New York: Random House, 2013); and Jeffrey D. Sachs, *Common Wealth: Economics for a Crowded Planet* (New York: Penguin Press, 2008).

242 **and destabilize economies:** Mohamed El-Erian, *The Only Game in Town: Central Banks, Instability, and Avoiding the Next Collapse* (New York: Random House, 2016).

243 **fail to act on warning signs:** Max H. Bazerman and Michael Watkins, *Predictable Surprises: The Disasters You Should Have Seen Coming, and How to Prevent Them* (Boston: Harvard Business School Press, 2004); and Michele Wucker, *The Gray Rhino: How to Recognize and Act on the Obvious Dangers We Ignore* (New York: St. Martin's Press, 2016).

243 **Homogeneous teams run some:** See, for example, Alliance for Board Diversity, "Missing Pieces Report: The 2016 Board Diversity Census of Women and Minorities on Fortune 500 Boards," http://www2.deloitte.com/us/en/pages/center-for -board-effectiveness/articles/board-diversity-census-missing-pieces.html; C. Todd Lopez, "Army Reviews Diversity in Combat Arms Leadership," July 19, 2016, https://www.army.mil/article/171727/army_reviews_diversity_in_combat_arms _leadership; and Gregory Krieg and Eugene Scott, "White Males Dominate Trump's Top Cabinet Posts," CNN, January 19, 2017, http://www.cnn.com/2016 /12/13/politics/donald-trump-cabinet-diversity/index.html.

243 **Our food supply chains are more:** See, for example, Aleda V. Roth, Andy A. Tsay, Madeleine E. Pullman, and John V. Gray, "Unraveling the Food Supply Chain: Strategic Insights from China and the 2007 Recalls," *Journal of Supply Chain Management* 44, no. 1 (2008): 22–39; Zoe Wood and Felicity Lawrence, "Horsemeat Scandal: Food Safety Expert Warns Issues Have Not Been Addressed," *Guardian*, September 4, 2014, https://www.theguardian.com/uk-news/2014/sep/04/horse meat-food-safety-expert-chris-elliott; and "Horsemeat Scandal: Food Supply Chain 'Too Complex'—Morrisons," BBC News, February 9, 2013, http://www.bbc.com /news/av/uk-21394451/horsemeat-scandal-food-supply-chain-too-complex -morrisons.

243 **manage and store nuclear weapons:** Eric Schlosser, *Command and Control: Nuclear Weapons, the Damascus Accident, and the Illusion of Safety* (New York: Penguin Press, 2013).

244 **plenty of research showing:** See, for example, Dan Lovallo and Olivier Sibony, "The Case for Behavioral Strategy," *McKinsey Quarterly*, March 2010, http://www .mckinsey.com/business-functions/strategy-and-corporate-finance/our-insights /the-case-for-behavioral-strategy; Günter K. Stahl, Martha L. Maznevski, Andreas Voigt, and Karsten Jonsen, "Unraveling the Effects of Cultural Diversity in Teams: A Meta-Analysis of Research on Multicultural Work Groups," *Journal of International Business Studies* 41, no. 4 (2010): 690–709; and Edmondson, "Psychological Safety and Learning Behavior in Work Teams."

244 **humanity faced a grave threat:** Ole J. Benedictow, "The Black Death: The Greatest Catastrophe Ever," *History Today* 55, no. 3 (2005): 42; and Barbara Tuchman, *A Distant Mirror: The Calamitous 14th Century* (New York: Alfred A. Knopf, 1978).

244 **catapulting infected bodies:** Mark Wheelis, "Biological Warfare at the 1346 Siege of Caffa," *Emerging Infectious Diseases* 8, no. 9 (2002): 971.

245 **The world was ripe:** For our understanding of the competing theories on these issues, we are indebted to Professor Samuel K. Cohn at the University of Glasgow (personal interview on May 2, 2017) and his article "Book Review: The Black Death 1346–1353: The Complete History," *New England Journal of Medicine* 352 (2005): 1054–55.

245 **"the golden age of bacteria":** Benedictow, "The Black Death."

# INDEX